The Feminine Subject

The Feminine Subject

Susan Hekman

polity

First published in 2014 by Polity Press

Polity Press
65 Bridge Street
Cambridge CB2 1UR, UK

Polity Press
350 Main Street
Malden, MA 02148, USA

ISBN-13: 978-0-7456-8783-4
ISBN-13: 978-0-7456-8784-1(pb)

A catalogue record for this book is available from the British Library.

Typeset in 11 on 13 pt Sabon
by Toppan Best-set Premedia Limited
Printed and bound in Great Britain by T.J. International, Padstow, Cornwall

The publisher has used its best endeavours to ensure that the URLs for external websites referred to in this book are correct and active at the time of going to press. However, the publisher has no responsibility for the websites and can make no guarantee that a site will remain live or that the content is or will remain appropriate.

Every effort has been made to trace all copyright holders, but if any have been inadvertently overlooked the publisher will be pleased to include any necessary credits in any subsequent reprint or edition.

For further information on Polity, visit our website: politybooks.com

Contents

Acknowledgments   vi

**1 Simone de Beauvoir and the
  Beginnings of the Feminine Subject**   1

2 Difference I: The "French Feminists"   27

**3 Difference II: Radical Feminism and the
  Relational Self**   48

**4 Continuing the Tradition: Liberalism
  and Marxism**   77

**5 From Difference to Differences:
  Postmodernism, Race, Ethnicity,
  and Intersectionality**   113

6 The Material Subject   147

Notes   186

Bibliography   191

Index   212

Acknowledgments

This book began at the Netherlands Institute for Advanced Studies in Wassenaar, Netherlands, in the fall of 2010. It is hard to imagine a more perfect setting for scholarly work. Scholars from an array of disciplines in the social sciences and humanities are housed in an idyllic setting in a small town near The Hague and the North Sea. I was greatly enriched by the intellectual interaction with a diverse group of international scholars in residence at NIAS. I am deeply grateful for the experience.

The book was completed during a Faculty Development Leave from the University of Texas at Arlington in the fall of 2013. Along the way portions of the book were presented at conferences in Los Angeles, Stockholm, Utrecht, and Umea, Sweden. My thanks to the scholars who commented on my work at these conferences.

Throughout the years I have been sustained by the friendship and scholarly support of a group of close friends at UTA. Laurie Porter, Wendy Faris, and, particularly, Stacy Alaimo helped me through a difficult time in my life as well as encouraging my work. My sincere thanks to them. But my deepest thanks go to John for giving me a new life. Together with our equine companions, Pepper and Shiner, as well as our canine friends, Honey and Glory, we have created a life together that is rich and full. In gratitude I dedicate this book to them.

– 1 –
Simone de Beauvoir and the Beginnings of the Feminine Subject

I. Introduction

The recent re-translation of Simone de Beauvoir's *The Second Sex* begins with a simple declarative sentence: in 1946 Simone de Beauvoir began to outline what she thought would be an autobiographical essay explaining why, when she tried to define herself, the first sentence that came to mind was "I am a woman" (Thurman 2010: ix). In the course of writing the book Beauvoir soon discovered that trying to explain what it meant to be a woman was far from simple. Somewhat to her surprise, what started as an autobiographical essay turned into a two-volume, nearly 800-page analysis that ranges widely over a disparate group of elements that define "woman" in society. It made Simone de Beauvoir both famous and infamous, and is commonly described as launching the contemporary feminist movement.

It is hard to imagine that anything new can or should be written at this point either on Simone de Beauvoir or *The Second Sex*. The book and its author excited intense interest, both positive and negative, after its initial publication. Since then its reception among feminists has gone through several phases. From the outset feminists recognized the book as the first radical statement of the situation of women. As the feminist movement matured, however, many feminists had second thoughts about Beauvoir. She was accused of masculinism, blind acceptance of Sartrean existentialism, even a rejection of the female body and maternity. Then, beginning in the late 1980s, a spate of books and articles re-evaluating Beauvoir and *The Second Sex* brought the book back into the feminist limelight. Many of these works are attempts to define Beauvoir's philosophical orientation and to place her work in a more positive light than that of the previous commentaries.

My goal in the following is not to evaluate, one more time, Beauvoir's work in general and *The Second Sex* in particular. Nor is it to refute all the previous interpretations of her work. It is, rather, to go back to Beauvoir's original question and evaluate her work in light of the answer that she gave to it. Beauvoir asked the question that has and must orient feminist theory: what, really, does it mean to say "I am a woman"? How do we go about answering that question and where does that answer lead us? What I want to emphasize in the following is that the question of the identity of "woman" is the central question in the tradition of feminist theory that has evolved in the wake of Beauvoir's work. Beauvoir, obviously, has much to say about this question. And so do all the feminist theorists that follow her. The identity of "woman" is at the center of all the feminisms that have developed in the 60 years since *The Second Sex*. From liberal to psychoanalytic, to socialist, to postmodern, to the current rage, material feminism, "woman" hovers over each one of them. Each begins and ends with an understanding of the identity of woman both philosophically and socially. In other words, Beauvoir asked the question that would define the tradition of feminist theory that she quite literally initiated.

It is misleading, however, to characterize feminist theory since Beauvoir as a simple linear development following in the footsteps of her theory. It would be more accurate to describe feminist theory since Beauvoir as attempts to get "woman" right and, in the process, to show the errors of previous theories. As feminism evolved, the proponents of each new iteration of "woman" claimed that previous attempts to define "woman" were, at the very least, seriously flawed and that the definition of "woman" now being advanced has, finally, gotten it right. I think that this approach is seriously wrong-headed. It is much more productive and, I would argue, incumbent on feminist theorists to look at the last 60 years of theories about "woman" as a positive cumulative enterprise, each theory building on the one that went before and adding to our understanding of "woman." I do not think that feminist theorists should be in the business of refuting previous feminist theorists but should, rather, be looking for elements in their work that have added to our understanding of "woman." Our goal, in other words, should not be to, finally, get "woman" right but, rather, to explore in contemporary terms what we can contribute to our understanding of this central concept, an understanding grounded in previous theories.

Much of the commentary on Beauvoir and *The Second Sex* revolves around placing her philosophically, examining her reliance, or lack thereof, on the philosophical currents of her time. I am going to advance a different thesis here. Although it is undeniable that Beauvoir was deeply influenced by the philosophies of her day, I will argue that in taking on the question of "woman" Beauvoir encountered an obstacle that effectively exploded the boundaries of these philosophies. The question of "woman" did not fit into the vocabularies of any of the philosophical positions that were available to her. As a consequence she had to make her own way, to forge a new method in order to deal with the unique question of woman, a question that the tradition of western philosophy had hitherto avoided. I am not going to claim that Beauvoir's method was flawless or even that she articulated her rejection of previous philosophies clearly. But I am going to claim that what Beauvoir proposes is unique and, most importantly, that she articulated a position that would define feminist theory in the aftermath of *The Second Sex*: the introduction of "woman" into the philosophical tradition requires a radical change in method, a change that alters the tradition of philosophy as we know it.

Another way of putting this is that many feminist theorists have lost sight of the radical nature of Beauvoir's thought. We tend to get caught up in the heated arguments between the proponents of different approaches. Those who espouse a particular approach to the subject spend too much of their theoretical energy trying to prove their opponents wrong. We do not see the forest but get lost in the trees. What we lose sight of is that Beauvoir invites us to enter, in Althusser's words, a new continent of thought. Although throughout the course of feminist theory we have approached this project from different perspectives, our goal is the same: transforming "woman."

In subsequent chapters this understanding of Beauvoir's work will ground my examination of the evolving tradition of feminist theory. In chapter 2, I look at the French feminists that came after Beauvoir. I interpret them not, as they sometimes claim, as repudiating her conception of "woman," but as continuing to explore how "woman" explodes the categories of philosophical thought. Despite the differences between the work of Beauvoir and that of Irigaray, Cixous, and Kristeva, and their differences from each other, they are continuing Beauvoir's legacy. Irigaray's concept of "jamming the theoretical machinery" summarizes not only her work, but the course of feminist theory that is emerging. In chapter 3, I interpret the emphasis on difference that characterizes radical feminism and the relational self in the same light. The "difference feminists" were, in a Beauvoirian spirit, exploring a definition of "woman" outside the boundaries of the masculine paradigm and, in so doing, adding new dimensions to the concept. I focus specifically on the work of Carol Gilligan, a theorist who has been, I think, unfairly pushed to the sidelines in contemporary feminism. Gilligan accomplishes an amazing feat: redefining the basis of western moral theory. I do not believe she has received full credit for this. In addition, her work on the development of adolescent girls is pathbreaking. Beauvoir suggested that it is in adolescence that girls acquire the sense of inferiority that characterizes the feminine. Gilligan's research proves this to be the case.

In chapter 4 I take a different tack. I argue that feminists who attempted to fit "woman" into the traditions of liberalism or Marxism effectively proved Beauvoir's thesis that "woman" does not fit into masculine traditions. Despite the valiant efforts of these feminists, they failed in their attempts to find a common ground with these theories. In both cases, introducing "woman" into these theories necessarily changes their fundamental assumptions. We have learned an important lesson from the efforts of these theorists: no tweaking of the tradition will suffice; we have to move beyond the parameters of western thought to redefine "woman."

The era of differences I examine in chapter 5 presents distinctive challenges. Previous feminists, including Beauvoir, assumed that they were trying to define a unitary conception of "woman." Postmodern feminists, theorists of race and ethnicity, and those who embrace intersectional analysis challenged this assumption. They argued that "woman" is multiple, that no one definition will fit all women. For some feminists this was a difficult transition, but it soon became clear that it was necessary to accommodate the diversity of women's lives. It also became clear that there was no going back to the era of difference.

I conclude with a discussion of the present era in which feminists are returning to the material after the linguistic turn of postmodernism. A widespread understanding of this approach is that it corrects the over-emphasis on the linguistic that defines postmodernism. Although this is not inaccurate, it also over-simplifies the relationship. A better characterization is that the turn to the material brings in issues, most notably the body and biology, that were side-lined in the linguistic turn. This approach has made a significant contribution to feminist theory. It has opened up new avenues of research that will enhance our understanding of the feminine subject.

My analysis of all of these theorists is driven by three theses. First, our exploration of the subject is a radical project that explodes the boundaries of previous theories. Beauvoir began this project by asking "what is 'woman'"? and we are still exploring this question. Second, our effort is cumulative – each theory builds on what has gone before rather than repudiating previous theories. My third thesis is closely related: we should not assume that our goal is to, once and for all, get "woman" right. Looking for essences is a central aspect of masculinist thought that we should abandon. The search for "woman" is an ongoing process begun by Beauvoir that continues to evolve.

II. *The Ethics of Ambiguity*

Beauvoir first expresses the ideas that will guide her discussion of women in *The Second Sex* in her collection of essays, *The Ethics of Ambiguity*.[1] Her concern in these essays is to get at the essence of the human subject, what it means to be a human being. At the beginning of the first essay she states that:

> This privilege, which he alone possesses, of being a sovereign and unique subject amidst a universe of subjects, is what he shares with all his fellow men. In turn an object for others, he is nothing more than an individual in the collectivization on which he depends. (1948: 7)

She goes on to assert that as long as men have lived they have felt this "tragic ambiguity of their condition" (1948: 7), ambiguity that, she later asserts, we must assume

(1948: 9). To attain his truth, man must not attempt to dispel the ambiguity of his being, but, on the contrary, accept the task of realizing it (1948: 13).

These statements set the tone for the analysis that follows, an analysis that, at least initially, follows the lines of Sartrean existentialism. The first implication of man's ambiguous status is that there are not "foreign absolutes," no "inhuman objectivity" but, rather, it is human existence that makes values spring up in the world (1948: 14–15). Another way of expressing this ambiguity is that the fact of being a subject is a universal fact; the Cartesian cogito expresses both the most individual experience and the most objective truth, but the ethics of ambiguity denies that separate existents can be bound to each other and their individual freedom can forge laws valid for all (1948: 17–18).

So far so good. Life, and particularly ethics, is ambiguous in that we are both separate and collective beings. But, as Beauvoir works through her theory, this ambiguity gets more complicated. Freedom is the source from which all signification and values spring. To will oneself moral and to will oneself free are one and the same decision. This theory places all human beings on a moral plane as seekers of freedom. But, as Beauvoir develops her theory, problems arise for this neat formulation. There are, Beauvoir asserts, exceptions to this principle. There are beings whose life slips by in an infantile world because, having been kept in a state of servitude and ignorance, they have no means of breaking the ceiling which is shielded over their bodies. Beauvoir first cites the example of women and slaves to illustrate her point, but as her argument progresses she turns her attention exclusively to women. Women in western countries, she asserts, lack an apprenticeship in freedom and, what is worse, consent to their servitude (1948: 37–8).

Women, in short, present a problem for the theory she is advancing. They do not fit neatly into the parameters of the ethics of ambiguity. In this context, however, Beauvoir seems unwilling to deal with this problem and pulls back from the difficulties it poses. Instead she plunges into the issue of freedom and what it means for this theory. Freedom, she asserts, must project itself toward its own reality through a content whose value it establishes. It is not necessary for the object to seek to be, but it must desire that there *be* being. To will oneself free is to will that there be being as one and the same choice; they both imply the bond on each man with all others. It follows that "To will that there be being is also to will that there be men by and for whom the world is endowed with human significations...To make being 'be' is to communicate with others by means of being" (1948: 71). Freedom cannot will itself without aiming at an open future.

It follows, Beauvoir asserts, that existentialism is not solipsism: "Man can find a justification in his own existence only in the existence of other men" (1948: 72); "To will oneself free is also to will others free" (1948: 73). It also follows that there is a concrete bond between freedom and existence. To will man free is to will there to *be* being; it is to will the disclosure of being in the joy of existence (1948: 135).

In later years, Beauvoir described *The Ethics of Ambiguity* as the book that irritated her the most (Moi 2008: 168). Reading the book today from the perspective of *The Second Sex* is irritating because the position she articulates here lacks the clarity she will achieve in *TSS*. A number of things, however, are clear at this stage. First, Beauvoir is distinguishing her position from the implicit solipsism of early Sartrean existentialism. As many commentators have pointed out, Beauvoir's concept of subjectivity and freedom in *The Ethics of Ambiguity* is specifically social; we cannot be without the being of others (Kruks 1990: 93; Tidd 1999: 15). Second, it begins to emerge that the key to this social identity of "man" is his *existence*, the specifics of his individual place in the society that gives him his being and his freedom. This point will become a major focus of the analysis in *The Second Sex*. What will then be identified as "situation" will take center stage in the analysis, whereas here it is still on the margins.

What is not clear, however, is how women fit into this scenario. In her commentary on *The Ethics of Ambiguity*, Toril Moi claims that for Beauvoir the human condition is characterized by ambiguity and conflict and that women embody this more than men. Thus, women incarnate the human condition more fully than men (2008: 195). I agree, but I think that the problem goes deeper than this. I think that what Beauvoir is beginning to realize is that women change everything. Yes, women do not fit into the philosophical position she is developing, but at this point she does not realize what follows from this. The philosophical position she is espousing cannot be adjusted to meet this problem. Women lack an apprenticeship in freedom. They cannot fit into the definitions of freedom and existence that Beauvoir is so carefully laying out in *The Ethics of Ambiguity*. And the reason for this failure lies in women's unique situation, what she here calls their "infantile world." In *The Ethics of Ambiguity* Beauvoir essentially sidesteps this problem. She mentions women, makes her central point regarding the sociality of human existence, and moves on. It is not until *The Second Sex* that she is forced to confront the problem of women directly. And there it becomes clear that the "ambiguity" of women's situation is of an entirely different order from that of men. It also becomes clear that dealing with the "problem" of women will necessitate a radically different approach.

III. *The Second Sex*

Following in the footsteps of many feminist critics of Beauvoir, I initially dismissed her approach as masculinist and epistemologically inconsistent. Focusing on her concept of the Other as it is presented in *The Second Sex*, I argued that Beauvoir's claim that the One/Other relationship is primordial and that the One is gendered masculine precludes women from full subjectivity. Women cannot be the One, the fully human transcendent subject, and therefore Beauvoir in effect denies woman full subjectivity (Hekman 1999).

It is very easy to read Beauvoir this way. The first few pages of *The Second Sex* present the One/Other relationship as a fundamental and an inescapable aspect of the human condition. Read outside the context of the rest of the book, it is not difficult to come to the conclusion that this relationship holds out little hope for women. There we learn that man represents both the positive and the neuter. Masculine and feminine are not symmetrical. Men, who define themselves in opposition to women, are the One, the positive pole. But men are also the neutral standard that defines humanness itself; woman is both a negative and a lack: "[woman] is the inessential in front of the essential. He is the Subject; he is the Absolute; she is the Other" (2010: 6). The category of the Other is as original as consciousness itself: alterity is the fundamental category of human thought (2010: 6); "the subject posits itself only in opposition, it asserts itself as the essential and sets up the Other as inessential, as the object" (2010: 7). Women's position in this scenario is unambiguously inferior. Women do not posit themselves essentially as subjects. Worse, they do not protest male sovereignty; they are complicit in their definition of Other, they have done nothing to bring about a change. They have more in common with the men of their class than with other women. Furthermore, women derive advantages from this status as Other; to decline to be Other would be to renounce those advantages. The division of the sexes, Beauvoir concludes, is a biological given, not a moment in human history: "Their opposition took place in an original *Mitsein*, and she has not broken it." The fundamental characteristic of woman is that "she is the Other at the heart of a whole whose two components are necessary to each Other" (2010: 9).

I, and many other feminists, read these passages as an assessment of the hopeless condition in which women find themselves. "Fundamental" and "primordial" seem to offer no escape for women. Beauvoir herself declared that the purpose of her book was to assess the condition of women. These passages go a long way toward doing just that, revealing the underlying cause of women's inferiority in society. But there is another way to read these passages, an interpretation that is more consistent with the subsequent arguments in the book and with Beauvoir's overall approach to the problem of "woman." What if we read these passages not as a brutally accurate description of the roots of woman's inferiority in society, but rather as the challenge that women must meet and transcend? What if Beauvoir is saying, in effect, that the One/Other dichotomy gives women no way out, and thus it is incumbent on us to develop a new approach – a feminist approach – to find that way out? And, finally, what if Beauvoir is saying that the tradition of philosophy in the west fails to provide a way out, that introducing women into philosophy entails radical changes and reveals the poverty of those philosophical conceptions?

I think that Beauvoir is arguing precisely this, although she does not say so directly in this or any other context. But discussions of the Other that recur with frequency throughout *The Second Sex* point in this direction. Early on she asserts that the perspective she will adopt is one of existentialist morality, a perspective that assumes that every subject posits itself concretely through projects:

> It accomplishes its freedom only by perpetually surpassing toward other freedoms; there is no other justification for present existence than its expansion toward an infinitely open future. Every time transcendence lapses into immanence there is a degradation of existence into in-itself, of freedom into facticity; this fall is a moral fault if the subject consents to it; if the fall is inflicted on the subject, it takes the form of frustration and oppression; in both cases it is an absolute evil. Every individual concerned with justifying his existence experiences his existence as an infinite need to transcend himself. (2010: 16–17)

This, then, defines the situation into which woman is thrust. The uniqueness of woman is that she discovers and chooses herself in a world where men force her to assume herself as Other: "Woman's drama lies in this conflict between the fundamental claim of every subject, which always posits itself as an essential and the demands of a situation that posits herself as an inessential" (2010: 17).

Beauvoir then asks a number of questions. How in the feminine condition can a human being accomplish herself? How can she find independence with dependence? Answering these questions, Beauvoir claims, is the task of the analysis ahead. But although she does not make the argument explicit in this context, the logic of her argument compels the reader to ask further questions. Do the presuppositions of the philosophical approach Beauvoir has articulated make it impossible to "solve" the question of women? Does the topic of woman necessitate jettisoning this philosophy and, indeed, all previously articulated philosophical approaches? Does "woman" change everything and necessitate something entirely new?

Beauvoir returns to the concept of the Other frequently in the course of *The Second Sex*.[2] Some of these comments are consistent with the discussion of the Other that opens the book. Thus she states that woman emerged as the inessential who returned to the essential. But as the absolute Other she lacked reciprocity (2010: 160). This is then followed by the statement that "the more women assert themselves as human beings, the more the marvelous quality of Other dies in them" (2010: 162). She concludes, however, that it exists today in the hearts of all men. But then another theme emerges: ambiguity.

> And her ambiguity is that of the very idea of Other: it is that of the human condition as defined in its relation with the Other. It has already been said that the Other is Evil; but as it is necessary for the Good, it reverts to the Good... through the Other, I accede to the Whole, but it separates me from the Whole; it is the door to infinity and the measure of my finitude. (2010: 163)

Again, there are various ways to read this passage. In *The Ethics of Ambiguity* Beauvoir told us that all human life is ambiguous; thus we should not find it surprising that woman's life is also ambiguous. But it is also possible to read this passage as a critique of the philosophical presuppositions of the Other. Woman doesn't fit into the One/Other schema; she violates its boundaries, ruptures its ethics. Good becomes evil and evil good. Later, in discussing the myth of femininity that has defined women's condition, Beauvoir comments that "There is no question of expressing eternal truths here, but of describing the common ground from which all singular feminine existence stems" (2010: 279). This entails an even more radical critique. What is the point of philosophy except to seek eternal truths? Without the goal of eternal truth philosophy loses much of its meaning. What Beauvoir seems to be suggesting in these remarks is that the question of women does not fit within the parameters of the philosophical positions she has been espousing. What this entails is that the question of woman requires a radically new approach that jettisons previous philosophical methods.

This conclusion is born out in the introduction to volume II that begins with the famous line, "One is not born but rather becomes a woman" (2010: 283). It is unfortunate that most commentators stop with this sentence. The following sentences, however, supply the context of Beauvoir's famous statement and throw a different light on its meaning:

> No biological, psychic or economic destiny defines the figure that the human female takes on in society; it is civilization as a whole that elaborates this intermediary product between the male and the eunuch that is called feminine. Only the mediation of another can constitute an individual as an *Other*. (2010: 283)

Beauvoir's point here is clear: in order to understand woman and, particularly her constitution as Other, we

Foucaultian

need to look at the broad array of factors that contribute to that constitution. No one factor defines her destiny; their interaction and interdependence construct her identity. It follows that to understand – and overthrow – the status of Other we need to examine all of these factors. And, most importantly, we must consider woman in interaction with others.

Examining these elements occupies Beauvoir's attention in the course of the book. I will not provide a survey of these factors here, but rather concentrate on a number of issues that impinge on my investigation of Beauvoir's subject. First is the question of method. Beauvoir never defines her method explicitly. But as she moves through the elements of her analysis – the biological, the psychoanalytic, the historical, the economic – her method emerges in practice if not in theory. At the end of her chapter on biology she states that "we will clarify the biological data by examining them in light of ontological, economic, social, and psychological contexts" (2010: 48). What Beauvoir calls woman's enslavement to the species is, she declares, of extreme importance. Woman's body is one of the essential elements of the situation she occupies in the world. "But" (and this but has great significance in this context) "her body is not enough to define her; it is a lived reality only as taken on by consciousness through actions and within a society" (2010: 48). Biology alone does not define women but neither do psychology or economics. As Beauvoir analyzes psychoanalysis, history, and historical materialism, she consistently rejects a monistic approach. Her method is composite. Woman is not defined by one thing but by the confluence of elements that constitute her place in society.

These statements not only define Beauvoir's method in *The Second Sex*; they also effectively refute the biological essentialism of which she has been accused by some interpreters (Evans 1985: 61–2). Part I, chapter 1 of volume I of *The Second Sex* is "Biological Data." But Beauvoir makes it clear from the outset that woman not only is not defined by her body, but the body is not a fixed entity.

However we want to regard the differences between men and women, she asserts, they do obviously exist (2010: 41). Woman is different biologically from man but it doesn't follow from this that her biology is her destiny. In a series of arguments that is consistent with the rejection of universals throughout the book, Beauvoir agrees that woman, like man, is her body, but claims that her body is something other than herself (2010: 41). Woman is not a fixed reality, but a becoming (2010: 44). This aspect of Beauvoir's work is immensely important, not only in her work but in subsequent feminist analyses. She is countering the abstraction that is at the center of the western philosophical tradition and opposing it with an understanding of woman as located, particularly in her body, without presupposing essentialism.

Beauvoir has much to say about the stages of woman's life: childhood, adolescence, marriage, motherhood. Many feminists have condemned her for her apparent disdain for traditional female activities. But it is worth noting that much of what Beauvoir argues in these sections of *The Second Sex* became the basis for subsequent feminist theory and practice. Beauvoir's discussion of girls' development, for example, has striking parallels to that articulated by Carol Gilligan in the 1980s. Like Gilligan, she identifies a crucial stage in girls' development in which they have to give up their childhood independence and embrace femininity, what Gilligan calls hitting the wall of western culture. The dilemma for the girl, Beauvoir argues, is that "she spontaneously grasps herself as the essential: How will she decide to become the inessential? If I can accomplish myself only as the *Other* how will I renounce my *Self*?" She is suspended between the moment of childish independence and feminine submission (2010: 348). It is significant that Beauvoir's discussion here not only presages much second-wave feminist thought, but is also disturbingly current.[3]

Toward the end of the book, in a chapter on women's situation and character, Beauvoir states:

The woman does not positively think that the truth is *other* than what men claim: rather, she holds that there *is* no truth. It is not only life's becoming that makes her suspicious of the principle of identity, nor the magic phenomena surrounding her that ruin the notion of causality: it is at the heart of the masculine world itself, it is in her as belonging to this world, that she grasps the ambiguity of all principles, of all values, of all that exists. She knows that when it comes to her, masculine morality is a vast mystification. (2010: 651)

This is pretty strong stuff. Taken out of context, it offers an almost perfect proof of the thesis that I am advancing regarding Beauvoir: that her consideration of woman compels her to jettison masculine philosophy and adopt a radically different approach. But, unfortunately for the neatness of my thesis, this is not an accurate interpretation of this particular passage. The context of Beauvoir's remarks is a discussion of the powerlessness women experience at the hands of men, the degree to which their lives are totally controlled by masculine institutions. It is a condemnation of particular practices rather than an overall indictment of the poverty of masculine thought. It is an indication, however, of the direction of Beauvoir's thought concerning masculinist philosophies. Although she does not state her position as clearly as we might like, she is beginning to question the validity of all philosophical systems for understanding the position of women.

In the conclusion to the book Beauvoir reverts to the philosophical position that she, at least ostensibly, employed throughout the course of her analysis. She begins with a summary of what that analysis has established: that there is no "original curse" that condemns men and women to tear each other apart or a psychological destiny imposed on women (2010: 753). She then turns to an assessment of women today and their hopes for a life of equality with men, an assessment cast in the philosophical terminology with which she began the book. Woman today, she claims, seeks to emerge into the light of transcendence. But she stands in front of man not as a subject, but as an object paradoxically endowed with subjectivity. She assumes herself as both self and other, which is a contradiction with disconcerting consequences. The vicious cycle is difficult to break out of because each sex is victim both of the other and of itself (2010: 754–5).

Change will come, Beauvoir concludes, not from individual women, but from society itself: girls and boys must be raised by the same standards. What will this change bring about? Men and women will recognize each other as subjects while at the same time remaining an other for the other. Reciprocity will not do away with the "miracles" that the division of human beings into two separate categories engenders (2010: 766). Thus, when the slavery of half of humanity is abolished, the division of humanity will reveal its authentic meaning and the human couple will discover its true form. And, finally, to unequivocally affirm their "brotherhood," the relation of man to woman will emerge:

> It therefore reveals the extent to which man's *natural* behavior has become *human* or the extent to which the human essence in him has become a natural essence – the extent to which his *human nature* has come to be *natural* to him. (2010: 766)

It is hard to take these passages seriously. It seems as if Beauvoir has lapsed into romantic dreams of a better world that have little relationship to her preceding analysis. But, again, another interpretation is possible. The fact that these passages verge on incoherence once more suggests that Beauvoir realizes the impossibility of the philosophical position she claims to espouse. The terminology of subject and object leaves us in the impossible position in which men and women are both and neither. Surely this is not the solution that Beauvoir is seeking. This is borne out in the final passage in which Beauvoir suggests an intriguing possibility that has not previously surfaced in her discussions: the collapse of the natural/human dichotomy. What Beauvoir seems to be saying here is that we should stop looking for the natural essence that grounds human existence and accept that human nature *is* natural. This has all kinds of echoes in contemporary thought, but even aside from this it once more leads to the conclusion that Beauvoir is looking beyond the categories of her philosophical heritage. Even though Beauvoir stubbornly clings to that philosophical heritage, the import of her book is to reveal its inability to deal with the advent of women into philosophy.

IV. Interpreting Beauvoir

How Beauvoir's extensive writings should be assessed has been a controversial issue since they first came to the attention of feminists. Even if one focuses on the philosophical writings, as I do here, it is difficult to sort through the different waves of criticism that have emerged over the years. It is obvious to anyone who wades through these criticisms that feminists have not arrived at a consensus on her work. My intent in the following is not to establish the true meaning of Beauvoir's corpus but to try to make sense out of what Beauvoir has to say about the feminine subject and how that understanding has shaped ours.

One of the recurring themes in Beauvoir criticism is the charge of masculinism. Beauvoir, it is claimed, uncritically adopts the philosophical heritage of her contemporaries, particularly that of Sartre, and, most importantly, fails to contest the masculinism that pervades these philosophies. On one level this criticism is irrefutable. Beauvoir clearly starts from the basic premises of existentialism and phenomenology to frame her discussions. But, as I have tried to illustrate above, this is only one aspect of her approach. She begins with the basic terminology of these masculinist philosophies but, in the course of her analysis, finds them wanting. What emerges from this is by no means clear-cut. It does not result in a definite rejection of her philosophical heritage or her articulation of an alternative, but, rather, a destabilizing of the assumptions and categories of the original philosophies.

Much of the discussion of Beauvoir's philosophical position revolves around an analysis of where she stands relative to the influential philosophies of her day. Lundgren-Gothlin, for example, argues that *The Second Sex* should be interpreted from the perspective of Sartrean philosophy, but also as influenced by Hegelianism, Marxism, and phenomenological existentialism (1996: 3). Thus, there is much discussion in the Beauvoir literature about her relationship to these various schools of thought, noting the elements in her work that relate to each respectively.[4] Again, there is a sense in which these commentaries are correct; the influence of these philosophical positions is irrefutable. What is significant about Beauvoir's work, however, is how she departs from the masculinist philosophical tradition, not how she conforms to it. This departure is, I am arguing, at the heart of Beauvoir's approach.

It should not be surprising that many commentators on Beauvoir and *The Second Sex* focus on her relationship to Sartrean existentialism. Here there does seem to be a consensus of sorts: that Beauvoir has moved away from the strict existentialist ontology that Sartre articulated. There is a veritable chorus of critics who place Beauvoir outside of Sartrean existentialism. Pilardi claims that *The Second Sex* "greatly weakens existential ontology" (1991: 148). Grosholz asserts that Beauvoir's consideration of women's oppression "draws her out of existentialism" (2009: 202). Karen Vintges goes so far as to claim that Beauvoir's departure from Sartre places her close to the postmoderns (1996: 5).[5]

What these critics claim, in short, is that Beauvoir starts with Sartrean existentialism but she does not end with it. What is important about these criticisms is what the critics identify as the locus of Beauvoir's departure from Sartre. Beauvoir finds a particular aspect of Sartre's ontology wanting: the abstract subject. At the heart of Sartre's

[handwritten marginal note: defining her by the man in her life . . .]

existentialism, particularly as articulated in *Being and Nothingness*, is an isolated consciousness who is the source of knowledge.[6] It is this aspect of Sartre's ontology that Beauvoir comes to reject. For her, subjects are situated (I will have more to say about this later), and necessarily connected to other subjects. The subject that emerges from the analysis of *The Second Sex* is situated, connected, and embodied, not isolated and alone. Sonia Kruks states this very forcibly: "The embodied subject of *The Second Sex* is social through and through, a gendered subject whose freedom is situated, at best partial, at worst rendered immanent" (2001: 49).

In 1987, Toril Moi commented that if we were to escape the current political and theoretical dead ends, feminism in the 1990s could not afford to ignore Beauvoir's pioneering insights (1987: 204). At the heart of Beauvoir's relevance is a concept that permeates *The Second Sex* and defines its departure not only from Sartre, but from the other philosophical influences at work in her writings: situation. In *The Prime of Life* Beauvoir wrote: "I have attempted to show in my book *The Second Sex* why a woman's situation still, even today, prevents her from exploring the world's basic problems" (1962: 38). There is a lot packed into this apparently simple statement. The consideration of women brings about profound changes. Their unique situation in human society necessitates a concept of freedom that departs not only from Sartre's individualism, but, more broadly, from the pillar of modern philosophy, the Cartesian cogito. What is required is a philosophy that begins with humans in particular situations, not individuals as abstract entities. But it goes deeper than this. Since its inception, philosophy has sought to tackle human beings' "basic problems," to develop a universal, absolute theory that defines knowledge itself. What Beauvoir seems to be suggesting here is that this may not be possible, or, alternately, may not be the appropriate task of philosophy. And, again, it is her reflection on women's situation that has led her to this conclusion. In an interview with Margaret Simons, Beauvoir asserts that she is not a philosopher because a philosopher is someone who creates a system, which, she asserts, she has not done. Her intent lies not in the big picture but in the specifics of woman's situation (Simons 1999: 11).

I am not alone in focusing on the concept of situation in Beauvoir's work.[7] Among these commentators, the works of Sonia Kruks and Toril Moi stand out. Kruks argues that in *Being and Nothingness* Sartre cannot account for the existence of social groups of various kinds, of social organizations and structures. In contrast, Beauvoir as early as *The Ethics of Ambiguity* argues that freedom needs an open future that only others can give me, that subjectivity cannot exist without intersubjectivity (Kruks 1990: 92). As a consequence, in *The Second Sex* Beauvoir develops a concept of being as embodied subjectivity that is always intersubjective. Kruks argues that Beauvoir's work implied that the notion of subjectivity must be rethought in terms of the significance of the body and the weight of social institutions for human situation (Kruks 1990: 17). I want to take Kruk's insight a step farther and assert that Beauvoir did indeed rethink subjectivity on the basis of her analysis of the situation of women in *The Second Sex*. She found that woman's situation prevents her from embracing the kind of freedom that Sartrean existentialism identified. What Beauvoir discovered in her analysis of women's situation is that there are situations against which individual action is powerless. Sartre is wrong. There are situations, and that of women is one of them, in which the individual is so constrained by circumstances that she cannot achieve freedom. It follows that we need a radically different concept of freedom to encompass this.

Moi's discussion of situation in Beauvoir is even more pointed. Moi argues that Beauvoir's statement that the body is a situation is a completely original contribution to feminist theory that provides an alternative to contemporary sex and gender theories (1999: 59). The body as situation is deeply related to the individual's subjectivity; it is not outside of her, but is bound up with the way she uses her freedom. The body is engaged in a dialectical interaction with its surroundings. For Moi, Beauvoir is at root an existentialist: we must take the fact of women's concrete existence as our starting point for philosophy (1999: 189). Again, I agree, but I want to push this thesis further. As Kruks points out, although Beauvoir started with existentialism, she ultimately found it wanting. Her move into more original philosophical territory constitutes the significance of her position.

In her commentary on Beauvoir's *The Second Sex* Judith Butler echoes these arguments. "Beauvoir's dialectic of self and other argues the limits of a Cartesian version of disembodied freedom and criticizes implicitly the model of autonomy upheld by these masculine gender norms" (1987: 133). She goes on to assert that Beauvoir suggests an alternative to the gender polarity of masculine disembodiment and feminine enslavement to the body with the notion of body as a situation. On this reading, the body is a material reality that has already been located within a social control; the body is the situation of having to take up and interpret that set of received interpretations (1987: 133).

Butler then goes on to take her interpretation of Beauvoir into territory that has become the central focus of her own work. For Beauvoir, Butler claims, we are culturally constructed but in some sense we also construct ourselves. For Beauvoir, becoming a woman is a project, a set of acts. The problem becomes, then, how gender can be a matter of choice *and* a cultural construction. To address this problem, Butler turns again to the issue of situation. One *is* one's body from the start and one becomes one's gender; the movement from sex to gender is internal to embodied life, a sculpting of the original body into a cultural form. It does not follow, however, that gender is traceable to a definable origin because gender is an originating activity incessantly taking place. Gender is a way of organizing past and future cultural norms, a way of situating oneself in those norms, a style of living as one's body in the world.

To choose a gender is to interpret received gender norms in a way that reproduces and organizes them anew (Butler 1987: 128–31).

Anyone familiar with Butler's arguments in *Gender Trouble* (1990a) will see a striking similarity between her interpretation of Beauvoir and the discussion of sex and gender in that book. It is tempting to write off Butler's argument as an attempt to enlist a powerful ally for her position. But there is more to Butler's argument than this intention. The elements of Beauvoir's understanding that Butler cites are not her invention. Beauvoir's analysis of the relationship between sex and gender is complex. She does not define the dichotomy between sex and gender as mirroring that between nature and culture, a position frequently attributed to her.[8] Rather, she begins with the situated character of women's lives as a way of understanding the possibility of freedom for women. Her conclusion is that women cannot remove themselves from this situation but instead are forced to conform to the norms that structure that situation. Although Beauvoir would not go so far as to assert, as Butler does in *Gender Trouble*, that gender produces sex rather than vice versa, Butler is right to see the elements of her argument in Beauvoir's theory.

V. Conclusion

In *All Said and Done*, Beauvoir asserts:

> If I were to write *The Second Sex* today I should provide a materialistic, not an idealistic, theoretical foundation for the opposition between the Same and the Other. I should base the rejection and oppression of the Other not on antagonistic awareness but upon the economic explanation of scarcity. (1974: 483–4)

Much has been written about the problem of transcendence in Beauvoir's work. There are passages in *TSS* in which she seems to be arguing that women must transcend the problems created by the Same/Other. This passage seems to repudiate that argument. A better reading, however, might be that Beauvoir was conflicted about this issue but, in her later work, tended more toward a materialist view. In the current era of the "new materialism" this passage resonates strongly with contemporary feminists.[9] After decades of linguistic monism, feminists are bringing the material back into feminist theory and practice and, we hope, thereby enriching feminist theory. This passage evokes the theme that characterizes this latest wave of feminist theory. But, of course, it would be a serious anachronism to label Beauvoir a materialist in the sense we mean it today. It would not be anachronistic to assert, however, that Beauvoir, like the new materialists, defines the identity of women as a complex mix of cultural and material factors. The fact her position has much in common with that of the new materialists, thus, is significant. It is important to our contemporary understanding of both Beauvoir's position and the feminine subject.

At the beginning of this chapter I posed the question of why we should still read Beauvoir and whether we can say anything significant about her work in a contemporary context. On the basis of the foregoing analysis I can now answer those questions. First, what I think is of enduring significance in Beauvoir's work is that, through her analysis, she revealed that bringing the question of woman into the philosophical canon essentially deconstructs that canon. Women don't fit. They explode the categories that have defined philosophy since its inception. Beauvoir never states this directly and her work can seem, and is, confused on basic issues. But this confusion has a cause and that cause is the radical nature of what she is doing. Although it is possible to see glimpses of the radical direction necessitated by the topic of women in previous thinkers, Beauvoir brings this out in the open and makes it the centerpiece of her work.

I am not alone in making this argument. Linda Singer asserts that by naming sex and sex differences as repressed structures of philosophical discourse, Beauvoir recasts the nature and scope of philosophical discourse (Singer 1990: 324). Nancy Bauer argues that in *The Second Sex* Beauvoir dramatizes the extent to which being a woman poses a *philosophical* problem (2001: 1).[10] But overall I do not think that the revolutionary character of Beauvoir's work has been fully appreciated. Ever since Beauvoir, feminists have been arguing about the identity of the subject, how we can best characterize the conundrum of woman. I think that Beauvoir's work reveals clearly and forcefully why "woman" has been so problematic. We can approach the question from the perspective of various philosophers, but none of them will be satisfactory because "woman" does not fit into the work of any of them. We are forced, in a sense, to start over, to reinvent what we are doing as women in philosophy, and, perhaps, in the process to reinvent philosophy.

The second advantage of reading Beauvoir today is closely connected to the first: her emphasis on situation. What Beauvoir found at the center of her investigation of women was that it was impossible to separate woman from her situation in society. This situation defines everything: her identity, the possibility of freedom, the possibility of change. Situation gives feminist investigation, particularly feminist investigation of the subject, its grounding. Although other philosophers – most notably the embodied subjectivity of Merleau-Ponty – also had a focus in situation, Beauvoir's approach is distinctive. Woman's situatedness is the starting point of feminist philosophy, an endeavor that defines a whole new approach in philosophy.

Finally, it is impossible not to connect Beauvoir's focus on situation to the contemporary feminist interest in the material. I am not arguing that Beauvoir's approach presages that of material feminism, but only that there is an affinity between the two and that this affinity is significant. Beauvoir's approach is multifaceted rather than monolithic. Her analysis in *The Second Sex* rejects the monism of biology, economics, anthropology, or any other single approach. This rejection of monism also characterizes the current approach of material feminism. As philosopher of science Andrew Pickering puts it, knowledge is a mangle, a complex mix of disparate forces in which no one element predominates. In *The Second Sex* Beauvoir teaches us that the identity of woman is a mangle, that no one element of her identity is alone constitutive, that the factors intra-act to form the whole. Today's new materialists are relearning this maxim.

In what follows I will use this interpretation of Beauvoir as a springboard for my analysis of subsequent theorists. In every case I will ask how these theorists continue Beauvoir's legacy of radically redefining "woman" outside the philosophical canon. I will also ask how this redefinition effects the definition of the political subject. My argument is that redefining "woman" is a cumulative process begun by Beauvoir and one that is ongoing. What "woman" is will continue to evolve as feminism itself evolves.

– 2 –

Difference I
The "French Feminists"

Strictly speaking, "women" cannot be said to exist.

Julia Kristeva

Woman does not have a sex.

Luce Irigaray

I. Introduction

Beauvoir's *The Second Sex* set the agenda for subsequent feminist theory: redefine "woman" outside the parameters of western thought. That this was a monumental task was clear to Beauvoir. It became even more clear to those who followed her. Where should we start? Without the grounding of western thought, feminists were adrift, lacking direction. This is particularly true with regard to the subject. Rejecting the pillar of modernist thought – the Cartesian subject – left a void in feminist thought. How it could be filled was the task of those who followed Beauvoir.

I begin my analysis with what has been dubbed the "Holy Trinity" of French feminists, those theorists who took up the mantle of feminism immediately after Beauvoir.

Luce Irigaray, Julia Kristeva, and Helene Cixous saw themselves as correcting Beauvoir's errors and boldly moving into new territory. They claimed that Beauvoir had not sufficiently broken away from the tradition but, rather, was still bound to its humanist assumptions. They also objected to Beauvoir's disdain for psychoanalysis. Unlike Beauvoir, they put psychoanalysis at the center of their work. These theorists thus fit into one aspect of my thesis very neatly: they define Beauvoir's conception of "woman" as flawed and their own as correcting her errors. But it is also possible to interpret these theorists in another light: as picking up where Beauvoir left off. As one of the commentators on these theorists argues: "One of the primary objectives of *TSS* was to demonstrate the inadequacies of all existing systems of thought when they addressed themselves to the woman question" (Marks and Courtivron 1980: 8). This leaves the field wide open for a new definition; the French feminists moved quickly into that field. They embraced the realization, also shared by Beauvoir, that the feminist vision required, quite literally, a new form of life (Fraser 1992: 2).

To say that much has been written about the French feminists (a misnomer because none were born in France and all had an ambiguous relationship to feminism) is a huge understatement. My intent here is not to survey all they have written and all that has been written about them, an impossible task in any event. My goal, rather, is to sketch how they take up Beauvoir's challenge to create the feminine subject outside the confines of western thought. My argument is that Irigaray, Kristeva, and Cixous continue Beauvoir's legacy by exploring what she only sketches: a radically new approach to "woman." Although each of these theorists claims to be rejecting or at least transcending Beauvoir's thought, in a broader sense they are following the path that Beauvoir defined. All would concur with Marguerite Duras's summary of their task: "Reverse everything. Make women the point of departure in judging; make darkness the point of departure in what men call light, make obscurity the point of judging what men call clarity" (1980: 174).

Two assumptions unite the work of these thinkers, assumptions that are implicit rather than explicit in Beauvoir's work. The first is that the phallocratic system of western culture is fundamentally oppressive and leaves no place for woman to be a subject. This, of course, was the principal thesis of *TSS*. The French feminists concur. Irigaray in particular devotes much of her early work to painstakingly detailing the phallocratic nature of western culture. The second assumption is entailed by the first: we must start over, create a "new history" in which women are coming into history as women (Gauthier 1980: 200). Alice Jardine, characterizing the French feminists' task as "gynesis," asserts that these feminists were diving into the wreck of western culture (1985: 153): "The demise of the Subject, of the Dialectic, of Truth has left modernity with a *void* that it is vaguely aware must be spoken differently and strangely: as women through gynesis" (1985: 154). The philosopher Michele Le Doeuff breaks the task down into two questions. Can we make philosophy accept its intrinsic incompleteness? And is it possible to transform the relationship of the subject to the philosophical enterprise (1987: 206–7)?

The French feminists who followed Beauvoir, then, realized, as she did, the enormity of the task before them. This goes a long way toward explaining not only the differences among them but also what, from the perspective of the twenty-first century, appear to be the oddities of their work. There is a paradox here. On one hand, the path is clear: reject phallocentric thought and devise a radically new way of conceptualizing "woman." On the other hand, the path is directionless and thus far from clear. All we know is that we should avoid phallocentrism. But what we should embrace has yet to be defined.

There are two issues prominent in the commentary on the French feminists that I will sidestep. The first is their reliance on psychoanalysis in light of Beauvoir's suspicion of it. Irigaray and Kristeva were practicing psychoanalysts

and put psychoanalysis in the forefront of their work;
Cixous relies heavily on Freud. I do not perceive this as a
problem for my thesis. Beauvoir left the path out of phallocentrism open. That one direction of this path should
include psychoanalysis is not contradictory despite the fact
that she did not favor this direction.[1] The second issue is
essentialism. I will not make a sustained argument against
the many commentators who have claimed that these theorists are essentialist. Instead, as I go through their theories,
it will become clear that their understanding of "woman"
is not essentialist but, rather, deconstructs the very notion
of essentialism. If, as these theorists clearly state, they are
rejecting western thought then they are also, of necessity,
rejecting the essentialism which is one of the central pillars
of that thought. This issue, despite its prominence in the
literature, is wrong-headed.

II. Irigaray

Irigaray begins *Speculum of the Other Woman* with a
quote from Freud: "Ladies and Gentlemen...Throughout
history people have knocked their heads against the riddle
of the nature of femininity" (1985a: 13). This quote sets
the tone for all of Irigaray's work. The pattern of that work
can be described very simply despite its complexity. Her
first trajectory is a detailed analysis of the work of some
of the pillars of western thought – here Freud and Plato,
in other places the major figures of the western canon – and
an explication of how their work approaches the question
of woman. Her answer is always the same: woman is the
Other, a void, a lack, a marginalized element. There is,
quite simply, no place for woman in western thought.
Her second trajectory is just as straightforward: what is
required is to:

Turn everything upside down, inside out, back to
front. Rack it with radical convulsions...Insist also and

silencing + rendering invisible of
women makes trad. W thought
(by default) cultural "work"
Difference I: The "French Feminists" 31

deliberately on those *blanks* in discourse that recall the
place of exclusion and which by their *silent plasticity*,
ensure the collusion, the articulation, the coherent expan-
sion of established forms. (1985a: 142)

If the ontological status of woman makes her incomplete
and incompletable (1985a: 165) then we need to start over
again. We need to radically alter the philosophical heritage
that we have received and find another way.

It is central to Irigaray's approach, however, that we
fully understand the nature of this philosophical heritage,
to explore the "blanks" in the discourse, before we can
move beyond it. So much of her work is devoted to a
careful analysis of the tradition she is rejecting. *Speculum*
begins with an extended analysis of Freud. One of her
themes here and elsewhere is what she calls "The Old
Dream of Symmetry," the assumption of male/female symmetry that dominates western thought. One of the consequences of this dream is that "any theory of the subject
has always been appropriated by the masculine" (1985a:
133). When her analysis turns to Plato she emphasizes the
deep-rootedness of the conception of Truth that grounds
the western tradition, the removal of Truth from the sensible world. All of this leads to her conviction that the
sensible, maternal feminine does not fit into this tradition:
it is a "hole." The philosopher is

Detached from human passions that hold others captive
still, but left in contemplation that wall him in on every
side, separating him from everything by projection screens;
and he can no longer perceive that they are playing a part.
(1985a: 363)

Irigaray continues these themes in *This Sex Which Is
Not One*. What was left for me to do, she comments, was
to "have an orgy with the philosophers" (1985b: 147).
Combining what I have defined as her two trajectories, she
asserts that by beginning with Freud and proceeding to
Plato she confounds the linearity of an outline, the

teleology of discourse. Her goal is not to topple the order or replace it, but to disrupt and modify it from an outside that is exempt from phallocratic law (1985b: 68). It is necessary to reopen the figures of philosophical discourse in order to pry out of them what they have borrowed that is feminine.

Initially, she claims, there is only one path: mimicry. We must convert a form of subordination into affirmation and thus begin to thwart it (1985b: 74–6). To speak about women entails a recuperation of the feminine within a logic that maintains its representation (1985b: 78).

> The issue is not one of elaborating a new theory of which woman could be the *subject* or the *object*, but of jamming the theoretical machinery itself, of suspending its pretension to the production of truth and of a meaning that are excessively univocal. (1985b: 78)

Key to jamming the theoretical machinery is language. The focus on language is a common theme among the French feminists. This alone is significant. But it is significant as well for future feminist theory that will turn increasingly to the issue of language. Our task, Irigaray claims, is to redefine language in such a way that it leaves space for the feminine. Every dichotomy must be disrupted. We must proceed in such a way that linear reading is no longer possible (1985b: 79–80). We can do without models, standards, examples. Let's never claim to be right; if one of us sits in judgment our existence comes to an end (1985b: 217). Women's relationship to language is not the same as that of men. Women make their entry by producing a river, a dance, a rhythm, a song. It follows that we have to be creative, to carve out a space for the feminine in language that does not now exist. What this amounts to is the most profound danger imaginable: the overturning of philosophical discourse itself.

Irigaray is keenly aware of the enormity of her task. Her outline of how we might effect this change is, however, very sketchy. But she does indicate where this change must start: by emphasizing sexual difference. "Sexual difference is one of the important questions of our age, if not in fact the burning issue" (1987: 118). It is, in a Heideggerian sense, the issue that defines our age; it is probably that issue in our own age that could be our salvation on an intellectual level. "Sexual difference would represent the advent of new fertile regions as yet unwitnessed at all events in the West" (1987: 118). "For the work of sexual difference to take place a revelation in thought and ethics is needed" (1987: 119). The transition to this new age, furthermore, also requires a new understanding of time and space; time must redeploy space.

At the root of the problem of sexual difference is the fact that woman as subject is missing from the western tradition. That tradition presupposed the symmetry of the sexes, the "old dream of symmetry," that obliterated the identity of women. Rejecting this, Irigary tries to define the female subject as distinct, different. We must reinterpret the relationship between the subject and discourse, the subject and the world, in the new world we are creating (1987: 119). Irigaray's goal, as Elizabeth Grosz puts it, is to represent woman "otherwise" than in phallocratic terms (1989: 110).

In *This Sex Which Is Not One* (1985b) Irigaray famously defines this "otherwise" of woman as "not one" because she does not have one sex organ, one sexuality. Rather, she touches herself all the time because her genitals are formed with two lips that are always in contact. Thus, within herself, she is already two (1985b: 24). When a woman touches herself, furthermore, this self-touching gives her a form that is infinitely transformed – metamorphoses occur (1985a: 233). It follows that women's desire, which has been submerged by the logic that has dominated the west, speaks a different language from men's. The key to this desire is touching, not seeing. It is a desire that is both nothing and at the same time everything (1985b: 25–30).

[margin handwritten note: western tradition of presupposing symmetry obliterates identity of women]

The nature of woman's desire, however, is thwarted by women's relationship to language. Since woman's only access to language is through masculine systems of representation, there is no possible law for their pleasure. What is needed, Irigaray claims, is a feminine syntax, a syntax that would have neither subject nor object, no proper meanings, names, or attributes. By speaking as woman, one may attempt to provide a place for the other as feminine (1985b: 95, 132–5). What I want, Irigaray concludes, is not to create a theory of woman, but to secure a place for the feminine in sexual difference. Women must *practice* this difference (1985b: 159). "If we don't invent a language, if we don't find our body's language, it will have too few gestures to accompany our story" (1985b: 214). And: let us hurry and invent our own phrases (1985b: 215).

The discussion thus far describes the aspect of Irigaray's work that is most familiar to Anglo-American feminists. The two lips, jamming the theoretical machinery, and the creation of a feminine syntax have become the icons of Irigaray scholarship. But if we trace the logic of these concepts the next step in Irigaray's trajectory is obvious: she needs to outline the nature of the transformation that she has declared as necessary. If we jam the theoretical machinery, what do we do next? What will a feminine syntax look like? In the work that Irigaray has produced since the mid-1990s she has begun to answer these questions. In *Sexes and Genealogies* Irigaray proclaims: "To achieve a different social order women need a religion, a language, and a currency of exchange, or else a non-market economy" (1993c: 79). Also needed are ethical and cultural transformations of our attitudes to sexual difference (1993c: 172). In *An Ethics of Sexual Difference* this comes out as the need to construct a world in all its dimensions. A world for women has never existed, she concludes, yet it is already present though repressed (1993a: 109).

Again, the logic of Irigaray's thought propels her to go in a particular direction. If we need to create a new order the obvious place to start is politics. And this is exactly where Irigaray goes. What Irigaray has claimed all along is that we need a new definition of the female subject that is not subsumed under the masculine. Now this redefinition takes a new turn. We must redefine the subject, she asserts, as at least two and not one. The difference between men and women, the recognition that the subject is two, not one, appears as a model for a new era in history. At this crossroads humanity can be reborn (2001: 6–29).

This is where politics comes in: "The step that women have to take is to obtain positive rights of citizenship in female mode" (2001: 38). Democracy begins through a civil relationship, protected by rights, between a man and a woman, a male citizen and a female citizen. Women's natural form of identity in the family must be transformed into a civil identity. "A real democracy must take as its basis, today, a just relationship between man and woman" (2001: 118). Interestingly, Irigaray faults Beauvoir on this point. Beauvoir, she claims, by accepting the singularity of the masculine subject, can find no place for the truth. What Irigaray is arguing is that if we posit two subjects rather than one, the problem of the other disappears (2001: 123).

Irigaray assures us that reaffirming that man and woman are really two different subjects does not bring them back to biological destiny. Her point is that men and women have a relational, cultural identity that is held between nature and culture (2002: 128–9). One of the chapters in *Democracy Begins Between Two* is "A Two-Subject Culture." The "being two" that Irigaray advocates results in a new way of being together for the community and for society; it represents a new ontology, a new ethics, and a new politics (2001: 141).

Creating this new civil identity for women would require legal changes, specifically a constitution that recognizes two kinds of citizens. Irigaray participated in a movement to change the constitution of the European Union to recognize dual citizenship. She also advocated steps to promote recognition for a relationship that, she claims, is

central to the creation of a new order: the mother–
daughter relationship. She advocated putting up images –
photographs, paintings, sculpture – of mother–daughter
couples in all public places. Her conviction is that to re-
establish elementary social justice, to save the earth from
subjugation to males, we must restore the missing pillar of
our culture: the mother–daughter relationship (1994: 112).

In a recent collection, *Returning to Irigaray* (Cimitile
and Miller 2007), the editors asked the authors in the collection to answer this question: is there a unity in Irigaray's
work or a "turn" from the early psychoanalytic writings
to the more political later writings? Most of the authors
in the collection argue against a turn in Irigaray's thought
and for its unity. I think this assessment is correct. Calling
for a radically transformed world, Irigaray was forced to
turn to politics to effect that transformation. But I think
the authors missed an opportunity to ask a more important question: what is the value and/or validity of her later
work? In today's intellectual climate, particularly for feminists, arguing for universality, even if it is divided in two,
is difficult to accept. Early in *Democracy Begins Between
Two*, Irigaray argues that recognizing that men and women
are different from each other leads to the recognition of
other forms of diversity (2001: 12). But this nod to diversity is lost in her subsequent work: the emphasis is on a
universality of two. This position flies in the face of contemporary feminist thought. It is difficult if not impossible
to maintain this universality in light of the evident and
abundant diversity of both men and women. There are
many good reasons why diversity is at the forefront of
contemporary feminist thought. Sidestepping this diversity,
as Irigaray does here, is hard to justify.

Another objection is the practicality of her political
approach. It is not surprising that the EU rejected the suggestion of dual citizenship and dual rights. I shudder to
think what kind of reception this would have received in
the US. And putting up images of mothers and daughters
is unlikely to have the effect Irigaray desired. In the US it

would likely only cause confusion and derision. I think a better assessment of Irigaray's recent work is that it is not as valuable as her early, pathbreaking work on the subject.

Finally, what have we learned from that early work on the subject? What is Irigaray's legacy? Irigaray's major contribution is to clearly distinguish this subject from the masculine subject: "she is beyond all pairs, all opposites, all distinctions between actual and passive, or past and future" (1985a: 230). She is neither open nor closed and this incompleteness allows her to become something else (1985a: 229). What we are left with is what we might call a "blurred" identity, an identity that is indistinct and never "right" (Quick 1992). This identity is, furthermore, the antithesis of the essential identity with which Irigaray is sometimes associated. Women are different from men, "otherwise," and it is imperative that women practice this difference. They do so, among other things, by creating a feminine syntax, a language that is apart from the masculine.

On the positive side, Irigaray's subject realizes the goal that both she and Beauvoir set for themselves: creating a distinctively feminine subject apart from the masculine. Irigaray's distinction is clear and forcefully argued; it is bold and inspiring. On the negative side, however, it is also indistinct. It is difficult to say who this subject is, what her qualities are, where her agency lies. What we know about her is primarily what she is *not*. Perhaps this is inevitable since the task Irigaray gave herself involved such a new area. But it is clear that there is still much work to be done on this subject, work that will be the focus of subsequent theorists.

III. Kristeva

Kristeva, like Irigaray, begins with the premise that the western tradition offers women no place to be subjects. Both follow Beauvoir in trying to find a way beyond the impasse of woman as "other." But, while Irigaray is much more concerned with a critique of the philosophical tradition, Kristeva focuses her attention almost exclusively on the psychoanalytic. Although one of her central concepts, the chora, is borrowed from Plato, it is located within a Freudian outline of subjectivity. Kristeva's work is immensely complex and extensive. I am interested in only a narrow slice of that work in which she makes what I see to be the most significant contribution to the redefinition of the feminine subject: the relationship between the semiotic and symbolic that she develops in *Revolution in Poetic Language* (1984) and other works from this period. In this work she offers a bold new understanding of the subject that escapes the trap of woman as "other" that Beauvoir defined.

Kristeva's text is a complex interweaving of three topics: poetic texts, political revolution, and the subject. Her thesis is that these elements are similar in important ways, ways that we can build on to produce radical change. She begins her analysis with the assertion that she will make use of notions from Freudian psychoanalytic theory to give the advances of dialectical logic a materialist foundation, a theory of signification based on the subject, his [sic] formation, and his corporeal, linguistic, and social dialectic (1984: 14). The parallel she wants to establish is stated at the outset: the text is a practice that brings about in the subject what political revolution brings about in society. The question she asks about the literary practice will be aimed at the political horizon from which this practice, she claims, is inseparable (1984: 17).

At the center of Kristeva's theory are four concepts: the symbolic, the semiotic, the chora, and the thetic. Defining these terms and explaining how they interact in Kristeva's theory is far from simple. The most straightforward is the symbolic. This is the realm of signification, of logic, of language, the linear world of rational thought. The semiotic, in contrast, introduces "wandering or fuzziness" into language. It is a mark of the working of drives, at the same

Reread + thetic, chora, etc

time instinctual and maternal; semiotic processes prepare
the future speaker for entrance into meaning, signification,
the symbolic (1980: 136). Semiotic processes constitute
what Kristeva calls a "presubject" (1987: 8). Kristeva is
adamant in insisting that because the subject is always
both semiotic and symbolic, no signifying system he [sic]
produces can be either exclusively semiotic or exclusively
symbolic (1984: 24). It is always a product of both.

The chora complicates this neat division. The drives,
Kristeva begins, articulate what we call a chora, a non-
repressive totality formed by the drives and their stases in
a motility that is as full of movement as it is regulated.
The chora is "essentially mobile and extremely provisional
articulation constituted by movements and their ephem-
eral stases" (1984: 25). All discourse moves with and
against the chora – it simultaneously depends upon and
refuses it. The chora is a rhythmic space which has no
thesis and no position. The chora is subject to a regulatory
process, but is different from symbolic law (1984: 26). The
genesis of the functions organizing the semiotic process
can be accurately elucidated only within a theory of the
subject that does not reduce the subject to one of understanding but rather opens up within the subject this other
scene of pre-symbolic functions (1984: 27).

Finally, the thetic: the thetic phase is the precondition
for the positing of language. The thetic phase marks the
threshold between the semiotic and the symbolic. The
semiotic chora is not the failure of the thetic but its precondition (1984: 48–50). The break in the signifying
process, the realm of signification, is the thetic. This break
produces the positing of signification; all enunciation is
thetic (1984: 43).

Where this leaves us, Kristeva asserts, is a "subject-in-
process/on trial" (1984: 37). It is never fixed, settled, but
always fluid. This is where the link to poetic language
comes in. Poetic language puts the subject-in-process/on
trial through a network of marks and semiotic facilita-
tions (1984: 58). But the most important product of the

subject-in-process is that it allows us to view the subject in language as decentering the transcendental ego. Kristeva's speaking subject is neither a phenomenological transcendental ego nor the Cartesian ego (1984: 30, 37). The stratified conception of signification that Kristeva develops enables us to articulate a powerful model of the human in which language is not divorced from the body. Kristeva argues that as speaking beings we have been divided, separated from nature. This split has left us with traces of pre- or translinguistic semiotic processes that are our only access to species memory (1987: 6–8).

The theme that runs through Kristeva's account is one of heterogeneity and destabilization. She points out that at the beginning of philosophy, before thought was constricted by the notion that language must reflect ideas, Plato spoke about the chora, a mobile, unstable receptacle prior to the One, metaphysically suggesting something nourishing and maternal (1987: 5). What she wants to do, ultimately, is to build on this heterogeneity, this instability. She wants to destabilize the Cartesian subject, reveal its underbelly, so to speak. Many critics of Kristeva have argued that she is positing a dualistic subject make-up of male (symbolic) and female (semiotic) elements. This is a much too simplistic reading of her work. Although there are some feminine elements in the semiotic and the chora, this is not their identity. Identity is always in process, on trial. What Kristeva is doing is, like Irigaray, mixing everything up, jamming the theoretical machinery. It is a different jamming from that proposed by Irigaray, but it is a jamming nonetheless. What we are left with is a subject that knocks the Cartesian subject off his pedestal. And this is what we are after as feminists in the tradition of Beauvoir.

There is, obviously, much more to Kristeva's work than this theory of the subject developed in her early work. As Kelly Oliver points out, more of Kristeva's work has been translated into English than any other of the "Holy Trinity" of French feminists (1993). For my specific purposes, however, this early theory is the most relevant, especially since the themes of destabilization and heterogeneity characterize the entirety of her work. In her famous essay "Woman's Time" Kristeva identifies a feminism that situates itself outside the linear time of identities and communicates through projection and revindication (1986b: 194). This is the feminism of the subject-in-process.

There are, obviously, significant similarities between Kristeva's subject and that of Irigaray. Both define a subject apart from the masculine realm of the western tradition. It is significant, however, that for Kristeva this subject pre-exists the masculine subject. This sets her subject apart from that of Irigaray and gives it a clearer definition. Her theory of the complex interplay among the symbolic, semiotic, thetic, and chora gives a shape to the subject that Irigaray's theory is lacking. The subject-in-process, like the blurred subject of Irigaray, does not have a definable identity. It is also, like Irigaray's subject, far from essentialist. But it has some substance, even materiality, that Irigaray's subject lacks.

IV. Cixous

Woman must write through their bodies, they must invent the impregnable language that will wreck partitions, classes, and rhetorics, regularities and codes, they must submerge, cut through, get beyond the ultimate reserve-discourse, including the one that, aiming for the impossible, stops short before the word "impossible" and writes it as "the end." (Cixous 1980: 256)

If woman has always functioned "within" the discourse of man, a signifier that has always referred back to the opposite signifier which annihilates its specific energy and diminishes or stifles its very different sounds, it is time for her to dislocate the "within," to explode it, turn it around, and seize it; to make it hers, containing it, taking it in her

own mouth, biting that tongue with her very own teeth
to invent for herself a language to get inside of. (Cixous
1980: 257)

Irigaray and Kristeva both assert that central to the redefinition of the female subject is creating a feminine language,
a feminine syntax that allows women to write the body.
They insist that we need to find a way around the hegemony of phallocentrism to give a voice to women. In the
work of Helene Cixous this insistence takes center stage.
While Irigaray and Kristeva focus on philosophy and psychoanalysis, Cixous focuses on writing. Freud is present
in her work, but her emphasis is going beyond phallocentrism to a place that we have yet to conceive. As Verena
Conley puts it, Cixous' move is related to a position of
excess. To free oneself from social and legal constraints
one has to gather courage to leap into the absolute. This
leap breaks us off from received social values (Conley
1992: 41–2).

The themes that Cixous pursues, particularly in *The
Newly Born Woman* (Cixous and Clement 1986), echo
those of Irigaray and Kristeva: the hegemony of phallocentrism, the absence of women, and the exploration of a
world without phallocentrism. But in Cixous there is an
anarchic quality to her exploration of these themes that is
missing in the other theorists. She states that woman, "like
the sorceress, is going to fly away. But this time no one
will know what she becomes" (Cixous and Clement 1986:
57). In Cixous there is danger present: when the line is
crossed, contagion is produced (ibid. 1986: 34).

Cixous begins, as do the other theorists, with Freud. She
asserts: "The Dark Continent is neither dark nor unexplorable" (1986: 68). She defines her task as moving beyond
Freud rather than, as he did, giving up on the nature of
women. Her first point is that the differences between men
and women are cultural, not anatomical. But then in a
move that would seem to contradict this, she refers to
woman's *jouissance* as woman's instinctual economy that

cannot be identified by man. This is very emblematic of the work of Cixous. If, on our way to the creation of a woman's language, we reject the rules of logic, this should not concern us. It becomes clear that Cixous' intent is to break down neat dichotomies like nature and culture. There is destiny (Freud's term) no more than there is nature. Rather, there are living structures caught in rigidly set historical limits so that it is impossible to imagine an elsewhere. We are currently living in a transitional period, she concludes. What we need to do is to invent another history (1986: 82–3).

But change cannot come without political transformation: "Difference would be a bunch of real differences" (1986: 83). In a move that is not popular with many feminists, Cixous asserts that the way out is bisexuality, an apparently paradoxical way of displacing and reviving the question of difference, of writing difference as feminine or masculine. Women's writing, in contrast to that of phallocentrism, goes on and on. It does not inscribe or distinguish contours. It refuses life nothing. At present defining a practice of writing is impossible. It will never be possible for this practice to be theorized, enclosed, coded.

> Women must write her body, must make up the unimpeded tongue that bursts partitions, classes, and rhetorics, orders and codes, must inundate, run through, go beyond the discourse with its last reserves, including the one of laughing off the word "silence." (1986: 94–5)

It is in these passages on women's writing that Cixous' anarchic tendencies come through most clearly. Woman " has always functioned within man's discourse, but now it is time to displace this within, to explode it, to overturn it, to grab it, to make it hers. Shoot through and smash the walls, she admonishes, run away with syntax: "To fly/steal is woman's gesture, to steal into language, to make it fly" (1986: 96). And, finally, there will not be *one* feminine discourse; there will be thousands of different kinds

The identity of "woman" created by man

of feminine words. There will be a code for general communication, philosophical discourse, rhetoric, like now, but with a great deal of subversive discourse (1986: 137).

Cixous first came to the attention of many American feminists in her rightly famous "Laugh of the Medusa," published in *Signs* in 1976. Apparent contradiction and rejection of dichotomies are strongly present in this work. Woman must write herself, Cixous declares. She must write about women and bring women to writing. Women have been driven away from writing as they have been from their bodies – with the same fatal goal. Woman must put herself into the text; the new breaks away from the old. I write this, she asserts, toward a "universal woman" subject – but there is no general woman. *Woman* must write woman (1976: 876–7).

And, again, the theme of transformation: woman must write herself because this is the invention of a new insurgent. Woman must carry out the indispensable rupture and transformations from her history. Defining a feminine practice of writing, she declares again, is impossible. But it will surpass the enclosure of the phallocratic system. We were told that the dark continent of woman is unexplorable – but we are exploring it and we find that everything has yet to be written about women and femininity. Feminine texts explode and dislocate; a feminine text cannot fail to be subversive (1976: 886–8).

It is significant that Cixous appeals to the image of Medusa in this essay. Her intent is obvious: to be subversive, startling, insurgent. Like Irigaray and Kristeva, Cixous is following Beauvoir's injunction to move beyond phallocratic discourse. Cixous' way of moving beyond – appealing to woman's language – is arresting but effective. Writing the body is not essentialist; it is disruptive. There is no universal woman or a single woman's language because there is no single woman's body. Male discourse ignores bodies. By bringing them into discourse she is in effect transforming that discourse.

What Cixous gives us, then, is yet another take on the feminine subject. Her subject is speaking, a move that is significant in the context of the hegemony of phallocentrism. She is speaking in a syntax that rejects linearity and the strictures of rationality and logic. She speaks from her body without appealing to the body's essence. But, like Irigaray's subject, her identity is blurred. We find out what she is *not* rather than what she is. In one sense, of course, this is appropriate. Fixed identities are the purview of the masculine, not the emerging feminine subject. But we are still left with a subject about whom we have more questions than answers.

V. Conclusion

In retrospect it is curious that the French feminists, as they have come to be known, have been identified as in opposition to Beauvoir. Both in their own work and in that of their critics they have been defined as moving away from Beauvoir's position and repudiating her erroneous stance, particularly as it regards the subject. There are several explanations for this. One is that the tone of their writing differs significantly from that of Beauvoir. While Beauvoir speaks in an existentialist/humanist syntax, these thinkers turn to psychoanalysis and literary theory to make their arguments. The work of Irigaray has much in common with the emerging perspective of deconstruction. Another explanation is generational. Several critics have suggested that these theorists felt the necessity of rebelling against the mother, particularly a mother with the status of Beauvoir. They had to define their work in opposition to hers in order to give it legitimacy.

As I have tried to demonstrate in the foregoing, however, this interpretation is shortsighted. If we define Beauvoir's work as, in a sense, throwing down the gauntlet by declaring the bankruptcy of the western tradition for women, then it seems obvious that what these theorists are doing is taking up that gauntlet. The task, as Beauvoir defined it, is enormous. We must jam the theoretical machinery and invent our own. We must disrupt and transform, create a new history and redefine "woman" in a radically new way. And this is precisely what these theorists do. They bravely set out on the new course defined by Beauvoir, although there are no guidelines for the path. Beauvoir defined the objective but not how we might achieve that objective.

It should come as no surprise, then, that these theorists differ from each other as much as they do from Beauvoir. Irigaray focuses on philosophy and psychoanalysis. She begins to explore the political implications of the transformed subject, a theme that will be taken up more strongly in subsequent work. Kristeva reinvents Freud's theory and Cixous tries to define a feminine syntax. But they all share, along with Beauvoir, two fundamental assumptions: that we must abandon the western tradition and that we must reinvent "woman" in radically new ways. It is easy to focus on the differences among these theorists as well as their departure from Beauvoir. These differences are real and significant. What I am suggesting here is another interpretation. All of these theorists are embarking on the daunting task of redefining woman. It will be a task that occupies feminist theory until the present. Instead of assuming that we will eventually get woman "right," it is more productive to see each attempt to define woman as adding another element to the conception that can be built on in future conceptions. Like constructing a structure in which additional rooms are added along the way, the conception of "woman" is additive: each new element fills in an element that was missing in previous conceptions.

An element that was glaringly missing in Beauvoir's account is politics. Although it is possible to extrapolate from her thesis that there is no place in the western tradition for women that this applies to politics as well, she does not make this specific. The theorists discussed here address this lack. Irigaray is the most specific. Her concept of dual citizenship, although not viable, is an attempt to deal with the exclusion of women from politics. Kristeva and Cixous do not specifically address politics, but there are political implications of their work. The instability and anarchy that mark their conceptions of the subject emphasize women's exclusion from politics. If women as defined in the western tradition have no place in politics, then our only alternative is anarchy. In an anarchic world men would not be in ascendency; nor would women be inferior. In the transformed world they imagine there would be no place for hierarchy, political or otherwise. That much more definition of the feminine political subject is needed, however, is obvious. And, as we move into the next stage of feminist theory, that definition will take center stage.

– 3 –

Difference II
Radical Feminism and the
Relational Self

(handwritten margin notes: Fundamentally different? or are we looking at (intersectionality))

(handwritten margin notes: hype w/ setting back to (woman))

I. Introduction

In 1985 Iris Marion Young published an article entitled
"Humanism, Gynocentrism, and Feminist Politics." The
thesis of her article is that, in the 1980s, feminism was in
the process of shifting from a Beauvoirian humanist feminism to what she calls a gynocentric feminism. She defines
humanist feminism as the belief that women's oppression
is rooted in the inhibition and distortion of woman's
human potential by men. Gynocentric feminism, on the
other hand, defines women's oppression as the devaluation
and repression of woman's experience by a masculinist
culture that exalts violence and individualism. It argues for
the superiority of values embodied in the traditional female
experience and rejects masculine values. Thus gynocentric
feminism, she concludes, is a more radical critique of
male-dominated society than humanist feminism. While
humanist feminism constitutes a revolt against femininity,
gynocentric feminism finds women's bodies and traditional
feminine activities as sources of value. It seeks to transform
the epistemology that created phallocentricity.

It should be clear from my analysis of Beauvoir in chapter 1 that I disagree with Young's characterization of Beauvoir as a humanist. Far from promoting a humanist feminism, Beauvoir rejects the masculinist (including humanist) tradition and argues for the redefinition of the subject in radically new terms. But I agree with Young that feminist thought shifted significantly in the late 1970s. While the French feminists who directly succeeded Beauvoir were "jamming the theoretical machinery" in distinctive ways, American feminists were taking another path to difference. Radical feminists were exploring issues such as gender and sexuality, reproduction, and biological motherhood, defining them as the source of women's oppression. Their approach to women's difference, in contrast to previous approaches, was oppositional and highly political. In another vein theorists such as Carol Gilligan, Mary Belenky, Sarah Ruddick, Nancy Chodorow, Joan Tronto, and Nel Noddings attempted to define women outside the masculine paradigm. The "relational self" that emerges from the work of these theorists shares two fundamental assumptions: that the self is formed in relationship to others and that this relational self stands in sharp contrast to the autonomous, separate, masculinist self. There is a great deal of overlap between these two trajectories of feminist thought and also a great deal of difference. What unites them is the effort to focus exclusively on "woman" and to celebrate the difference that woman represents.

II. Radical Feminism

"The personal is political."

Perhaps more than any other movement in feminism, radical feminism made an indelible mark on public consciousness. For many people outside the feminist movement radical feminism, even today, *is* feminism. It represents what feminism is all about and defines what a feminist is. Although this definition is, particularly today, far from accurate, the influence of the movement has been undeniable.

Why this is the case is the result of several related issues. Radical feminism is distinctive in its turn to the political to address feminist issues. But their approach to the political was far from typical. Their slogan, "the personal is political," attacked one of the sacred cows of liberalism: the separation of the public and the private. Radical feminists claimed that many, if not all, of the personal problems that women face are rooted in political institutions. This led them to assert that unless we break down the public/private distinction we will be unable to get at the underlying causes of women's oppression. But doing so would entail a radical restructuring of those political institutions.

In the spirit of Beauvoir, then, the radical feminists were exploring the roots of women's oppression, probing its underlying causes. But by turning to the political and linking it to the personal, their analysis goes deeper than that of Beauvoir. By identifying women's oppression as political – understood in a broad sense – the radical feminists reveal another aspect of that oppression that explains why it is so deep-seated. As Marilyn Frye puts it:

> There are reasons... why you should want to know whether the person filling your water glass or your tooth is male or female and why that person wants to know what you are, but those reasons are woven invisibly into the fabric of social structure and they do not have to do with the bare mechanics of things being filled. (1983: 27)

What is needed to remedy this is, as Mary Daly asserts, a transvaluation of values.

If there is any aspect of women's lives that seems quintessentially private it is to be found in the spheres of reproduction and sexuality. The radical feminists' exploration of these issues constitutes their most distinctive contribution to feminist thought. Overall, their thesis is that these "personal" areas of women's lives are not only the fundamental source of women's oppression, but also under strict patriarchal control. Beginning with Shulamith Firestone's *The Dialectic of Sex* (1970), many radical feminists focused on male control of women's reproduction and sexuality, identifying this control as the root cause of women's subordination. While Firestone argued that women should abandon motherhood to escape patriarchy, others argued that we need to reclaim motherhood and celebrate it as a uniquely valuable aspect of women's existence.[1] But in either case the argument was the same: women must wrest control of the most intimate aspects of their lives from males.

Closely connected to male control of reproduction is male control of female sexuality itself. Central to the radical feminist approach is the claim that men have constructed women's sexuality to serve men's, not women's, needs. This thesis became the centerpiece of what is probably the most famous, or infamous, aspect of radical feminism: Catherine MacKinnon's assault on pornography. MacKinnon argued that pornography, far from being a marginal aspect of social life, is the root cause of the inferior status of women in our society. The depiction of women as sexual objects in pornography, MacKinnon argued, affects all women, establishing and maintaining their subordination.

Although MacKinnon's attack on pornography is valuable politically, there is another aspect of her thesis that constitutes a significant insight into the feminine subject. In *Feminism Unmodified* MacKinnon asserts:

> To the extent pornography succeeds in constructing social reality, it becomes invisible as harm. If we live in a world that pornography creates through the power of men in a male-dominated situation, the issue is not what the harm of pornography is, but how that harm is to become visible. (1987: 174)

This statement, buttressed by numerous descriptions of how women are portrayed in pornography, takes the social construction of women into new territory. If, as

MacKinnon claims, reality is constructed by men's concepts, then displacing that reality becomes an almost insuperable task. If, as MacKinnon states elsewhere, sex is what women are *for*, how can women contest this reality? This is the question that Marilyn Frye addresses in *The Politics of Reality* (1983). Frye argues that what we know as reality is "that which pertains to the one in power" (1983: 155). To develop this thesis, she turns to J. L. Austin who describes this phenomenon in linguistic terms: "Our common stock of words embodies all the distinctions men have found worth drawing" (1983: 160). Frye unpacks this statement in feminist terms by pointing out, first, that it is *men* who create this common stock of words and, second, that those words are what construct reality for all of us. It follows that if that common stock of words defines women as sexual objects, then that creates reality for women. Furthermore, if that common stock of words ignores the existence of a particular group of women, lesbians, then lesbians do not exist and "speaking of women who have sex with other women is like speaking of ducks who engage in arm wrestling" (1983: 157).

Frye uses the metaphor of a play to illustrate her thesis. Men and what they do are in the foreground and constitute the reality of the play. Women are in the background, off the stage and invisible. Men, not women, act; what women do is not seen or conceptualized. The question Frye addresses is how to alter this situation, how to bring women into the foreground and make them participants in the action of the play. Frye does not have a simple answer to this question. Phallocratic reality, she asserts, is all powerful:

> All eyes, all attention, all attachment must be focused on the play, which is Phallocratic Reality. Any notice of the stagehands must be oblique and filtered through interest in the play. Anything which threatens the fixation of attention on the play threatens a cataclysmic dissolution of Reality into Chaos. (1983: 170)

The only option for woman, she concludes, is to become a "seer" – one whose eye is attracted to the ones working as stagehands: the women. A seer is disloyal to phallocratic reality; her disloyalty threatens it with utter dissolution. "Reality afloat begins to disintegrate" (1983: 171).

> The maintenance of phallocratic reality requires that the attention of women be focused on men and men's projects – the play; and that attention not be focused on women – the stagehands. Woman-loving, as a spontaneous and habitual orientation of attention is then, both directly and indirectly, inimical to the maintenance of that reality. And therein lies the reason for the thoroughness of the ontological closure against lesbians, the power of those closed out, and perhaps the key to the liberation of women from oppression in a male-dominated culture. (1983: 172)

The radical feminists' discussion of reality constitutes an important step in the understanding of "woman" but also introduces a disturbing complexity. While Beauvoir and those who followed her explored the myriad ways in which women are denigrated in the western tradition, Frye and MacKinnon add depth to this understanding. The language that, as Austin argues, creates reality for us either excludes women entirely or defines them solely in terms of what uses men can put them to. This thesis defines the problem women face as nearly insurmountable. As Frye makes clear, attacking Reality itself threatens Chaos. Perhaps Freud was right when he claimed that women are the enemies of civilization. Radical feminists have made this disturbingly clear.

III. The Relational Subject: Object Relations Theory

The grounding of many versions of the relational self lies in an unlikely source: male theorists of moral development writing in the mid-twentieth century. A number of psychologists loosely categorized under the label "object relations theorists" developed an approach to the subject that challenges the separate self of the psychological tradition rooted in Freud. Object relations theory seeks to describe a self that has no separate, essential core but, rather, becomes a "self" through relations with others. This concept of self jettisons the notion of a pre-existent ego. But, more radically still, object relations theory maintains that the separate, autonomous self that is the cornerstone of the modernist self is itself a product of relational forces.

Object relations theory clearly represents a departure in psychoanalysis and moral development theory. From a feminist perspective what is most significant about this theory is that it foregrounds the definition of self that has been defined as feminine, a connected, relational self. The separate self that represents the norm of selfhood in traditional theories is here defined as, like the relational self, a result of relational forces. Feminists, particularly feminist psychoanalysts, soon grasped the radical implications of object relations theory for the understanding of the female *and* male subject. Perhaps the most comprehensive analysis of object relations theory from a feminist perspective is that of Nancy Chodorow. In *The Reproduction of Mothering* (1978) Chodorow argues that the contemporary reproduction of mothering occurs through social structurally induced psychological processes. It is not biological or intentional role-taking that produces this effect but, rather, a process that draws on a psychoanalytic account of female and male personality development. Women, as mothers, produce daughters with mothering capacities and the desire to mother and produce sons whose nurturent capacities are curtailed. The conclusion of her analysis is sweeping: women's mothering reproduces the sexual and financial division of labor that structures our society (1978: 7).

To establish her theory Chodorow turns explicitly to object relations theory, filling in the implications for the feminine subject that its (male) proponents ignored. Object relations theory differs from other psychoanalytic theories, she asserts, because it claims that the child's social, relational experience from early infancy determines its psychological growth and personality foundation: "All aspects of psychic structure are socially constructed through a history of 'object choices'" (1978: 50). Because females and males experience different interpersonal environments as they grow up, feminine and masculine personality will develop differently. Women mother, but their mothering occurs in a social structure that defines the mother's gender expectations. Mothers develop mothering skills in their daughters but not their sons. This is a result of the differential object-relational experiences and the ways those experiences are internalized and organized. Because of their mothering by women, girls come to experience themselves as less separate than boys, as having more permeable ego boundaries. Because they are of the same gender, mothers do not experience daughters as separate from themselves; because they are of a different gender, however, they experience sons as separate (1978: 86–110).

Chodorow concludes that women's mothering produces asymmetries in the relational experiences of girls and boys that account for crucial differences in masculine and feminine personality and their relational capacities: "The basic feminine self is connected to the world, the basic masculine sense of self is separate" (1978: 169). Biology and instinct, she asserts, cannot account for why women mother: it is a result of social structure. "The relational basis for mothering is thus extended in women and inhibited in men, who experience themselves as more separate and distinct from others" (1978: 207).

Chodorow's thesis is focused around two claims. First, asserting that there is no biological or instinctual basis either for mothering or sexual identity challenges deeply ingrained assumptions in psychoanalysis. Second, asserting that the gender roles extant in our society are caused by the social structure of mothering radically alters our understanding of those gender relations. It entails that women – and men – are made rather than born. This understanding of the infant's relationship to the mother necessarily changes our understanding of gender relations, and, necessarily, gender asymmetry in our society. These are radical theses and Chodorow explores them effectively.

What she does not explore explicitly is an even more radical thesis: the displacement of the masculine subject as the norm of selfhood. If subjects are created through relational experiences in early childhood and if this is true for men as well as women, then the ascendancy of the masculine, autonomous, separate self is called into question. It is true that women's mothering, as Chodorow points out, causes asymmetries in adult gender relations, but the creation of the two genders is symmetrical. Both men's and women's gender identity is a result of relational experiences in early childhood. In this sense they are in a position of equality. But if this is the case it necessarily challenges the superiority of the separate self who turns out, ironically, not to be so separate after all. It will take another feminist, Carol Gilligan, to explore the full implications of this thesis.

IV. Gilligan and the Different Voice

In 1982 Carol Gilligan published an empirical and inter-pretive analysis of the decision-making process of a sample of girls and young women confronted with both hypotheti-cal and real-life moral dilemmas. Gilligan, a Harvard psy-chologist who specializes in moral development, challenged the influential approach of the moral development theorist Lawrence Kohlberg, who was also her teacher at Harvard. Against Kohlberg, Gilligan argued that the women and girls she interviewed articulated their moral dilemmas in a "different voice." Kohlberg's studies had concluded that women clustered at an inferior stage of moral develop-ment; few women attained what he defined as the highest stage of moral reasoning, Stage 6. In order to avoid the "distortion" that female subjects created, Kohlberg conducted his studies using primarily male subjects. Gilligan's study opposed Kohlberg's findings, as well as his interpretation of them. She attempted to define a separate but *different* equal moral sphere for the different voice and thus to *but equal* reform Kohlberg's theory by describing women as equals rather than inferiors.

It does not overstate the case to say that when it was published in 1982 Gilligan's work revolutionized discussions in moral theory, feminism, theories of the subject, and many related fields. *In a Different Voice* was unquestionably one of the most influential feminist books of the 1980s. It has been criticized and praised by feminists, moral philosophers, and moral psychologists. Gilligan's work has been hailed both as the harbinger of a new moral theory and as the final blow to the exhausted masculinist tradition of moral philosophy. It has also been condemned as methodologically unsound, theoretically confused, and even anti-feminist. Gilligan's critics and defenders have cast her, respectively, as either villain or savior in the ongoing intellectual debate of the 1980s and 1990s.

Thirty years after the publication of Gilligan's book and the commentary on it I would like to revisit her theory in light of the evolution of the subject in feminist theory. It is my contention that Gilligan, more so than the other relational theorists and the proponents of the object relations theory, offers a clear alternative to the masculine, autonomous subject and in effect removes that subject from its position of dominance. It is also my contention that Gilligan's contribution constitutes a significant step in the evolution of the feminine subject and deserves serious consideration by contemporary theorists. Gilligan does not explicitly attack the subject of modernist thought in her work. She is not a moral philosopher, she does not define her project in terms of a displacement of the Enlightenment moral subject. Yet her work contributes significantly to that displacement. Gilligan articulates a relational subject that is the product of relational experiences, a subject that undermines the very possibility of the autonomous, self-legislating agent.

Although Gilligan is not offering a new, fully developed moral philosophy, theory of the subject, methodology, or epistemology, the implications of her work have radical consequences in all these areas. She is not concerned with moral philosophy per se, yet her findings have led her to an understanding of the development of moral voices that undercuts the very foundation of modernist moral theory. Gilligan is not the only contemporary theorist to advance the concept of the relational subject; yet her description of the evolution of this subject's moral voice in gendered terms reveals the radical implications of the concept in unique ways. Her work is not explicitly methodological; yet her counter to Kohlberg's method suggests a definition of the relationship between truth and method that has implications for contemporary disputes in the philosophy of social science and feminist methodology. Gilligan, perhaps more than any other theorist since Beauvoir, is continuing in the tradition of Beauvoir by exploring how woman is made rather than born. Like Beauvoir, Gilligan challenges the hegemony of the masculine subject. Unlike Beauvoir, she takes the necessary next step: defining an alternative.

In the introduction to *In a Different Voice* (1982) Gilligan articulates the issues that will concern her both in that book and in her subsequent work. At the center of all these issues is what might be labeled the "woman problem": the fact that women fail to fit the existing models of human moral development (1982: 2). Beginning with Freud, theorists of moral development have cited the "failure" of woman's development (1982: 6). Piaget and other development theorists "solved" this problem by ignoring women and articulating a developmental theory based solely on the experience of men (1982: 10). Gilligan discusses how Erikson and Bettelheim skirted the issue by asserting that women's development is "different" from that of men, but showed little interest in defining the difference (1982: 12–13). It is precisely this "difference," however, that Gilligan wants to address. But the way in which she does so, even at this early stage in her thinking, indicates that she will be departing from the epistemological and methodological assumptions of her male predecessors. As her theory unfolds, it will emerge that she is not only challenging the hegemony of the masculine subject but also the understanding of truth and method that are tied to that hegemony. In the tradition of Beauvoir, Gilligan's work illustrates that subjectivity, truth, and method are inextricability intertwined. To challenge one is to challenge all.

The goal of the theories that Gilligan critiques is to find the "truth" of human moral development. Each of these theories employs the standard procedures of scientific method in order to attain this truth: hypotheses, factual evidence, empirical studies of representative subjects, and so forth. The most straightforward way to counter these theories from a feminist perspective is to assert that they are "biased" – that is, that they are incomplete – because they ignore the reality of women's experience. Following this line of argument, the solution to the problem appears to be quite simple: the theories should be completed by including women in the empirical studies, thereby supplying the missing element – women's development – and thus bringing them up to the standard of completeness and objectivity to which they aspire. Many passages of *In a Different Voice* suggest that this is precisely Gilligan's goal. She states that her intention is to yield a "more encompassing view of the lives of both of the sexes" (1982: 4), to find "the truth of women's experience" (1982: 62) and thus of human experience (1982: 63). She wants to force development theorists to "admit the truth of women's perspective" (1982: 98) because women's experience provides clues to the "central truth of adult life" (1982: 172). In what appears to be a direct appeal to the legitimizing force of standard scientific method, she argues that "by looking directly at women's lives over time, it becomes possible to test, in a preliminary way, whether the changes predicted by the theory fit the reality of what in fact takes place" (1982: 21). She concludes her study by asserting: "Yet in the different voice of women lies the truth of an ethic of care" (1982: 173).

Yet other elements in Gilligan's work suggest that her approach departs significantly from the methodological assumptions that inform the work of the theorists she examines and that her concepts of "truth" and "method" also differ significantly from theirs. At the outset, she notes that recent trends in social science have called into question the "presumed neutrality of science," recognizing instead that "the categories of knowledge are human constructions" (1982: 6). This almost offhand reference to an epistemology of science starkly opposed to that employed by standard developmental theorists continues to be a theme throughout the book. Gilligan defines woman's voice as "an alternative concept of maturity" (1982: 22) and a "new line of interpretation" (1982: 26). Women's experience, she asserts, is a "vision" that "illuminates" a hitherto unseen realm (1982: 62–3). At the end of the book she brings these reflections together with the assertion that women's "underdevelopment" according to previous, male-biased theories was a result of the construction of those theories and not of "truth" (1982: 171). She claims that her work on the different voice results in a "new perspective" on relationships, which changes the basic constructs of interpretation and consequently expands the moral domain (1982: 173).

These passages require a good deal of unpacking. Gilligan is here appealing to an alternative conception of scientific analysis, which radically shifts the terms of the debate in which she is engaged. Advocates of this alternative conception assert that the categories of analysis create the parameters of the data analyzed. Gilligan applies this perspective to moral development theory with startling results. She asserts that defining moral development in terms of the evolution of autonomous, separate selves who are eventually capable of applying abstract universal principles to moral problems produces a particular definition of the moral realm. This definition entails that only such autonomous subjects applying such abstract principles can be considered fully moral. It defines the "truth" of moral development as the evolution of moral subjects who meet these criteria. It also relegates the different voice of women to, at the very least, moral inferiority. A strict application of this theory yields an even harsher conclusion: that women, who fail to meet the criteria of fully moral subjects, do not inhabit the moral realm at all. What Gilligan proposes in her work is a radically different perspective on moral development, which results in an alternative definition of the moral realm. By developing this new concept of the moral subject, she redefines the "truth" of moral development and the constitution of morality itself. She proposes a dual vision of the moral realm, one in which two interacting and intertwining voices replace the unitary view.

This way of reading Gilligan contrasts sharply with the first reading I have suggested. On the first reading, Gilligan seems to be arguing that she is replacing one truth with another, attempting to correct the biased and incomplete masculinist theories of moral development by introducing a truer, more objective theory. On the second reading, however, she is doing something quite different. On this reading she is introducing a new interpretation of the moral realm, which wholly reconstitutes it. She is opposing the "truth" of the masculinist theories with other "truths." But if we interpret this statement in the context of the alternative scientific methodology, the conclusions that follow differ from those entailed by the first reading. Most important, it follows that Gilligan cannot claim that her interpretation is truer or more objective, because she has defined truth as a function of theoretical perspective. The "truth" that Gilligan claims for her perspective is thus a truth that is internal to the theoretical perspective itself, just as the "truth" of the dominant conception is internal to that perspective.

It is possible to interpret *In a Different Voice* from the perspective of either of these two readings. I employ the second reading in my analysis of Gilligan for a number of reasons. First, in the studies she has published since *In a Different Voice*, Gilligan quite explicitly adopts what I am calling the second reading, embracing an alternative scientific methodology that departs from standard empiricism. In these works she employs what, in the jargon of the philosophy of science, amounts to a coherentist scientific method. Second, employing the second reading of Gilligan accomplishes a redefinition of the moral realm and the reconstitution of moral theory. Defining the moral realm as constituted by conceptions of the moral subject and of morality itself fosters an approach that is pluralistic and non-hierarchical, an approach that highlights the constitution of moral voices. Third, the second reading emphasizes the necessary connection between method and truth – that is, that the method employed in the analysis of morality cannot be divorced from the moral truths that the method produces.

In chapter 3 of *In a Different Voice*, entitled "Concepts of Self and Morality," Gilligan ties her redefinition of the moral realm to a concept of self that challenges the autonomous self of the masculinist tradition. One of the major themes of Gilligan's work – and also one of her most significant contributions – is the claim that selfhood and morality are intimately linked. Gilligan argues that subjects develop moral voices as a function of the emergence of selfhood and that the definition of the moral realm is necessarily structured by the concept of self that informs it. Moral development theory as defined by Piaget and Kohlberg is grounded in the separate, autonomous self of the modernist tradition. This separate self is both the precondition and the goal of the moral stages that Kohlberg posits. Against this, Gilligan proposes a version of the relational self. She defines a self that is formed through relational patterns with others, particularly in the early years of childhood. Following the psychological approach of object relations theory, she describes the way in which girls, because they are not encouraged to separate from their mothers, develop a sense of self in which relationships are primary. Boys, by contrast, because they succeed in separating from their mothers, develop a sense of self as separate and autonomous. Thus, as a result of their different relationships with their mothers, girls develop relational skills and find autonomy problematic, while boys fear relationships but develop autonomy skills.

It is tempting to read Gilligan's argument about the constitution of the self in an empiricist vein. She seems to be proposing a corrective to the incomplete, erroneous, and biased view of the self propounded by masculinist theorists. These theorists listened to the accounts of male subjects only; Gilligan, by listening to women as well, can be interpreted as completing the faulty accounts of masculinist theorists. As is evident from the passages quoted above, there is evidence in the text for this interpretation: Gilligan several times refers to her goal as uncovering the "truth" of human development. But here, too, there are grounds for a second reading. At the very beginning of her account, Gilligan states that she is interested in listening to the "stories" that women tell about their lives (1982: 2). Her emphasis on narrative, listening, and voices introduces a different approach to the study of moral development, an approach that is incompatible with the empiricist studies she challenges.

Two points are crucial here. First, Gilligan is well aware that theorists such as Kohlberg have listened to women's stories, but, because they employed the interpretive framework of separate selves, they were forced to classify these stories as deficient and those who told them as lacking the qualities necessary for moral agency. What Gilligan is proposing is an alternative framework in which these women's stories are interpreted as genuine moral statements. If, as Gilligan proposes, we interpret relationship, care, and connection as integral to human life and development, then we will interpret women's stories as genuinely moral narratives, distinct from, but every bit as moral as, those based on abstract principles. Implicit in Gilligan's articulation of the different voice is the assumption that what we, as listeners, hear is a function of the different interpretation of the same moral experiences. These moral experiences, the voices of women that Kohlberg dismissed as deficient, Gilligan hears as genuine moral statements.

Second, Gilligan's use of the term "stories" here is significant. Kohlberg does not claim to be telling a "story" about moral development. The word "story" connotes fiction, whereas Kohlberg claims to be discovering an antecedently given truth. "Stories" suggests multiplicity, invention, interpretation; Kohlberg is searching for facts and evidence. By claiming that she is listening to women's "stories," Gilligan is advancing two key theses: first, that we need to alter our interpretive framework in order to hear these stories as moral stories, and, second, that women (and men) make sense of their lives by telling stories about themselves. Gilligan does not elaborate on the role of narrative in her theory. It is clear, however, that viewing subjectivity as a function of narrative is incompatible with the empiricist accounts she is challenging. Two themes emerge from her account: that women's moral stories were not heard by her male colleagues as *moral* and that it is her intention to replace their interpretive framework with one that does not ignore or silence the moral voice of women.

how can that be read into public representation?

What, then, is the story that Gilligan wants to tell about human experiences, a story that includes the moral voice of women? And, most important, how does this story relate to the story of separate selves that has dominated accounts of moral development? In the course of her work, Gilligan proposes several different understandings of this narrative. In *In a Different Voice* her account can best be described as additive or dialogic: she proposes that women's relational, caring voice be added to the voice of the separate self. Thus she asserts that "Adding a new line of interpretation, based on the imagery of the girls' thought, makes it possible not only to see development where previously development was not discerned, but also to consider differences in the understanding of relationships without scaling these differences from better to worse" (1982: 26). She suggests that both voices are integral to the human life cycle, that "we know ourselves as separate only insofar as we live in connection with others, and that we experience relationships only insofar as we differentiate other from self" (1982: 63). The result, she claims, is a "dialogue between fairness and care" (1982: 174), a kind of complementarity of the two voices.

The themes introduced in *In a Different Voice* also inform Gilligan's subsequent work, but in the later work these themes have been expanded and, in some cases, even transformed. My interpretation of this later work is guided by two theses. The first is that it is impossible to separate questions of substance from questions of method in Gilligan's discussions. In working through this literature it becomes evident that her substantive claims about justice and care are a function of the method with which she approaches the issue of moral development. Second, although Gilligan continues to claim that she is merely adding another "voice" to existing moral theory, I argue that in an epistemological sense this is not an adequate description of the theoretical import of her work. Her concepts of the moral domain and the moral subject are incompatible with the definition of morality found in modernist moral theory; thus she cannot add the different voice to that theory. Gilligan frequently backs away from an outright rejection of contemporary moral theory; she claims that she wants to reform rather than reconstitute it. But the elements of a radically different approach to moral theory are nevertheless present in her work.

At the center of this radically different approach is the relationship between the two moral voices, justice and care. It is not an exaggeration to assert that both critics and defenders of Gilligan's work are obsessed with the question of the hierarchy of justice and care. Defenders of modernist moral theory have argued that justice subsumes care; feminist critics of Gilligan have argued that emphasizing women's traditional differences perpetuates their inferiority. And, most notably, feminist defenders of Gilligan have tried to enlist her as an ally in their attempts to argue for the superiority of the care voice. She neatly sidesteps this controversy, however, first, by advancing a non-oppositional understanding of justice and care through the use of musical metaphors and, second, by asserting that both justice and care are universal elements of the human condition. There is only one passage in Gilligan's work in which she succumbs to the temptation to privilege care over justice. At a conference on women and moral theory she asserted: "The promise of joining women and moral theory lies in the fact that human survival, in the late twentieth century, may depend less on formal agreement than on human connection" (1987: 32). This passage, however, is exceptional. In all other instances Gilligan steadfastly maintains the equality of justice and care. In an interview in which she was asked whether the care voice was the "better" voice, she replied that thinking about issues of care and responsibility is better than ignoring them and that seeing detachment as morally problematic is better than not seeing it in this light. She concluded: "My argument, therefore, about better voice/different voice, is that you really are going to have a new understanding of both attachment and equality. They're both vitally important. Attachment and equality will always be with us. They're built into the human experience" (Gilligan, in Marcus and Spiegelman 1985: 61).

One of the central issues that occupied Gilligan's attention after the publication of *In a Different Voice* was the development of adolescent girls. Like Beauvoir, Gilligan believed that adolescence is a crucial time in the life of women. In her first series of articles on adolescent girls, Gilligan argued that adolescence is "a time when girls are in danger of drowning or disappearing" (1990b: 10). Whereas 11- and 12-year-old girls tend to be outspoken and sure of themselves, adolescent girls are conforming, less resistant, and more hesitant (1990a: 514). The explanation that Gilligan offers initially for this transition in girls' lives is that it is at this point that they meet what she calls the "wall of western culture" (1990a: 502). What she means by this is that girls begin to realize that being a "good woman" in this society means becoming selfless. It follows that the adolescent girl must renounce the clear sense of self that the 11- or 12-year-old has developed; continuing to assert this self will result in her being labeled selfish (1990b: 10). The crisis that this produces in girls' sense of self is devastating. But Gilligan theorizes that this crisis also produces resistance. Adolescent girls develop a resistance because they are being asked to renounce the knowledge they have acquired, a knowledge of the body and of relationships (1990a: 504). When Gilligan first theorizes about this resistance, her goal is to devise ways in which it can be healthy, rather than corrosive, to allow girls to stay in "the open air of relationships," rather than turn inward (1990a: 533).

[handwritten margin note: → not in the positive sense -self less → lack of self]

In a subsequent study of adolescent girls, however, Brown and Gilligan (1992) articulate a more radical approach to girls' "development," one that constitutes a fundamental challenge to development theory. Gilligan and her colleagues followed a group of girls from the age of seven or eight to their mid-teens. The seven- and eight-year-olds whom they interviewed expressed the strong belief that they knew what was going on in their relational world and were willing to act on that knowledge. They expressed a wish for honest dialogue that was not always "nice" but was full of genuine disagreements and feelings; they did not feel that these disagreements jeopardized their relationships (1992: 44–53). But as early as age eight, the girls began to come up against "the wall of conventional female behavior" and were expected to give up their strong feelings. By the time they were 10 or 11, the girls were struggling against the growing pressure not to speak what they knew and to repress their strong feelings (1992: 91).

Brown and Gilligan define the nature of this crisis in a
unique way. They argue that the 7- to 11-year-olds' knowledge of relationships is one in which strong feelings are
expressed and disagreements occur. As they approach "the
wall," however, they are asked to accept a *very* different
model of relationship, one in which they must remain
silent and be "selfless" rather than "selfish." As Brown and
Gilligan put it, girls take themselves out of relationship for
the sake of relationship (1992: 106). The result is that the
girls yearn for honest, open relationships, but fear such
relationships as dangerous because they conflict with the
image of the good, that is, "selfless" woman (1992: 175).

A number of significant conclusions emerge from these
studies. Gilligan is suggesting an understanding of "development" that constitutes a radical departure from that
of Kohlberg. Kohlberg's theory of moral development
defined development as a progression from dependence to
independence, from reliance on relationships to autonomous selfhood. Gilligan's observations of adolescent girls,
however, led her to a different interpretation. In her first
studies, Gilligan noted that many of the girls she interviewed resisted the move to detachment from relationships, a move that, they were told, constitutes mature
selfhood. Instead, they attempted to remain attached, to
continue their relationships, but to change the character
of their attachments. Gilligan found that adolescent girls
defined "dependence" as positive, not negative; they found
that depending on someone is a good thing (1988: 14–15).
From this, Gilligan concluded that adolescent girls' resistance to detachment may not signal a failure of individua-
tion but "may lead to a different vision of progress and
civilization" (1988: 14). She reminds her readers that,
since Freud, detachment has been identified as the key to
civilization, that the individual's move to disengagement
from relationships signaled his entry into mature selfhood.
The alternative that Gilligan derives from her study of
adolescent girls is one in which psychological health is
defined not as disengagement but, rather, as staying in

relationships: with oneself, with others, and with the world (1991: 23). In a closely related study, one of Gilligan's colleagues, Lori Stern, showed that adolescent girls resisted the opposition of separation and connection; instead, they wanted to define separation and independence in the context of relationship (Stern 1990).

The conclusions that Gilligan and her colleagues drew from these first studies were relatively optimistic: they defined a developmental pattern for girls that identified relationships in positive terms. This optimism was abandoned, however, in *Meeting at the Crossroads*. Although Brown and Gilligan have not relinquished the latter's earlier claim that girls' development constitutes "a different vision," the choice that girls make to stay in relationships is now defined more negatively. At the end of *Meeting at the Crossroads*, Brown and Gilligan conclude that the movement experienced by girls from outspoken to "selfless" relationships is "movement into the sea of western culture and a profound psychological loss" (1992: 180).

Gilligan's position entails, first, that the dominant tradition of moral development, a tradition that defines detachment and separation as the hallmarks of mature selfhood, creates severe psychological problems for women, who define themselves in relational terms. In one of her most pessimistic passages, Gilligan admits that women are excluded from the male definition of selfhood, a definition that labels them inferior because of their inability to separate themselves from others. Women cannot be mature moral agents, according to this tradition, because they fail to achieve the autonomy it demands: "The wind of tradition blowing through women is a chill wind, because it brings a message of exclusion – stay out; because it brings a message of subordination – stay under; because it brings a message of objectification – become the object of another's worship or desire, see yourself as you have been seen for centuries through a male gaze" (1990b: 20).

The second theoretically significant aspect of Gilligan's position emerges most clearly in *Meeting at the Crossroads*.

Gilligan's initial optimism with regard to defining a relational developmental pattern for girls is abandoned in this work. What was earlier defined as a progression in the development of girls toward a mature selfhood defined in terms of relationship is now redefined as a regression. The kind of relationships women are encouraged to form, the authors now argue, are psychologically unhealthy. Gilligan's initial understanding of the developmental pattern of girls offered an alternative of sorts: mature selfhood defined in terms of relationship rather than autonomy. This new study closes off that option. The authors' conclusion is now that women are doubly handicapped: they are excluded both from the masculine model of autonomous selfhood and from the kind of open, honest relationships that they knew as pre-adolescent girls.

Gilligan's research on adolescent girls, then, reinforces the thesis of *In a Different Voice*. For the masculinist tradition of moral theory the separate self is given, whereas relationships are, by definition, incidental rather than constitutive. The relational self that Gilligan articulates, by contrast, claims that relationships are constitutive of the self, that there is no given core that is definitive. One of the most significant aspects of the object relations theory on which Gilligan depends is the claim that the existence of autonomous selves is itself a product of relationships. According to object relations, a boy develops into an autonomous self because his mother forces him to separate from her. A girl, on the other hand, because her mother does not enforce such a separation, fails to develop the autonomy that is fostered in her brothers. There is a cruel irony in this state of affairs; for when these girls become women, they are told that autonomy is the natural and proper state of mature selfhood, a selfhood that they cannot hope to attain. The relational pattern that produces the masculine autonomous self is thus privileged over that which produces the feminine relational self. What this comes to, and what constitutes the import of Gilligan's work, is that it displaces the separate self tradition by asserting that the allegedly given autonomous self is itself a product of relationships.

This conclusion is hugely significant for the evolution of our understanding of "woman." Perhaps more than any other theorist after Beauvoir, Gilligan has challenged the hegemony of the masculine subject and defined an alternative. Gilligan's work is also significant in that it, in a sense, takes up where Beauvoir's analysis leaves off. In *The Second Sex* Beauvoir explores the question of the sources of women's inferiority in our society. Although her analysis is wide-ranging, it is also incomplete. She does not successfully explain how women become the passive and submissive selves that define "woman." Gilligan fills in this gap. Both in *In a Different Voice* and her analysis of adolescent girls, Gilligan gives us an explanation of this development. Her relational self does much of the work only implicit in Beauvoir, completing the concept that Beauvoir merely sketched.

V. After the Different Voice

The storm created in the feminist community by the publication of *In a Different Voice* ranged across the theoretical spectrum. Many feminists criticized Gilligan's methodology, claiming that her assertion of a distinctively female moral voice is empirically unsupportable. Others examined the ethics of the different voice, assessing whether the assertion of a distinctively female moral voice is an advantage or a disadvantage for moral theory. However, 30 years after the publication of Gilligan's work, this controversy has not so much died down as disappeared.

But there is one aspect of Gilligan's work that has endured: her discussion of the ethics of care. Much of this literature, however, is not consistent with Gilligan's approach. Gilligan does not want to replace the justice voice with the care voice, substituting one truth with another. Rather, she wants to argue for the equality of the two voices, replacing a unitary moral theory with a dualistic one. Although this in effect undermines the basis of western moral theory, her approach deviates from that of most care ethicists.

Despite this, there is much of value in the literature of care ethics. Focusing on women's "ways of knowing" and women's distinctive ethical stance affirms their validity and importance. Nel Noddings' *Caring* (1984), published immediately after Gilligan's book, is one of the definitive statements of care ethics. Noddings advances the thesis that an ethic built on caring is essentially feminine, arising out of our experience as women (1984: 8). At the center of Noddings's analysis of the ethic of care is its contrast to the justice voice. Unlike a masculinist morality, it is not rule-bound, but molds itself to individual situations. Rational-objective thinking has only limited use in care situations: "Thus we keep our objective thinking tied to a relational stake at the heart of caring" (1984: 36). She even questions whether caring is really an ethic at all. Ethics has been defined as the study of justified action, but women were never a party to that definition (1984: 95). Noddings makes it very clear that the care ethic offers a distinctive alternative to the justice voice and, most significantly, a superior one.

In *Women's Way of Knowing* (1986) Mary Belenky and her co-authors pursue similar themes, with an emphasis on epistemology rather than moral theory. In the preface they state:

> In this book we describe the ways of knowing that women have cultivated and learned to value, ways we have come to believe are powerful but have been neglected and denigrated in the intellectual ethos of our time. (1986: preface)

The authors assert that women's sense of self and their ways of knowing are intertwined and that women's conception of knowledge and truth – what they know and who they know themselves to be – have been shaped through history by male-dominated culture. Like Gilligan, the authors attempt to counter this by listening to women, overcoming the silence that has been imposed on them by the dominant culture. And, also like Gilligan, they find that, for women, the "real" lessons of their lives are rooted in relationships, not intellectual learning (1986: 4).

Sarah Ruddick's *Maternal Thinking* (1989) takes the discussion in a different direction. Focusing on the activity of women as mothers, Ruddick tries to construct a care ethic based on this model. As mothers, women are continually involved in ethical decisions with regard to their children, deciding how to act in the best interests of the child. In a detailed argument, she develops the parameters of maternal thinking and contrasts this ethical stance to that of the justice voice. She is careful to include men in the category "mother" when men perform the nurturing activities that she defines as maternal. What is a departure in Ruddick's work, however, is her refusal to claim truth or superiority for maternal thinking. For Ruddick, neither maternal thinking nor the standpoint of which it is a part represents "True" or "Total discourse" (1989: 136). Her claim is only that there is a peacefulness latent in maternal practice, not that it can or should replace the justice voice or that it establishes the truth of morality.

The theorist who approaches care ethics from a perspective most similar to that of Gilligan is Joan Tronto. In *Moral Boundaries* (1993) Tronto, like Gilligan, defines the perspective of care ethics as offering a radical challenge to our understanding of the ethical subject. Taking seriously the value of caring, she argues, requires a radical transformation in the way we conceive the nature and boundaries of morality. Tronto's goal is to offer a vision of the good society that draws on feminist sensibilities and traditional women's morality. Her contention is that the care ethic as it has been developed in the feminist literature has not succeeded in effecting this transformation; it has failed to challenge the boundaries of moral life. Against this, Tronto argues that the world would look very different if we moved care from its current peripheral location to a place near the center of human life (1993: 101).

Tronto goes a long way toward defining what this different world looks like:

> On the most general level, we suggest that caring be viewed as a species activity that includes *everything we do to maintain, continue and repair our "world" so that we can live in it as well as possible.* That world includes our bodies, ourselves, and our environment, all of which we seek to interweave in a complex, life-sustaining web. (1993: 103)

> To live by an ethic of care means that a person strives to meet the demands of caring in his/her life. Likewise, for a society to be judged moral it must adequately provide for the care of its members (1993: 126).

> The key to the care perspective is a conception of human beings as not fully autonomous, but as needing care throughout their lives. When we embrace this different conception of human nature as interdependent we can see care not as a parochial concern of women but as a central concern of human life (1993: 162–80).[2]

Although most care theorists focus on ethics, it is also clear that these arguments have huge political implications. Ruddick talks about the possibility of a maternal politics, using maternal practice as a guide for political practice. Tronto does not specifically refer to politics, although her effort to define a different world constitutes a political project. Significantly, Gilligan herself outlines the political implications of an ethic of care. In a recent work she states:

> [The ethic of care] is a human ethic, integral to the practice of democracy and to the functioning of a global society. More controversially, it is a feminist ethic, an ethic that

(margin handwriting) How can there be morality w/out caring?

guides the historical struggle to free democracy from patri-
archy. (2011: 175).   *brings in, rather than shuts out

VI. Gilligan's Radical Displacement

[Women's] super-ego is never so inexorable, so impersonal,
so independent of its emotional origins as we require it to
be in men. Character traits which critics of every epoch
have brought up against women – that they show less sense
of justice than men, that they are less ready to submit to
the great exigencies of life, that they are more often influenced in their judgment by feelings of affection or hostility
– all these would be amply accounted for by the modifica-
tion in the formation of their super-egos which we have
inferred above. (Freud 1961: 257–8)

The individual, left to himself, remains egocentric... The
individual begins by understanding and feeling everything
through the medium of himself... It is only through contact
with the judgment of others that this anomie will gradually
yield. (Piaget 1965: 400)

[Stage 6] is what it means to act morally. If you want to
play the moral game, if you want to make decisions which
anyone could agree upon in resolving conflicts, Stage 6 is
it. (Kohlberg 1981: 172)

What I have attempted to do in the foregoing is to establish
that Gilligan's research does not, as she herself suggests in
her early work, merely add another dimension to existing
moral theory. The moral dimension that she propounds
does not exist in the same epistemological space as that of
western moral theory. It stands not as a supplement to that
tradition but in another, incompatible theoretical space.
Her claim is that she is articulating a "different" moral
voice, a voice that has been silenced by the dominant tradition. But, strictly speaking, this is not the case. As the
quotation from Freud indicates, the "moral" voice of

women, a voice rooted in emotion rather than reason, in particularity rather than universality, has not been ignored by moral theorists. Plato excluded his Guardians from family life because he saw the emotional bonds involved in family attachments as detrimental to the unity he wished to foster among them. The equality of women that he proposed rested on a renunciation of such familial ties by both men and women. Enlightenment philosophers in general, and Kant and Hegel in particular, condemned women for their inferior moral sense. Significantly, they traced this inferiority to women's connectedness, to their inability to abstract from the particularity of situations. Even the nineteenth-century feminist John Stuart Mill argued that women are more biased than men and thus handicapped in the moral realm. Throughout the western tradition, then, women's moral voice has not been so much silenced as marginalized. That women's moral voice is distinctive, that it is inferior to that of men because it lacks objectivity, and that it is only marginally "moral" have been very much a part of western moral theory. And, of course, very much a part of western political theory.

It is no mean feat to take on the grounding of the western tradition, pulling the rug out from underneath the autonomous subject and the moral and political theory he [sic] grounds. But this is, in effect, what Gilligan has done. In the spirit of Beauvoir she has developed not so much an alternative to the masculinist, modernist subject but a radically different conception. Perhaps Gilligan's contribution has been overlooked today because she is not as explicit as she might be in her assertion of the radical nature of her theory. Maybe it is the case that as feminist theory moved into a new phase that emphasized differences rather than difference her perspective seemed irrelevant. Either way, the contemporary silence of feminists on Gilligan's theory is a loss for feminist theory.

– 4 –
Continuing the Tradition
Liberalism and Marxism

The master's tools can never dismantle the master's house.

Audre Lorde

Beauvoir asserted that woman changes everything – that introducing women to the western tradition requires a radical redefinition and transformation of that tradition. The theorists I have examined thus far have followed her lead, moving into new theoretical territory and recasting "woman" in radically new terms. But the hegemony of the western tradition has been and continues to be a powerful force. It is difficult to evade that tradition, particularly when there are elements of it that seem to speak directly to the situation of women.

This is particularly true in the cases of liberalism and Marxism. Liberalism has been closely connected to feminism since the rise of the modern feminist movement. From the outset is has seemed to hold out great promise for women. Its message, equality and freedom for all, appears to be precisely what women want and need. With some appropriate changes that extend this message to women as well as men, liberalism can be seen as an attractive option for feminism. Marxism has also held out a particular appeal to feminism. Marxism and feminism, it is frequently noted, "inhabit the same space." Both are liberatory doctrines that offer freedom from domination. It would seem to follow that capitalism and patriarchy can and should be attacked using the same theoretical tools.

That neither of these claims holds up to scrutiny is the thesis of this chapter. Great theoretical efforts on the part of both liberal and socialist (Marxist) feminists have attempted to adapt feminism to these powerful theories. But, in the end, these efforts fail. Feminist thought escapes the confines of these theories by transforming their basic premises. Despite heroic theoretical efforts, "woman" doesn't fit into either tradition.

I. Liberalism

A. Criticisms

In 1981 Zillah Eisenstein published a book that stands out in the crowded field of discussions of liberalism and feminism: *The Radical Future of Liberal Feminism*. Instead of taking a clear stance for or against liberalism as most feminists have done, she argues that the contradiction between liberalism, which is patriarchal and individualist, and feminism, which is sexually egalitarian and collectivist, lays the groundwork for a feminist movement beyond liberalism (1981: 3). She does not try to adapt feminism to liberalism or to reject liberalism out of hand as unacceptable to feminism but, rather, explores the complex relationship between the two.

Central to Eisenstein's account is her analysis of the historical and ongoing connection between liberalism and feminism. It is undeniable that the modern feminist movement has its roots in the liberal tradition of Wollstonecraft, Mill, and Elizabeth Cady Stanton. This tradition continues in more contemporary work such as that of Betty Friedan. Eisenstein wants to emphasize two aspects of this *liberalism: patriarchal, individualistic (capitalistic →fits w/classical morality*

conjunction. First, if we look carefully at the analysis of any of these authors, the conclusion that women don't quite fit is inescapable. Feminism is at root liberal in its claim that woman is an independent being. But the discovery, even as early as Wollstonecraft, that women are a sex class undermines this fundamental claim. Second, she reveals that in every instance of the intersection of feminism and liberalism, feminism necessarily moves beyond its liberal framework. The demand for the equality of women with men dislodges the patriarchal structure of liberalism and consequently transforms it (1981: 4–6).

What is notable about Eisenstein's work is that she does not simply reject liberalism out of hand as inadequate to feminism. Instead she explains both why liberal feminism evolved and why and how it inevitably moves beyond liberalism. In a very Beauvoirian spirit, she asserts that feminism does not merely redefine liberalism, it transcends it. The subject that emerges from feminism's encounter with liberalism is not the subject of liberalism, but a different entity altogether. It is a subject that embodies, as she puts it, the recognition of the individual character of our social nature and the social nature of our individuality (1981: 191).

incorporates/ recognizes the individual into the collective

The critiques of liberalism that have emerged in feminist theories are numerous and remarkably consistent. Most focus on the contradiction between the rational, autonomous subject of liberalism and the very different subject emerging from feminist critiques. This contradiction, several theorists have noted, goes as far back as the premier liberal feminist, John Stuart Mill. Mill's work is firmly rooted in the rational subject. For Mill, this subject is and must be the defining characteristic of both men and women and the basis of their equality. But when he considers the particular situation of women from this perspective his analysis becomes decidedly ambiguous. Although at some places in his work he declares that women can be as rational as men given the right education, he pulls back from identifying women wholly by this model. He wants to preserve woman's "difference" – her intuition, her

But then not quite equal

practicality, her ability to beautify. So the woman that emerges from Mill's account is not quite the rational subject of liberalism. She is half and half and therefore incoherent (Hekman 1990: 47–60).

The inability to reconcile the rational subject of liberalism with feminism defines a range of feminist critiques. In *Feminist Politics and Human Nature* (1983) Alison Jaggar faults liberalism for its rationalism, abstraction, and individualism. This has become a mantra in other feminist critiques. But perhaps the most forceful contemporary feminist critique of liberalism is that of Catherine MacKinnon. Although MacKinnon agrees with the critique of the liberal subject, her focus is on the role of the liberal state as it relates to women. She argues that liberalism applied to women has supported state intervention on behalf of women as abstract persons with abstract rights without scrutinizing the context and limitations of these notions in terms of gender (1989: 160). The liberal state, she asserts, is male: male objectivity is its norm. Specifically, the state is male jurisprudentially because it adopts the standpoint of male power on the relations between law and society. The neutrality of the law entails that it gives little to women that it cannot also give to men. The result is to maintain sex inequality (1989: 162–8).

MacKinnon's critique extends and reinforces the feminist critique of the individuality of liberalism. Liberalism enshrines the abstract individual into law, seeking to place men and women in the same mold. Liberalism defines equality as sameness (1987: 22). The absurdity of this position becomes particularly obvious when applied to the issue with which MacKinnon is most concerned: the law of obscenity. The "average person" on which that law rests is, she claims, a fiction; no gender-neutral person exists (1989: 202). The fiction of the gender-neutral individual that is the bedrock of liberalism skews all issues of equality as it relates to women. As feminists, she concludes, our issue is not gender difference but the difference that gender makes (1987: 23).

The key issue here is the constitution of the subject. Liberalism stands and falls on the rational, autonomous subject. Feminist critics of liberalism attack this subject not only as a fiction but as a dangerous one. Enshrined in the state, it perpetuates the sexual inequality that is the hallmark of the liberal state. As the radical feminists point out, it also erects a barrier between the public and the private that makes harm to women in the private sphere invisible. Feminist defenders of liberalism counter that for all its problems the concept of the liberal individual is good for women. It gives women the freedom and equality that must be the basis of feminism. These defenders want to redefine the liberal individual so that it is compatible with feminist goals without losing what they see to be the advantages of liberalism for women. The question is whether they succeed.

B. Defenses

I will focus on two contemporary defenses of liberal feminism that make the case for this redefinition as well as it can be made. Susan Moller Okin and Martha Nussbaum both acknowledge the feminist critiques of liberalism and particularly of the liberal subject. But they argue that the advantages of liberalism for women outweigh the problems with this subject. Both attempt to redefine the liberal subject by adding elements of social constitution. The key question in both of these efforts is whether the liberal subject survives this redefinition.

Even though Okin eventually repudiates Beauvoir's claim that feminists must move beyond the western tradition, it is ironic that in her first attempt to grapple with the question of women in western thought she takes a position that is very similar to that of Beauvoir. In *Women in Western Political Thought* (Okin 1979) she begins with the assumption that women cannot be simply added to the subject matter of existing political theory because the works of our philosophical heritage are to a great extent

Beauvoirdian

The "why" theory argument

issue: current public policy / of any institution

re: individualism

built on the assumption of the inequality of the sexes. In an argument reminiscent of Marilyn Frye, she asserts that when women who have been minor characters in political theory take major roles the entire play in which they are acting looks different (1979: 10–12). After an exhaustive survey of the treatment of women by western political theorists, Okin comes to the conclusion that the equality of women cannot be achieved in any political theory without the radical restructuring of the family. And the transformation of the family cannot occur without the transformation of the political order (1979: 289).

What is needed, Okin asserts, is the merging of the private and unproductive functions of family life and the public, productive work of the market economy. The key is child care: it can be done outside the home and employers must acknowledge that men also have responsibility for the care of children. Feminist political theorists concur, Okin argues, that the public and the private are inextricably connected. The crucial question, then, becomes whether such changes can be accomplished within the existing structure of capitalism. This, she concludes, is an open question (1979: 302–14).

But there is more to this open question than Okin acknowledges at this point. Although she never states it explicitly, the only issue is not whether capitalism can survive the deconstruction of the public/private distinction, but whether liberalism can. This question becomes the subtext of Okin's next attempt to deal with the issue of women and political theory, *Justice, Gender, and the Family* (1989). This book begins with the conclusion of her first book: the key to women's equality is restructuring the family. But her conviction that adding women to political theory would change the actors and the play itself has dimmed. And she seems to be less worried about the question of whether capitalism, and, implicitly, liberalism, can survive these changes.

Okin begins *Justice, Gender, and the Family* with the claim that "The injustice that results from the division of labor between the sexes affects virtually all women in our society, though not in the same ways" (1989: vii). The result is what she calls a "justice crisis" in contemporary society, arising from issues of gender. Contemporary political theory, she asserts, has ignored gender. Her intent is to rectify that oversight and develop a "more humanist theory of justice." The key to that effort, the "linchpin" of the gender structure, is the family. The key to the injustice of the family, furthermore, is the separation of public and private, which, she claims, is an "artificial dichotomy" and an "ideological construct" (1989: 7–23).

To accomplish her goal, Okin turns to what might seem an unlikely source: the work of John Rawls. Rawls is the twentieth century's most prominent liberal theorist. Liberalism, by any reasonable definition, is the source of what Okin has identified as an "artificial dichotomy" and an "ideological construct": the separation of the public and the private. It would seem, therefore, that liberalism, and particularly the liberalism of Rawls, would not be a useful tool for deconstructing this dichotomy. But Okin plunges ahead nonetheless, convinced that Rawls, properly reinterpreted, can be used to challenge the gender system of our society. Appealing to Rawls's veil of ignorance, Okin asserts that Rawls would have to require that the family be constituted according to the two principles of justice that he defines (1989: 89–105).

To complicate things further, Okin then sets out to defend one of the pillars of radical feminism: the claim that the personal is political. The family, she asserts, is rife with power relations and the division of labor in the family creates barriers for women in other spheres. Her analysis of the inequality in the family hinges on the specifically *socially constructed* barriers to women. Turning to a famous radical feminist, and vigorous critic of liberalism, Catherine MacKinnon, Okin declares that treating unequals as equal "has long been recognized as an obvious instance of injustice" (1989: 161–2).

Okin's analysis leads her to the conclusion that "a just future would be one without gender." She then proceeds to detail policies that would move us away from gender and the socially constructed inequalities that it produces. These policies are far-reaching: facilitating shared parental responsibility for child care; parental, not only maternal leave; subsidized high-quality child care; flexible work hours for both parents until children reach the age of seven; more sex equality for elementary school teachers and administrators; equal standards of living for both spouses after divorce; checks made out to worker *and* spouse (1989: 175–81).

Okin justifies all of these policies by appealing to Rawls's veil of ignorance. Behind the veil of ignorance, Okin argues, we would not know our gender and would therefore choose a world in which gender had no more relevance than eye color. Although the policies she advocates blur if not eliminate the public/private distinction, this does not seem to diminish Okin's adherence to liberalism. The liberal state, she asserts, already invades the privacy of the family. The policies she suggests are consistent with these invasions but, unlike the previous policies, they are just (1989: 182).

In "Humanist Liberalism" (1998) Okin's commitment to feminism pushes liberalism even further from its classical principles. Taking aim at the inegalitarian trend of US society, she asserts that the aims of liberalism are much more likely to be achieved in a society considerably more egalitarian than the US today. She then goes on to claim that liberalism is compatible with a significant degree of socialization in the means of production and redistribution of wealth, and indeed requires it. If liberalism is to include all of us, furthermore, it must address the feminist challenge that the personal is political. The deficit of liberalism is that it does not deal with socialization. Liberal theorists who take socialization by gender seriously, she concludes, cannot continue to see the family as irrelevant to the political (1998: 40–1).

Okin's justification for what would appear to be an obvious departure from liberal principles is the same as that which she offered in *Justice, Gender, and the Family*: under liberalism the state has always controlled the family. Liberal family law has never been neutral and should not try to be. She concludes: "We can have a liberalism that fully includes women only if we can devise a theoretical basis for public policies that recognize the family as a fundamental political institution, extend standards of justice to life within it" (1998: 53). The liberal state cannot dictate and enforce the abolition of gender but it cannot favor gender either. Family law under the liberal state, she asserts, must provide for alternative conceptions of marriage.

In this article Okin strays even further from liberalism than she has in previous work. But her tendency to go beyond liberalism to accomplish her feminist goals has been evident since *Women in Western Political Thought*, where she questioned whether the changes necessary to feminism could be accomplished under capitalism and, by implication, liberalism. What emerges in the evolution of Okin's thought is a form of feminism that has only tenuous connections to liberalism. Her commitment to the social constitution of the self is the first significant element of her departure from liberalism. The rational, autonomous self of the liberal tradition is almost absent in her work. It is hard to imagine the socially constructed woman of Okin's work constructing a life plan, a concept central to the work of Rawls, the theorist whose work she claims to be adopting. For Okin, women, and by implication, all humans, are products of the social forces that shape us. It is these social forces that Okin wants to alter in her feminist program. Liberalism's rational individual, however, is nowhere to be found in this program.

The second significant element in Okin's departure from liberalism is her adherence to the radical feminist principle: the personal is political. The policy suggestions she makes in *Justice, Gender, and the Family* are clear violations of the liberal principle of the separation of the public and the private. In "Humanist Liberalism" she makes that departure explicit: as feminists we must leave this principle behind. She justifies the intrusion into the family that she advocates by citing past liberal policies that regulated the family. But this justification is ineffective. Arguing that liberal states have always regulated families simply establishes that, in the past, they have violated their own principles. It does nothing to change the fact that this intrusion is anti-liberal.

It is hard not to conclude, then, that Eisenstein is right: feminists who embrace liberalism in order to achieve feminist goals necessarily transform liberalism. Okin's work shows, and she herself admits, that the liberal doctrines of the rational, autonomous individual and the separation of the public and the private are not compatible with feminism. MacKinnon is right: liberalism's self is a male concept and feminism necessitates a rejection of that self. Women, and men, are formed in the complex interaction of the public and the private. Feminists understand this; liberals, as Okin admits, do not. The liberal feminism that Okin develops is, indeed, feminist, but it is not, on any reasonable definition, liberal.[1]

Okin's defense of liberalism focuses on the analysis of women in contemporary American society and is rooted in the contemporary work of Rawls. Another contemporary defender of a liberal feminism, Martha Nussbaum, takes a more global perspective and relies on the work of Mill and Kant. Nussbaum defends liberal feminism on the grounds that women throughout the world, and particularly women in non-western countries, need the principles of liberalism in order to achieve better lives. Nussbaum, like Okin, finds it necessary to redefine liberalism to accomplish this goal. It is significant that her redefinition is remarkably similar to that of Okin.

Nussbaum's most explicit defense of a liberal feminism, or, perhaps more accurately, a feminist liberalism, is in *Sex and Social Justice* (1999b). She begins by appealing to what she calls the core of modern liberal democratic thought: that human beings have a dignity that deserves respect from laws and social institutions. She goes on to argue that we need a universalistic theory of what she defines as "human capabilities" in order to improve the lives of women worldwide. Rejecting the notion that any universalistic theory is male-biased and western, she asserts that this theory provides support for basic *human* capabilities. She then links this conception to liberalism: "Any universalism that has a chance to be persuasive in the modern world must, it seems to me, to be a form of political liberalism" (1999b: 9).

Later in the book Nussbaum takes on feminist critiques of liberalism more directly. It is paradoxical, she notes, that around the world the terms of liberalism – autonomy, dignity, self-respect, and rights – are used by women, yet many feminists reject liberalism as a strategy for feminism. Nussbaum's rejoinder is that not all liberalism is the same and that of Kant and Rawls is most compatible with feminist goals. The core of this tradition is that all human beings are of equal worth and that the source of this equal worth is the power of moral choice – specifically, the power to plan a life according to one's own ends (1999b: 56–7).

Nussbaum then goes on to counter what she identifies as the central feminist objections to liberalism. Against the claim that liberalism is too individualistic, she asserts that neither Kant nor Rawls is individualist and that ethical self-sufficiency is a worthwhile goal not necessarily linked to individualism. Liberal individualism entails the separateness of human beings, not egoism or normative self-sufficiency. Her counter to the second charge, that the ideal of equality in liberalism is too abstract, is related. Here she asserts that seeing women in more particular terms is better for them. Finally, she rejects the notion that liberalism is too focused on reason, by asserting that reason and emotion, far from being antithetical, are closely linked (1999b: 58–73). She concludes that "a liberal individualism, consistently followed through, entails a *radical feminist program*" (1999b: 67).

Eisenstein argues that because liberal feminism leads us to radical feminism we should leave liberalism behind. Despite her advocacy of what she calls a "radical feminist program," Nussbaum is not ready to abandon liberalism. But in her more recent work she appears to be pushing liberalism even further from its core principles. In *Women and Human Development* (2000) she asserts that her liberal account of basic capabilities is explicitly committed to a prominent place for love and care as important goals for social planning. And, most significantly, it does not define any institution as "private." Liberal individualism, she asserts, emphasizes the intrinsic worth of love and care (2000: 245–6). From this, Nussbaum concludes that the state should give family actors considerable liberty but within the constraints imposed by the central capabilities she has defined. Like Okin, she argues that since the state already regulates the family it is appropriate that it should do so more self-consciously and, implicitly, more justly (2000: 275–8).

In an article significantly titled "The Future of Feminist Liberalism" (2004), Nussbaum takes on the central core of liberalism: the rational, autonomous individual. In the context of a discussion of how to incorporate care into liberalism, she argues that we need to redesign the political conception of the person by bringing the rational and the animal into a more intimate relation. We want to bring in the dignity of all: disabled, children, elderly, and so on. What we need is a political conception of the person that is more Aristotelian than Kantian. The guiding principle of this person should be an Aristotelian-Marxist conception of the person as in need of a rich plurality of life-activities. This, she claims, would result in a political conception that is close to that of Rawls (2004: 111–12). Despite her advocacy of a radically different subject, however, Nussbaum concludes that her solution "lies squarely within the liberal tradition" and is still basically liberal (2004: 112–13). Liberal political thought, she asserts, has not yet realized its full potential. Although she concedes that there are basic problems with liberal doctrines as they relate to women's equality, she insists that what we need to do is to try out new liberal alternatives, specifically a neo-Aristotelian liberalism based on the idea of human capabilities (2004: 123).[2]

Once more it is tempting to appeal to Eisenstein. Is an Aristotelian-Marxist liberalism a liberalism at all? In her 2004 article, Nussbaum comes close to conceding that liberalism as it currently exists is inadequate to the needs of feminism and that we need to radically redesign it in order to advance a feminist program.[3] It is a small step from this position to the conclusion that we need to abandon it entirely. Obviously, neither Nussbaum nor Okin want to take this step. But the logic of both arguments clearly leads to this conclusion.

It is significant that both Nussbaum's and Okin's redefinition of liberalism focus on the two pillars of liberalism: the rational, autonomous individual and the public/private distinction. Both replace the liberal individual with a socially constructed, plural subject who is far from the liberal mold. Despite Nussbaum's protestations, this individual constitutes a transformation of the liberal self. The deconstruction of the public/private distinction is just as clear. Both Nussbaum and Okin assert unambiguously that there *is* no private sphere; they accept the radical feminist dictum that the personal is political and try to redefine liberalism in its terms.

That these two issues are a stumbling block to a feminist redefinition of liberalism is evident in the work of another contemporary theorist, Diana Meyers. Meyers attempts to reconcile the apparent contradictions between the rational, autonomous liberal self and the socially constructed self. Meyers's goal is to define what she calls autonomy competency in a way that can account for social conditioning. Her initial definition of autonomy competency appears to be completely consistent with the liberal individual:

> The self of the person who exercises autonomy compe-
> tency, then, is an authentic self – a self-chosen identity
> rooted in an individual's most abiding feelings and firmest
> convictions, yet subject to the central perspective auton-
> omy competency affords. (1989: 61)

She asserts, furthermore, that this self is compatible with
Rawls's concept of a life plan. But then she goes on to
claim that this self is not an asocial core and that autonomy is impossible without socialization. People are born
with the potential to become competent in certain ways,
but this must be realized through education (1989: 135).

It is at this point that things get interesting. Socialization
does not foster the same capacity for autonomy in men
and women: more women than men are likely to be mini-
mally autonomous. Liberal democratic states, Meyers
asserts, should make sure that pedagogical practices and
curricula in schools even-handedly develop that autonomy
in all people. But there is a problem with this strategy:
some parents would resist the fostering of autonomy competency in their homes, particularly for their daughters.
The state could only counter this by engaging "outrageously invasive policies that would ruin family bonds"
(1989: 260). Meyers concludes that the state should not
undertake these far-reaching measures.

There are two problems with Meyers's account, problems endemic to liberal feminism that reveal its underlying
liability. First, it is not explained how we can simultaneously have a socially constructed individual and an authentic self that possess a life plan that matches his/her authentic
self, a problem particularly acute in the case of women.
Nussbaum, Okin, and Meyers all embrace a version of
Rawls's concept of a life plan while also acknowledging
the social construction of the individual. Yet how a socially
constructed individual develops an "authentic" life plan is
never explained. Second, Meyers, more explicitly than
either Nussbaum or Okin, reveals the impotence of the
liberal state when it comes to addressing the lack of

autonomy in women. Education is the key, but Meyers makes it clear that education must stop at the door of the family. Insisting that families develop autonomy in all their children would entail "outrageously invasive policies." Yet without those policies women would still be vulnerable.

Okin, Nussbaum, and Meyers are not the only theorists who espouse a version of liberal feminism.[4] But the themes that these theorists advance are characteristic of most of the literature on liberal feminism. There is consensus that liberal feminism moves beyond liberalism in significant ways, transforming it in the process (Phillips 1991; Wendell 1987). Yet most of the authors of this literature, along with Okin, Nussbaum, and Meyers, stubbornly cling to the liberal tradition. The question then becomes whether a transformed liberalism is still liberalism. Eisenstein and Beauvoir claim that it is not and that trying to fit women into those structures is an exercise in futility.

C. Transforming liberalism

There is, however, another dimension to the intersection of feminism and liberalism that is not revealed in either the critiques or defenses of liberalism. In her feminist critique of liberalism Carole Pateman makes many of the same points as the theorists cited above. But she also moves beyond this to suggest precisely how feminism transforms liberalism and what a post-liberal politics would look like.

Key to Pateman's argument is her analysis of Rawls's *A Theory of Justice* (1971). The parties in Rawls's original position are defined as sexless but also, tellingly, as heads of families (Pateman 1988: 43). It would be easy to conclude from this that the most influential contemporary theorist of liberalism continues the tradition of defining the individual as masculine and presupposing a previous sexual contract. And this is not an illegitimate conclusion. But this is not the center of Pateman's argument. Rather, she advances an epistemological argument about the relationship between public and private that informs liberalism. Women are the opposite of the civil law. They represent what man must master to bring civil society into being (1988: 102). Thus "The civil sphere gains its universal meaning in opposition to the private sphere of natural subjection and womanly capacities" (1988: 113). And, more pointedly,

> The civil individual and the public realm appear universal only in relation to and in opposition to the private sphere, the natural foundation of civil life. Similarly, the meaning of civil liberty and equality, secured and distributed impartially to all "individuals" through the civil law, can be understood only in opposition to natural subjection (of women) in the private sphere. (1988: 114)

Another way of putting this is that liberty and equality are the attributes of the fraternity that exercises what Pateman calls "the law of male sex right" (1988: 114). As Pateman sees it, there is a double conjuring trick going on here. The sexual contract is hidden in the "natural" sphere and thus not examined or brought into the public sphere. But, in addition, the fraternity that constitutes the public sphere is defined as universal. As Pateman puts it: "What better notion to conjure with than 'fraternity' and what better conjuring trick than to insist that 'fraternity' is universal and nothing more than a metaphor for community" (1988: 114). The result of these conjuring tricks is that both the false universality of the citizen of the liberal polity and his preceding sexual contract are hidden from public view.

Pateman brings together the elements of her argument to assert what should now be obvious: that the construction of civil society defined by liberalism puts women in an impossible position. On one hand, a man's (citizen's) wife can be neither an "individual" nor a "citizen" (1988: 179). Pateman's conclusion here is both sweeping and unequivocal: "The conclusion is easy to draw that the denial of civil equality to women means the feminist aspiration must be to win acknowledgment for women as 'individuals.' Such an aspiration can never be fulfilled. The 'individual' is a patriarchal category" (1988: 184). Women can never be full members of the liberal polity. Liberal feminism is an oxymoron. On the other hand, however, women are also doomed to try to achieve this equality. When contract and the individual hold sway, Pateman argues, women are left with no alternative but to try to become replicas of men (1988: 187). But women are incorporated into civil society on a different basis from men. The private sphere of women is separated from civil society. It both is and is not a part of it. Thus women both are and are not a part of the civil order (1988: 181). Their status is inherently ambiguous.

Underlying Pateman's argument here, as well as her prescription for what we might do about the problem she defines, is a fundamental assumption: there is no "neutral" human individual. In her critique of liberal theorists' attempts to define such an individual she comments: "The attempt to set out the purely natural attributes of individuals is inevitably doomed to fail; all that is left if the attempt is consistent enough is a merely psychological biological or reasoning entity, not a human being" (1988: 41). Even Rawls's original position, she argues, is a logical construction; there is nothing human in it (1988: 43). If this is the case, then there is only one option for women: to enter civil society as *embodied* individuals:

> Women can attain the formal standing of civil individuals but as embodied female beings we can never be "individuals" in the same sense as men. To take embodied identity seriously demands the abandonment of the masculine, unitary individual to open up space for two figures: one masculine, one feminine. (1988: 224)

Unfortunately, Pateman offers only the briefest outline of what this possibility might entail. She identifies only two embodied citizens, one masculine, one feminine. But this is only the beginning of what is implied by allowing embodiment into citizenship. Gender is not the only form of embodiment and/or identity. Race, class, ethnicity, and many other factors enter into play as well. At the end of the book, Pateman seems to concede this by arguing that what she calls new social movements (presumably identity politics) raise similar issues as feminism but from a different perspective (1988: 223). In another context Pateman elaborates on this theme by arguing that feminists are trying to develop the first truly general theory in the western world, one that includes men as well as women. She claims that feminism looks forward to a differentiated social order which includes both men and women as biologically differentiated but not unequal creatures (1988: 135–6). Furthermore, she has no illusions as to how radical such a change would be. The theoretical and social transformation required if women and men are to be free and equal members of a democratic society, she argues, is as far-reaching as can be imagined (1989: 52).

Pateman's critique reveals the transformative power of bringing women into the public sphere. Liberalism both veils and forbids identity. The (masculine) identity of the citizen is denied because particular identities do not belong in the public sphere. If we tear away the veil, recognize and legitimize identity, the nature of the political is radically altered. Bringing identity into the liberal polity radically alters that polity. It challenges the abstract uniformity that defines liberalism and moves in the direction of radical pluralism. Tearing the veil from the abstract, neutral citizen of liberalism creates a polity in which identities are recognized and legitimated.

Although she does not refer to Beauvoir, Pateman's thesis is strikingly similar to the position Beauvoir develops in *The Second Sex*. Like Pateman, Beauvoir attacks the notion of the neutral citizen/human being. She challenges the masculine standard as the norm of citizenship. Beauvoir implies and Pateman asserts that a polity that jettisons this false neutrality, that embraces difference, would be a very different polity from that of liberalism. Beauvoir does not even attempt to outline the parameters of a transformed polity. Pateman gives us a sketch of that polity, but only a sketch.

Feminism and liberalism have been linked since the beginning of the modern feminist movement with Wollstonecraft and Mill. It has seemed to many feminists, and rightly so, that feminism can gain much from liberalism. But what Pateman's critique reveals is not only that this is not the case, but that, if we understand the full implications of liberalism, our only option, as women, is transformation. Like other aspects of the western tradition, liberalism is inherently masculine. Adding women changes everything. It is not clear what the embodied, plural citizen that Pateman outlines would look like. But it is clear that until we define this citizen, women cannot move as equals into the political sphere.

II. Marxism

The connection between Marxism and feminism, like that between liberalism and feminism, has seemed an obvious alliance from the outset. Both are focused on liberation from an oppressive social institution, capitalism and patriarchy respectively. Both movements claim, furthermore, that overcoming the oppression of these institutions will result in true liberation. For both movements, the solution to human oppression seems very straightforward: complete eradication of the determining social institution.

Another significant similarity unites the two movements: their conception of the subject. Marx is arguably the first major proponent of the conception of the subject that dominated the twentieth century: the socially constructed subject. Marx challenges the modernist subject by defining a subject that is constituted by social/historical/material conditions. As he so famously put it, "It is not the consciousness of men that determines their existence, but their existence that determines their social consciousness" (1970: 21). This precisely parallels Beauvoir's equally famous statement that women are made, not born. For Marx and Beauvoir, social conditions are what create identity, not innate qualities. The proletariat, like women, are made, not born.

The bond between Marxism and feminism, furthermore, was articulated before feminism became a social force by Marx's closest collaborator, Friedrich Engels. In *The Origins of the Family, Private Property and the State*, originally published in 1884, Engels argued for a close historical association between capitalism and patriarchy. Using faulty anthropological evidence, Engels argued that, following the demise of an original matriarchy, private property and patriarchy emerged in the same historical period as necessarily linked phenomena. His central argument was that without the control of women's sexuality, the core of patriarchy, the ownership and heredity of private property could not be assured. The two phenomena, Engels concluded, were indispensable to each other. For him it followed, furthermore, that their demise must also be linked: destroy private property, the backbone of capitalism, and patriarchy will follow in its wake.

Early Marxist feminists bought into Engels's argument. For them, it seemed obvious that capitalism and patriarchy, both oppressive social institutions, must rise and fall together. Evelyn Reed argued that women did not become subservient until the evolution of class society; before that they enjoyed higher position and equality. Reed did not follow Marxist orthodoxy by arguing that women are a class; she argues, rather, that women are multi-class sex. She does follow Engels's argument, however, in that she asserts that the sex competition that characterizes capitalist society is the result of the class struggle and will cease with the elimination of classes (1971).

Later Marxist feminists would reject the simplicity, and error, of these early views. But the conviction that feminism and Marxism are necessarily linked continued to dominate feminist discussions in the 1970s and early 1980s. An equally strong conviction, however, that the relationship between patriarchy and capitalism is much more complex than Engels and early Marxist feminists contended also emerged. The first element of that complexity revolves around the issue of labor. Marxism, at its core, is a theory of labor: labor makes man [*sic*] what he is and defines the parameters of human society. The problem for women is that women's connection to labor under capitalism is different from that of men. Women's labor in the home and her reproductive labor are ignored by both capitalism and Marxism. Because it is unpaid, women's labor in the home does not count as labor for either the Marxist or the capitalist. Furthermore, this labor also affects the woman's relationship to capitalism as a member of the working class. Because she, and not her husband, has a "second shift" in addition to her labor in the workforce, her relationship to labor is different from that of the male proletariat. This difference was not recognized or theorized by Marxists.

Sheila Rowbotham was concerned to address this silence. She asserted that feminists need to analyze women's labor in the home on its own terms and develop new concepts that can explain this labor (1973: 69). As if answering this call, Christine Delphy argued that housework's exclusion from the market is the cause, not the consequence, of its unpaid status. Her conceptual creation was the "domestic mode of production." Consumption in the family, she argued, must be studied if we are to understand what maintenance consists in and how it differs from a wage (1984: 16–18). Unlike Reed, she argued that women are a "sex-class." Just as Marx analyzed the proletariat's relationship to production, feminists must analyze the specific relationship to production experienced by women. We need, in effect, a class analysis of women (1984: 57–9).

This Delphy proceeded to develop. She argued that domestic service and childrearing are excluded from the realm of exchange and have no value. She theorizes that there are two modes of production in our society: goods produced in an industrial mode and domestic and childrearing services in the family mode. The first gives rise to capitalist exploitation; the second to patriarchal exploitation. The unpaid domestic labor of women, Delphy concludes, constitutes slavery; marriage is an oppression common to all women. The marriage contract is essentially a work contract and the discrimination that women suffer in the labor market is a result of the marriage contract (1984: 90–6). Anticipating arguments that will become central later, Delphy argues that oppression creates gender and that gender creates anatomical sex (1984: 144). She concludes:

> Women's consciousness of being oppressed changes the definition of oppression itself. [Materialist feminism] will not leave any aspect of reality, any domain of knowledge, any aspect of the world untouched ... The feminist theoretical point of view must also aim at a revolution in knowledge. (1984: 218)

This sounds eerily familiar. Once more feminists began by exploring the implications of a masculinist theory for women and found it inadequate. As a consequence Delphy, like many feminists before her, ends up calling for a transformation of knowledge. Women don't fit into Marxist theory; it follows that that theory must be transformed. Beauvoir could not have said it better.

The most notable statement of Marxist feminism is, of course, Hartmann's famous article on "The Unhappy Marriage of Marxism and Feminism" (1981). Perhaps the greatest advantage of Hartmann's article is that it brought to the forefront the uniqueness of the relationship between feminism and Marxism. Early Marxist feminists were all too ready to ally Marxism and feminism. Hartmann's article cautioned that this alliance was problematic. Her analysis of the "dual systems" of capitalism and patriarchy was an essential theoretical contribution in this discussion. But her thesis that we need new categories to understand the dual system, and that both Marxism and radical feminism are insufficient, is equally valuable. Her conclusion, that the socialism being struggled for by men and women is not the same, set the stage for subsequent discussions.

Iris Young objected to Hartmann's theory by arguing that we need one theory, not two, to comprehend capitalist patriarchy as one system (1981). For Young, feminists must transform Marxism into a theory in which the situation of women is a core element. The marginalization of women is an essential feature of capitalism; gender must be brought into the center of historical materialism. This thesis is echoed by Zillah Eisenstein, who argues that we need a synthesis of radical feminism and Marxism. If we join Marxist class analysis with radical feminist patriarchal analysis, the result, she claims, is socialist feminism (1990).

Catherine MacKinnon does not specifically refer to dual-systems theory. But MacKinnon, like the Marxist feminists that preceded her, argues that the effort to create a feminist theory of the state necessarily transforms Marxist theory (1989). MacKinnon begins from a Marxist perspective, asserting that sexuality is to feminism what work is to Marxism. But as her analysis progresses it becomes clear that she finds little in Marxism that is useful for feminist analysis. Most Marxist feminists focus on dialectical/historical materialism as the most valuable aspect of Marxism and try to build a Marxist feminism around this method. MacKinnon rejects even this strategy. Marxist method, she claims, is dialectical materialism, while feminist method is consciousness-raising, the collective critical reconstruction of the meaning of women's social experiences as women live through it. All revolutionary movements, she concludes, create their own way of seeing. Consciousness-raising is that way for feminism (1989: 83–4).

A pattern is emerging here. As it has evolved, Marxist feminism has moved progressively farther and farther from orthodox Marxism. Analyses of the inadequacies of Marxism turn into calls for a transformation of Marxist theory. This pattern is remarkably similar to that which characterized the development of liberal feminism. Liberal feminists began as committed liberals but gradually moved away from liberal doctrine as its inadequacies for feminism became more apparent. Similarly, as it has developed, Marxist feminism has become less and less Marxist and the theme of transformation has become more prominent.

In her *Feminist Politics and Human Nature* (1983), Alison Jaggar presents a survey of feminist theories extant at the time. She finds fault with all the approaches, including Marxist feminism. Her conclusion, however, is that a theory with its roots in Marxism, feminist standpoint theory, is the best chance for feminism: "Socialist feminism shows that to reconstruct reality from the standpoint of women requires a far more total transformation of our society and of ourselves than is dreamt of by a masculinist philosophy" (1983: 389).

Two versions of feminist standpoint theory emerged in the 1970s and 1980s: a philosophical version articulated by Nancy Hartsock and a sociological version articulated primarily by Dorothy Smith. I will focus on Hartsock's version primarily because it reveals more clearly the fundamental contradictions that characterize this version of Marxist feminism. In both her conception of reality and the subject, Hartsock's feminist standpoint theory, because it presupposes the social construction of both the subject and reality, transforms the Marxist conceptions of both. Although Hartsock herself does not acknowledge this transformation, her careful articulation of the feminist standpoint explodes the categories of the Marxism she espouses. Her approach points to a plural definition of the subject and reality that will characterize subsequent feminist theory.

In an article published in *Quest* in 1975, Hartsock wrote: "At bottom feminism is a mode of analysis, a method of approaching life and politics, rather than a set of political conclusions about the oppression of women" (1981a: 35). The power of feminist method, she asserts, grows out of the fact that it enables us to connect everyday life with the analysis of the social institutions that shape that life (1981a: 36). This early article reveals the presupposition that defines her later formulation of the feminist standpoint: the belief that feminism, while necessarily political, at the same time must be centrally concerned with method, truth, and epistemology. But this early article also raises an issue that will complicate Hartsock's search for truth in a feminist mode. She notes that the reality perceived by different segments of society is varied. Thus, she concludes, "Feminism as a mode of analysis leads us to respect experience and differences, to respect people enough to believe that they are in the best possible position to make their own revolution" (1981a: 40).

For Hartsock, activity is epistemology: women and men create their own realities through their different activities and experiences. If this were the whole story, however, then both truth and reality would be multiple, even "relative," and Hartsock is very concerned to avoid this conclusion. When she presents her theory of the feminist standpoint in *Money, Sex, and Power* (1983b), this is the focus of her attention. She insists that "the concept of a standpoint rests on the fact that there are some perspectives on society from which, however well-intentioned one may be, the real relations of humans with each other and with the natural world are not visible" (1983b: 117). Hartsock's goal in the book is to define the concept of a standpoint and apply it to the situation of women.

Hartsock outlines five criteria of a standpoint that she adapts from Marx's theory (1983b: 118). Two potentially contradictory definitions of reality structure this discussion. First, in an explicitly social constructionist argument, Hartsock asserts that material life structures and sets limits to an understanding of social relations. It follows that reality will be perceived differently as material situations differ. It also follows that the dominant (ruling) group in society will label its perspective as "real" and reject other definitions. Second, Hartsock insists that while the ruling group's perception of reality is "partial and perverse," that of the oppressed is not, that it exposes "real" relations among humans and is hence libertory. Throughout her work Hartsock struggles with the relationship between these two definitions of reality. It constitutes a kind of fault line that runs through her articulation of the feminist standpoint. Although her formulation changes over the years, she continues to maintain *both* that reality is socially and materially constructed *and* that some perceptions of reality are partial, others true and libertory.

What we need, Hartsock asserts, is a theory of women's oppression and exploitation that is both material and historical – material in the sense of explaining the relations that structure women's lives and historical in the sense that it involves examining the changes and concrete regularities that have persisted over time (1983b: 150). Her thesis is that, like the lives of the proletariat in Marxist theory, women's lives make available a particular and privileged vantage point on male supremacy, a vantage point that can be a powerful critique of phallocratic institutions and ideology that constitute the capitalist form of patriarchy. The structures that define women's activity as contributing to subsistence as mothers, and the sexual division of labor, provide the basis for the construction of a feminist standpoint on which to ground a specifically feminist historical materialism. Feminist standpoint can allow us to descend further into materiality to an epistemological level at which we can better understand why patriarchal institutions take such perverse forms, and how both theory and practice can be redirected in more libertory directions (1983b: 231).

Hartsock concludes that the vision of reality that grows from the female experience is deeper and more thorough-going than that available to the worker. Women are responsible for reproducing labor power. Men's contact with nature, on the other hand, is mediated by women. If life consists of sensuous activity, the vantage point available to women on the basis of their contribution to subsistence represents an intensification and deepening of the materialist worldview available to producers of commodities in capitalism (1983b: 234–6). Women's constitution of self, furthermore, is a direct result of their experience. Women construct themselves in relation to others; they oppose dualisms and value concrete life. In the end, "One can conclude then that women's life activity does form the basis of a specifically feminist materialism, a materialism that can provide a point from which to both critique and work against phallocratic ideology and institutions" (1983b: 247).

A slightly different take on the feminist standpoint emerges in Hartsock's well-known article, "The Feminist Standpoint" (1983a). Here Hartsock states that a specifically feminist historical materialism "might enable us to lay bare the laws of tendency which constitute the structure of patriarchy over time" (1983a: 283). Her dualistic concept of reality structures this discussion as well. On one hand, social constructionist themes recur throughout the argument: "I will sketch out a kind of ideal type of the social relations and world view characteristic of male and female activity in order to explore the epistemology contained in the institutionalized sexual division of labor" (1983a: 289). The feminist standpoint "expresses female experience at a particular time and place, located within a particular set of social relations" (1983a: 303). Quickly following this, however, is the statement that the feminist standpoint allows us to "go beneath the surface of appearances to reveal the real but concealed social relations" (1983a: 304). Her thesis is that "women's lives make available a particular and privileged vantage point on male supremacy" (1983a: 284).

In this article Hartsock introduces an approach that will become the hallmark of standpoint theory: object relations theory. The introduction of this theory, however, serves to highlight the tension inherent in her concept of reality – in a sense widening the fault line in that concept. In her discussion Hartsock appeals to object relations theory to explain the difference between the male and female experiences of the world (1983a: 296). Bringing object relations theory to bear on her Marxist assumptions, Hartsock argues that if material life structures consciousness, then women's relationally defined existence structures a life in which dichotomies are foreign and what she calls "abstract masculinity" is exposed as partial and perverse (1983a: 298–9). Implicit in Hartsock's discussion is the assumption that object relations theory is an appropriate and useful addition to feminist standpoint theory, not a major departure. In the context of her theory it seems to fit nicely with the Marxist thesis that reality is socially constructed and supplies a needed gendered component to that theory.

The incorporation of object relations theory, however, represents a major theoretical departure in the development of standpoint theory. Feminist standpoint theory's identification with object relations theory has changed the focus of the approach in three respects. First, object relations theory, unlike Marxist theory, lacks a distinction between socially constructed and "true" reality. As feminist theorists in the 1980s discovered, object relations theory effectively jettisons the concept of objective reality. Some advocates of feminist standpoint theory see this as an advantage, others as a disadvantage. But it becomes a problem that must be continually negotiated. Second, the incorporation of object relations theory further problematizes the issue of difference. What was merely a troubling issue in feminist standpoint theory is a major stumbling block in object relations theory. In object relations theory, the opposition between *the* experience of men and *the* experience of women is the centerpiece of the theory. The difficulty of theorizing differences among women and the variety of women's experiences will lead to critiques of object relations theory as well as feminist standpoint theory.[5] Third, the incorporation of object relations theory into Marxist-inspired feminist standpoint theory creates an internal contradiction in the theory. For Hartsock, the point of defining the difference of women from men is to promote resistance; it is a form of political opposition. Object relations theory, in contrast, lacks even a hint of resistance. It defines women as peaceful, caring, relational, and nurturing, as opposed to men who are aggressive and autonomous, but fails to draw any political implications from this opposition. The incompatibility of these two definitions will become a significant problem for feminist standpoint theory.

The fundamental problem for Hartsock's theory is that if material life structures consciousness, if the different experiences of different groups create different realities, then this must hold for the oppressed as well as the oppressor. Hartsock would reply that the oppressed's conception of reality is true because it is based on a correct perception of material reality, while that of the oppressor is false because it does not. But such an argument begs the question of how a correct perception of material reality is achieved. Ultimately, it must presuppose this reality as a given, as the standard by which truth and falsity are defined. Even in her early formulations of feminist standpoint theory, Hartsock is defensive about the accuracy of the oppressed/women's conception of reality. The incorporation of object relations theory makes her defense of this position far more difficult. If, as object relations theory claims, our relations with others define our perceptions, then selecting one of these perceptions as "real" is instantly suspect. But Hartsock also realizes the centrality of this point. Unless women's standpoint can be shown to be truer, a reflection of reality itself, why bother with feminist analysis at all?

This problem relates to the issue of the subject as well. If we jettison the concept of a true or truer reality, then we must also jettison the unitary concept of woman. If the material reality of women's lives structures their concept of self, if the relational self of object relations theory is socially constructed, then we must admit, even focus on, the differences among women. And, indeed, it is precisely this issue that is the major concern of feminist standpoint theory after Hartsock's initial formulation. Originally, feminist standpoint theorists claimed that the standpoint of women offers a privileged vantage point for knowledge. But as the theory evolved it became obvious that if the experiences of women create knowledge and reality, then it must be the case that this knowledge and reality are plural because the experiences of women are varied and diverse. The subsequent re-evaluation of feminist standpoint theory was an attempt to reconstitute the theory from the perspective of these differences.

This re-evaluation focused on two issues. First, if, as we must, we acknowledge that there are many realities that women inhabit, this necessarily affects the status of the truth claims that feminists advance. One cannot appeal to one true reality to ground claims about social reality if there is more than one such reality; if there are multiple realities then there must be multiple truths that correspond to them. Second, if we abandon a single axis of analysis, *the* standpoint of women, and instead try to accommodate the multiple, potentially infinite standpoints of diverse women, we are in danger of losing the analytic force of our argument. Or, in other words, if we try to accommodate an infinite number of axes of analysis, our arguments seem destined to slip into hopeless confusion.[6] These issues, as many commentators have noted, have more than methodological significance; they impinge on the possibility of a feminist politics. The political corollary to both issues is the concern that if we abandon the monolithic concept of "woman" implicit in *the* feminist standpoint, the possibility of a cohesive feminist politics is jeopardized.

The concern both to accommodate difference and preserve the analytic and political force of feminist theory, specifically feminist standpoint theory, is prominent in Hartsock's subsequent work. It is obvious that Hartsock cares very deeply about these issues. She is painfully aware of the evils of racism, particularly within the women's movement. She is also passionately committed to feminist social criticism as a force for social change and is determined not to let forces such as postmodernism erode that potential. These concerns emerge forcefully in her 1987 article, "Rethinking Modernism." The point of departure for Hartsock's argument is based on the differences among women. She asserts that we need to develop an understanding of difference by creating a politics in which previously marginalized groups can name themselves and participate in defining the terms that structure their world (1987: 189). Central to Hartsock's argument is the claim that unless we provide a systematic understanding of the world we will be unable to change it. The object of her polemic in this and several other articles is postmodernism. At the time of Hartsock's writing the issues of difference and multiplicity had come to be closely identified with postmodernism. Hartsock wants to reject this identification. She wants to valorize difference, to claim that the differences among women are significant both theoretically and practically, while at the same time rejecting postmodernism on the grounds that it obviates the possibility of the systemic knowledge that is necessary for social change.

Hartsock's efforts both to valorize difference and retain at least some notion of reality and truth, of the "way the world is," produce some odd results. In "Rethinking Modernism," she significantly alters the basic thesis of feminist standpoint theory by asserting that although women are not a unitary group, white, ruling class, Eurocentric men are (1987: 192). The ruling class, now referred to as the "center," is defined as unitary while those on the periphery, the "others," are defined as heterogeneous. Hartsock's argument is that we must create a politics that lets the "others" into the center, a center which, she claims, will "obviously" look different when occupied by women and men of color (1987: 201). Hartsock's solution raises some troubling questions. It posits a center that is heterogeneous rather than homogeneous, which suggests that it may not be a "center" at all. Further, positing the movement of the "others" into the center effectively eliminates the periphery. We can, I think, assume that Hartsock would not endorse a politics in which any groups were marginalized. But it is difficult to retain the concept of "center," as she does, without a corresponding concept of periphery.[7]

All of these questions could be quite easily eliminated by abandoning the center/periphery dichotomy. But Hartsock is adamantly opposed to such a move. She is also adamantly opposed to what she sees as a related danger: the disappearance of the subject. It is highly suspicious, she notes, that questions about the subject are arising now:

> Why is it that at the moment when so many of us who have been silenced begin to demand the right to name ourselves, to act as subjects rather than objects of history, just then the concept of subjecthood becomes problematic? (1998: 210)

The solution, Hartsock claims, is for those of us who have been constituted as other to insist on a vision of the world in which we are at the center, not the periphery (1998: 214). She concludes: we need to sort out who we really are and in the process dissolve the false "we" into its "real multiplicity and variety" (1998: 240). The result is what she calls "principled relativism" (1998: 245).

Hartsock's fear that the proliferation of differences in feminist theory threatens the basis of feminist theory and practice is not frivolous. It is a legitimate concern of feminist theory. If, as Hartsock realizes we must, feminism abandons *the* feminist standpoint and, with it, *the* correct view of reality, then we are in danger of abandoning the whole point of feminist analysis and politics: revealing the oppression of "women" and arguing for a less repressive society. If there are multiple feminist standpoints, then there must be multiple truths and multiple realities. This is a difficult position for those who want to change the world according to a new image, that is, for feminists.

Ultimately Hartsock finds herself in a difficult position. She wants to embrace the "situated knowledges" that are entailed by both feminist standpoint theory and object relations theory, but she cannot accept the logical conse- quence of this position: that no perspective/standpoint is epistemologically privileged. She wants to retain a notion of privileged knowledge that can accommodate both diver- sity and locatedness. But her attempts to achieve this goal are not successful. "Situated knowledges," she claims, are "located in a particular time and place. They are therefore partial. They do not see everything from nowhere but they do see some things from somewhere." Borrowing post- modern terminology, she refers to the knowledges pro- duced from the various subject positions of different women as "the epistemologies of these marked subjectivi- ties." She then goes on to argue: "The struggles they rep- resent and express, if made self-conscious, can go beyond efforts at survival to recognize the centrality of systemic power relations" (1989–90: 28–30). What this formula- tion requires is a sustained argument for how such sys- temic knowledge is possible. But Hartsock does not provide such an argument.

Hartsock is not the only feminist standpoint theorist to attempt to stem the tide of what is perceived as the onslaught of postmodernism. For feminist standpoint the- orists, the principal issue is how to accommodate differ- ences among women without losing the claim to uncover a truer reality. Dorothy Smith's approach is to look to "women's actual experience," arguing that this encom- passes the diversity of women's lives. Patricia Hill Collins abandons the notion of *the* feminist standpoint by arguing that black women's standpoint is only one angle of vision, thus rejecting both absolute truth and relativism. Sandra Harding defends feminist standpoint theory by endorsing "strong objectivity," a concept that accommodates the situatedness of knowledge without abandoning objectivity (Hekman 1997).[8] But, as with Hartsock, none of these accounts successfully addresses the problem she raises:

how do we accommodate difference without abandoning the claim to truth?

On one crucial point, however, Hartsock was right: the challenge for feminist theory in the 1990s and onward is how to accommodate difference without slipping into meaningless relativism. Postmodernism and related approaches become the focus of feminist theory in the 1990s, pushing Marxist/socialist/materialist feminists to the margins. But these feminists have continued to argue their cause. In the collection edited by Hansen and Philipson (1990) the authors argue that although socialist feminism is "dead," many of its ideas have been incorporated into feminist theory and practice. Writing in 1993, Rosemary Hennessy takes a different tack: she argues for a kind of synthesis between discursive approaches such as that of postmodernism and what she calls "materialist feminism." Her goal is to situate feminism within a postmodern Marxist problematic. Materialist feminism, she claims, can make use of postmodern notions of the subject that are congruent with feminism's political goals. Along with other materialist feminists (and Hartsock), Hennessy is concerned that, guided by postmodernism, feminism will devolve into difference for the sake of difference. What we need, she argues, is critical cultural studies that inquire into the histories of the organization of knowledges and their function in the formation of subjectivities. We must reveal the structural links between the disciplining of knowledge and larger social arrangements (1993: 11–12).

Like Hartsock, Hennessy's goal is to articulate a kind of middle ground between a totalizing Marxist perspective and what appears to be unrestrained eclecticism. Her goal is a global analytic that is systemic but not totalizing. This goal is particularly relevant to the issue of subjectivity. A feminism that aims to understand the discursive construction of "woman" across multiple modalities of difference – race, class, gender, sexuality – requires a problematic that can explain the connection between discursive constructions of difference and the exploitative social arrangements that shape them (1993: 65–6). Her thesis is that we cannot ignore totalities like patriarchy and heterosexuality that continue to organize people's lives in systemic and oppressive ways (1993: 90).[9]

What, then, is the legacy of Marxist/socialist/materialist feminism? First, as the work of Hartsock and the more recent Marxist feminists indicate, many of the issues taken up in their work are at the forefront of contemporary feminist thought. Hartsock was right: postmodernism, although immensely valuable to feminism in many ways, led us down a path of endless (rather than principled) relativism. Instead of deconstructing the discourse/reality dichotomy, postmoderns led us to focus exclusively on discourse to the exclusion of reality. Today's material feminists are concerned to redress this imbalance. They want to bring the material back in without losing the insights of discursive analysis. In some senses contemporary material feminists are following the lead of the materialist feminists who went before them.

Second, Marxist feminism illustrates yet again that women don't fit into masculinist theories and require a transformation of those theories. Women's labor is an anomaly that doesn't fit into either capitalist/liberal theories or Marxism. It requires a rethinking of the entire theory that is in essence an abandonment. Furthermore, as Hartsock's reliance on object relations theory indicates, the concept of woman must also be rethought. Women are diverse; we cannot theorize in terms of *the* women's standpoint. In order to accommodate the diversity of women we must reconceptualize "woman" once again. In order to do this we also need a new paradigm of knowledge.

In the end, however, the failure of liberal and Marxist feminism is not without its positive effects. First, it solidifies Beauvoir's argument that we must look beyond the western tradition for a redefinition of woman in the political sphere in particular. Second, specifically with the work of Pateman, it suggests a possible avenue for a feminist political praxis that is beholden neither to Marxism nor liberalism. It would be a praxis that jettisons the neutral citizen and replaces him [*sic*] with an embodied citizen that brings diversity into the political sphere. This praxis must be able to accommodate difference and diversity without hierarchy. It will be the task of subsequent theories to fill in this outline.

— 5 —

From Difference to Differences
Postmodernism, Race, Ethnicity, and Intersectionality

In 1988 Elizabeth Spelman's book, *Inessential Woman*, advanced a thesis that, ten years earlier, would have been heresy in feminist theory: that we should abandon the unitary definition of "woman" that has been at the center of the feminist movement since its inception. Spelman's argument was both practical and theoretical. "Woman," she claimed, inevitably leads to a hierarchy among women; a fixed definition of "woman" entails that some women are more "woman" than others. More specifically, the concept privileges white, middle-class, heterosexual women and relegates other women to the margins as "different." Spelman's challenge was a radical one: abandon the concept "woman," what she called the "Trojan Horse" of feminist theory, and embrace "women" in all their diversity. Spelman was fully aware that, for many feminists, such a move was almost unthinkable. It seemed obvious that a feminist politics without "woman" was inconceivable. In an effort to allay these fears, Spelman argued that we don't know that emphasizing difference is dangerous unless we try it.

By the time Spelman's book was published her argument, far from being heresy, was well on its way to being orthodoxy among feminists. Discontent with "woman" came from many sources: women of color who found that they had no place in feminist theory and practice; the rise of identity politics with its emphasis on multiple sources of identity; and postmodern/poststructuralist philosophy. Difference, it seemed, was suddenly everywhere. Moving from an emphasis on the difference between men and women to an emphasis on the differences among women constituted a sea change in feminist thought that profoundly changed feminism. It also produced a sea change in feminist conceptions of the subject. Feminists began the difficult process of trying to define the multiplicity of women's identities and placing that conception at the center of feminism.

I. Postmodernism[1]

Emblematic of the move from difference to differences that characterizes post-1980s feminism is postmodernism. To say that postmodernism overwhelmed the feminist community is an understatement. Whether feminists saw postmodernism as the perfect partner for feminism or as its most dangerous opponent, grappling with the approach was unavoidable. To those who espoused a postmodern feminism the commonalities of the two approaches were compelling. Both attack the fundamental roots of western thought, arguing that this philosophy is misconceived. Both assert that this tradition must be displaced and a radically different approach embraced. And both approaches, most notably, attack the centerpiece of the western tradition: the subject "man." As postmodern feminism evolved, it became clear that the reasons for these challenges to western thought varied significantly between postmoderns and feminists. The similarities of the challenges, however, are hard to ignore.

Another way of characterizing this affinity is from a Beauvoirian perspective. Beauvoir claimed that "woman" does not fit into the Western tradition and that women must seek a radical alternative to that tradition. On the face of it, it seems that postmodernism is the perfect vehicle for that transformation. If all aspects of western thought are found wanting because they define women as Other, then a philosophy that radically "deconstructs" that tradition seems to be precisely what feminism requires. As the story of postmodern feminism unfolds it will become clear that this perspective is too simplistic. But at the outset it appealed to many feminists.

It would be foolhardy to attempt to characterize postmodernism as a whole or to identify who, really, is or is not a postmodern. What I will do instead is to focus on one central aspect of postmodern thought that is particularly germane both to feminism as a whole and to the evolution of the feminine subject. Perhaps the most radical element of postmodern thought is what has come to be called "the death of the subject/man." For Michel Foucault and Jacques Derrida, the linchpin of western thought is the autonomous, Cartesian subject. The deconstruction of this subject as the source of all knowledge and truth is fundamental to the postmodern critique (if, indeed, postmodernism can be said to have a center). The postmoderns moved beyond one of the pillars of feminist thought, the socially constructed subject, to the position that the subject is quite literally constituted through discourse. For the postmoderns the subject is not, as the social constructionists understand it, a product of social influences imposed on an already existing subject. Rather, as one commentator famously put it, "there is no there there." There is no doer behind the deed (Nietzsche): it is all discourse.

The postmodern conception of subjectivity epitomizes both the attraction of postmodernism for feminists and the conflicts between them. The postmodern subject is consistent with Beauvoir's insight that woman is made, not born, but takes that insight further into the realm of the discursive. For postmodern feminists the discourse of "woman" both constitutes and subjugates women. This postmodern perspective has been immensely useful to feminists in their attempt to explore the sources of the inferiority of women. But the death of man is also problematic for feminism. Feminism has been and must be about resistance and change. But how does the subject that is wholly constituted by discourse resist that constitution? How can we understand agency in the constituted subject? These questions have haunted feminists since the advent of a postmodern feminism.

If the postmodern deconstruction of the subject eliminates "man," then all the issues that Beauvoir analyzes under the heading of woman as "Other" disappear as well. As Donna Haraway puts it, it took the politico-epistemological terrain of postmodernism to be able to insist on a co-text to Beauvoir: one is not born an organism. Organisms are made – they are constructs of a world-changing kind (Haraway 1991: 208). The postmodern feminist subject goes beyond Beauvoir by deconstructing the nature/culture dichotomy. For Beauvoir, women are "made" on the bodies of organisms – women. Haraway and the postmoderns take this a step further by asserting that both women and organisms are discursively constituted. Haraway's concept of the cyborg encapsulates this postmodern insight. For Haraway, the cyborg is "a fiction mapping our social and bodily reality as an imaginative resource suggesting some very fruitful couplings" (1990: 191). "The cyborg is a kind of disassembled and reassembled postmodern collective and personal self. This is the self feminists must code" (1990: 205). And, finally, "I would rather be a cyborg than a goddess" (1990: 223).

Haraway occupies an anomalous place in the discussion of postmodern feminism. On one hand, she is one of the earliest and most enthusiastic proponents of the usefulness of postmodernism in defining the feminine subject. But she will eventually find that subject wanting and move into different territory. Her work becomes a kind of cautionary tale as feminism's enthusiasm for postmodernism evolves.

There is little question about who has come to be most closely associated with the postmodern subject. Judith Butler, and particularly her work in *Gender Trouble* (1990a), is iconic. Although it would be an exaggeration to say that Butler's work single-handedly set feminism down the path of postmodernism, it is not an exaggeration to say that *Gender Trouble* took the feminist community by storm and became the dominant influence in feminist theory in the 1990s. Even today the influence of this book remains, if only as the necessary starting point for counter-arguments.

At the beginning of my study I asked whether there was any utility in analyzing, yet again, the work of Beauvoir. The same question could be asked with regard to Butler, particularly her position in *GT*. There are two ways of answering this question. First, whether we agree with her or not, Butler's position has had a profound effect on the evolution of the feminine subject. Ignoring her position on the grounds that it has been superseded would be fool-hardy; many contemporary positions are rooted in her conceptions. Second, Butler's position has evolved in very fruitful ways. Her present position, which has much in common with material feminism, builds on the foundation articulated in *GT*. This alone constitutes a significant reason to return to that work.

In 1999, *Gender Trouble* was reissued with a new intro-duction. In it, as one would expect, Butler tries to deal with the barrage of criticisms of her work by explaining her intent in the book. It is easy to dismiss this as an *ex post facto* reinterpretation of the work that distorts the original in order to refute her critics. I do not think this is the case. On the contrary, I think that many of the criti-cisms of *GT* are distorted. A careful reading of *GT* reveals that Butler addresses the key issues that were at the fore-front of the critiques of her work: the subject, agency, and resistance. Far from ignoring these issues, she offers cogent arguments in defense of her position.

Butler begins the new introduction by asserting that the mode of the book is in the tradition of immanent critique that seeks to provoke critical examination of the basic vocabulary of the movement of thought to which it belongs (1999: vii). The aim of her text, she claims, is to open up the field of possibility for gender without dictating which possibilities might be realized. Central to Butler's argument is the presupposition that feminists should not restrict the meaning of gender, thus producing new forms of exclusion and hierarchy. By bringing poststructuralist theory to bear on US theories of gender, Butler sought to explore how an epistemic/ontological regime can be brought into question (1999: viii–xi). Her goal, she claims, was to initiate a radical inquiry into the political constitution and regulation of identity, to investigate the political stakes in designating as an origin and cause those identity categories that are the effects of certain practices (1999: xxi–xxii).

One of the key criticisms of postmodern feminism in general and Butler in particular is that it precludes the possibility of a feminist politics of resistance. Yet here Butler is asserting that the whole purpose of her book is resistance – initiating a radical inquiry into the political constitution and regulation of identity with the aim of opening up new possibilities in the definition of gender. Her objection to the concept of "woman" as the subject of feminism is informed by this conviction: "woman" cannot provide the emancipation it promises because it is discursively constituted by the political system from which it seeks emancipation (1999: 3). It is clear from this that Butler's famous/infamous attack on the concept "woman" is motivated not by the desire to eradicate "woman" but by her goal of political resistance. Feminist critique, she asserts, must understand how the category "woman" is produced and restrained by the structures of power through which emancipation is sought (1999: 4).

It follows that since the category "woman" reifies gender relations what we need is a feminist genealogy of the concept "woman." To begin this genealogy, Butler takes on one of the sacred cows of feminist theory: the sex/gender distinction. She asserts that

> gender is not to culture as sex is to nature; gender is the discursive/cultural means by which "sexed nature" or a "natural sex" is produced and established as "prediscursive," prior to culture, a politically neutral surface *on which* culture acts. (1999: 10)

Butler's goal is to open up the category of gender by exploring gender identity that fails to conform to cultural norms. In order to accomplish this we need to abandon the notion that there is a subject who pre-exists the doing of gender:

> There is no gender identity behind the expressions of gender; that identity is performatively constituted by the very expressions that are said to be its results. (1999: 34)

And, once again, the theme is resistance: if the regulatory fictions of sex and gender are multiply contested sets of meaning, then their multiplicity holds out the possibility of their disruption (1999: 44).

To buttress her position, Butler then launches into an extensive discussion of Lacan, Freud, Irigaray, Wittig, and Kristeva. What Butler emphasizes in these discussions is that gender is a becoming, not a being. It follows that if to *be* a woman is to *become* a woman, then this process is not fixed and it is possible to become a being whom neither "man" nor "woman" describes (1999: 173). This leads Butler to a discussion of how we might destabilize the categories of gender and open up new possibilities, in other words, how we might foster political resistance. Her first suggestion is drag: drag reveals the imitative structure of gender as well as its contingency. Her second is pastiche, which goes one step further by mocking the very notion of an original (1999: 187–8).

Identifying drag and pastiche as the basis for a feminist politics of resistance was, to put it mildly, unsatisfactory to many of Butler's critics. It seemed a frivolous departure from what might be termed the real world of politics. Critics were equally dissatisfied with her approach to a closely related issue: agency. For many of Butler's critics, it was hard to imagine the discursively constituted subject possessing agency because they assumed that agency can only be established through recourse to a prediscursive "I." To answer this critique, Butler refers again to the "necessary failure" of the production of gender identity. These failures produce the possibility of a "complex reconfiguration and redeployment" of gender. There is not a transcendental subject that enables action in this deployment, but, rather, "There is only taking up of the tools where they lie, where the very 'taking up' is enabled by the tool lying there" (1999: 199). And, even more forcefully:

> Construction is not opposed to agency; it is the necessary scene of agency, the very terms in which agency is articulated and becomes culturally intelligible. (1999: 201)

Where, then, does this leave the possibility of resistance? If there is no possibility of agency outside of discursive practices, then our task is to engage in a radical proliferation of gender in order to displace the gender norms that enable repetition (1999: 202–3). The deconstruction of identity is thus not on Butler's view the deconstruction of politics, but the establishment as political the terms through which identity is established together with the proliferation of new configurations of gender. What this comes to is that Butler is indeed calling for political resistance but it is a politics that radically changes the definition of the political. It is wrong to claim that Butler obviates a feminist politics of resistance, but the "politics" she calls for is not recognizable to many of her critics; for them, it is not a politics that is "real."

The appeal to the real – the reality of women's bodies – was a second major criticism of Butler's position in *GT*. This criticism led, at least indirectly, to Butler's book *Bodies That Matter* (1993a). In the introduction to the book Butler addresses the real head on: "I began writing this book by trying to consider the materiality of the body only to find that the thought of materiality invariably moved me into other domains…I could not fix bodies as simple objects of thought" (1993a: ix).

At the root of all of these questions about her work – the materiality of bodies, the reality of politics, and the possibility of agency – is the issue of construction. And Butler's answer to all of these questions is that we must not define construction as leading inexorably to cultural determinism. To claim that sexual differences are indissociable from discursive demarcations is not to claim that discourse causes sexual difference. The regulatory norms of sex work in a performative fashion to constitute the materiality of bodies, to naturalize sexual difference (1993a: 2). What we need is not to bring back the transcendental subject but to foster a collective disidentification that can facilitate a reconceptualization of which bodies matter. To claim that the subject is constituted by gender norms does not do away with the subject or the possibility of resistance but allows us to examine the conditions under which it emerges (1993a: 7).

Rethinking construction will lead to a rethinking of subjects, agency, and bodies. All are constituted by discourse but not wholly determined by it. Two themes are emphasized here that were present in *GT* but now come to the foreground: performativity and the abject. Gender norms are constituted by their performance; destabilizing those norms can be effected by denying the performance. Gender norms determine what is and is not a valuable body. Bodies that are *not* valuable – the abject – can only be recognized if we expand what counts as a valuable body through a radical rearticulation of the symbolic horizon (1993a: 10–23).

> The task is to refigure this necessary "outside" as a future horizon, one in which the violence of exclusion is perpetually in the process of being overcome. (1993a: 53)

Central to Butler's argument is her claim that the iterability of performance is not determined in advance. Drag reveals the performativity of gender, but also the anxiety of heterosexual performativity (1993a: 128). If gender is established through performance then our best strategy is not to fix identity, but to reveal the political power of the performance and deploy a multitude of identities. Performativity allows us to turn power against itself to produce alternative modalities of power. The key question, however, is "How will we know the difference between the power we promote and the power we oppose." We are *in* power even as we oppose it. The incalculable effects of action are as much a part of their subversive promise as those that we plan in advance (1993a: 241).

Thus, finally, it all comes back to the subject: we need a new way of thinking about subjects and their agency, a way that begins with discursive constitution: "The subject is neither a ground nor a product, but the permanent possibility of a certain resignifying process" and "To take the construction of the subject as a political problematic is not the same as doing away with the subject; to deconstruct the subject is not to negate or throw away the concept" (1995a: 47–9).

I think that it is fair to say that, on the whole, Butler's critics could simply not accept the radical nature of this formulation.[2] To say that subjects could be both constituted and agentic seemed an impossibility for many feminists. But there is a sense in which what Butler is doing here is precisely what Beauvoir prescribed. "Woman," Beauvoir argued, was a dead-end for women; she doesn't fit into our conceptual schemes; she is forever the inferior

Other. Butler displaces this by redefining subjectivity and deconstructing the conceptual schemes that ground the subject. Without "man" there is no Other – woman – and we can rethink everything accordingly.

Although Butler's work dominated the 1990s discussion of postmodernism/poststructuralism and its relation to feminism, she was not the only defender of the alliance. The reaction to postmodernism among feminists was polarized between those who heartily embraced the approach and those who saw it as a danger to the very existence of feminism. Although there was no middle ground in these discussions, there was an agreement that, somehow, feminists had to react to the onslaught of postmodernism.[3] Toward the end of the 1980s a spate of books and articles appeared, embracing the new approach and proclaiming its usefulness for feminism. Many of these works focused on Foucault and specifically on the possibilities of resistance in his work. Most of the authors of a collection of articles by Diamond and Quinby that appeared in 1988 argued that Foucault's work was useful for feminist analysis, while acknowledging the tensions between feminism and postmodernism. In their introduction, Diamond and Quinby identify the convergences between feminism and Foucault in terms of their common emphasis on the body as a site of power, the local and intimate sources of power, the critical role of discourse, and the critique of western humanism (1988: x). Jana Sawicki (1990) likewise focuses on the possibilities of resistance in Foucault's work. The aim of her book, she declares, is to flesh out Foucault's underdeveloped remarks about resistance and struggle in order to show how his discourses can be used to support specific libertory political struggles (1990: 8). Chris Weedon's emphasis is on power rather than resistance. Feminist poststructuralism, she asserts, is a mode of knowledge production that uses poststructuralist theories of language, subjectivity, and power to understand existing power relations and to identify strategies for change (1987: 40).

I argued above that Butler's redefinition of the subject is consistent with Beauvoir's rejection of "Woman." Another defender of a feminist postmodernism also writes in this Beauvoirian spirit. In *Thinking Fragments* (1990) Jane Flax identifies feminism, psychoanalysis, and postmodernism as "transitional" modes of thinking that are, together, transforming our ways of thinking: each approach tries to understand the self, gender, knowledge, social relations, and cultural change without resorting to linear, teleological, hierarchical, holistic, or binary ways of thinking. Although she acknowledges the ambiguous origins of feminism, Flax nevertheless maintains that feminist notions of self, knowledge, and truth are too contradictory to the Enlightenment to be contained within its categories. She asserts:

> If we do our work well, "reality" will appear even more unstable, complex, and disorderly than it does now. In this sense perhaps Freud was right when he declared that women are the enemies of civilization. (1990: 183)

Although in *TF* Flax admits some skepticism about the postmodern subject, in her next book, *Disputed Subjects*, she seems to have overcome these hesitations: "I believe a unitary self is unnecessary, impossible, and a dangerous illusion" (1993: 93).

In her defense of a postmodern approach to feminism Margrit Shildrick argues that the openness of postmodernism should not be interpreted as a weakness but as the courage to refuse broad categories and a unidirectional fixed vision (1997: 3). But it was precisely this openness and lack of vision that became the focus of feminist critiques of postmodernism. Losing "woman" was more than some feminists were willing to accept. It seemed obvious to many critics that without "woman" feminism, and particularly a feminist politics, would be impossible. Nancy Hartsock found the timing of this questioning of "woman," furthermore, to be especially ironic. What we need to do,

Hartsock insists, is not to get rid of the subject and sub-jectivity, but to engage in the historical, political, and theo-retical process of constituting ourselves as subjects as well as objects of history (1990: 170).

Christine Di Stefano echoes this critique in her striking image of the "incredible shrinking woman" (1990). How, she asks, can fractured identities be the basis for politics (1990: 76)? In a similar vein, Seyla Benhabib argues that the postmodern subject leads to incoherence, not politics or emancipation (1995: 21). Susan Bordo takes the theme of incoherence to the methodological level. Feminist post-moderns want us to see identity as a tapestry and to examine the many aspects of women's identity. But, she asks, "how many axes can one include and still preserve analytic focus or argument" (1990: 139)? We are so afraid of falling into essentialism, she concludes, that we have become methodologically paralyzed.

It should not be surprising that the most vociferous criticisms of postmodernism come from theorists who identify themselves in Marxist terms. A number of related issues emanate from these critiques but they revolve around three key concerns: materiality, systemic social criticism, and emancipation. Because of its exclusive emphasis on discourse and difference, it is claimed, postmoderns "lose" the material world, the world in which the exploitation of women takes place.

Hartsock, again, is the most eloquent: "For those of us who want to understand the world systematically in order to change it, postmodern theories at their best give little guidance" (1990: 159). The Marxist orientation of this statement is obvious, but its challenge is specifically femi-nist. The whole point of feminism, Hartsock argues, is to understand the world so we can change it; emancipation is the goal of feminism just as it is for Marxism. Postmod-ernism, on her reading, is not only not a help, but is actu-ally a hindrance. Benhabib, speaking from a Habermasian perspective, concurs: "Can feminist theory be postmodern-ist and still retain an interest in emancipation?" she asks

(1995: 24). The answer for her, as it is for Hartsock, is obvious.

Perhaps the most forceful, if not vituperative, attack on postmodernism from at least a quasi-Marxist perspective is Teresa Ebert's *Ludic Feminism* (1996). From Ebert's perspective in the mid-1990s postmodernism had become the dominant force in feminist theory. Hence her critique has an added urgency. On her reading, it is necessary not only to reveal the errors of postmodern feminism but to dislodge it from its dominant position by offering an alternative. Her way of doing so is to divide postmodernism into ludic and resistance postmodernism. For Ebert, ludic feminism encompasses most of what is commonly identified as postmodern feminism. Her argument is that ludic feminism has abandoned the problems of class and exploitation and their relation to gender, sexuality, difference, desire, and subjectivity (1996: ix). Ludic feminism denies the possibility of reliable knowledge, replacing it with a concept of theory as play. Like Hartsock, she argues that this obviates the possibility of a coherent understanding of patriarchy and capitalism, and also the possibility of changing these institutions (1996: 5, 17). By rewriting the social as discursive, ludic feminism fails to provide the basis for a coherent feminism.

Resistance postmodernism on Ebert's definition is a strange hybrid. On the surface it looks very much like historical materialism. It is defined in terms of a historical materialist understanding of changing socio-cultural conditions and a new articulation of the relations of production. The historical materialist practice that it articulates identifies difference within a material system of exploitation. Ebert claims that resistance postmodernism constitutes a radical intervention in the relations of production and the superstructure (1996: 133, 148, 182). The difference between resistance postmodernism and classical historical materialism thus appears to be that its subject matter is the postmodern world of advanced capitalism. It is, in other words, the postmodern translation of Marx's theory. This,

Ebert claims, should be the future direction of feminist theory rather than the ludic variety that has prevailed.

These criticisms of postmodern feminism are far from frivolous. The postmoderns' radical critique deconstructs not only the basis of Enlightenment thought, but also the historical and epistemological basis of feminism. As Christine Di Stefano points out, feminism is thoroughly if ambivalently modern (1990). The critics of postmodern feminism are right: we do need a subject as well as knowledge, agency, and politics. The problem with these critiques is that they assume that it necessarily follows that we retain modernist concepts to achieve these goals. But we do not have to accept this assumption. What postmodernism has revealed is that the challenge, rather, is to recast these concepts in light of what we have learned from discursive analysis. Postmodernism does not, despite its critics, entail the death of the subject, but instead the death of the modernist subject, man. This death is a triumph for feminism and consistent with the project that Beauvoir initiated. Perhaps the reluctance of many feminists to accept postmodernism's radical critique is related to their reluctance to abandon the tradition that has such deep roots in our culture. What postmodernism revealed is that what feminists need to do is to construct a new way of defining subjects, agency, politics, and knowledge in the wake of the death of man.

It is possible to argue that this is precisely what material feminism has done and continues to do. But material feminism did not, in a sense, emerge full-blown from the criticisms of postmodernism. In the 1990s several feminist theorists made important contributions to the definition of the feminine subject that were informed by postmodernism and pointed to material feminism. Drucilla Cornell and Rosi Braidotti in particular advanced our understanding of feminist theory in the wake of the postmodern/discursive turn. Their work is important not only in clarifying the path that the postmoderns articulated, but also in pointing toward what was to follow.

In *Beyond Accommodation* (1999) and several other works, Cornell takes up the challenge that postmodernism poses to feminism. If there is to be a feminism at all, she asserts, we must rely on a feminine voice and feminine reality that can be identified as such and correlated with the lives of actual women. And we must do so in a way that does not deny the differences between women (1999: 3). The strategy she proposes to accomplish this is mimesis: the affirmation of the feminine as performance that can be restylized (1999: 19). Mimesis, she claims, allows us to move within the gender hierarchy to give it new meaning (1999: 148). Our goal cannot be to dethrone the myth of woman and create a neutral person. Beauvoir has shown that to be impossible. Our only option is to work within myth to reinterpret it (1999: 196). And, finally:

> Ontology of gender identity, then, has been deconstructed not just to expose the normative injunction that lies at its base, but to protect the possibility of a different destiny. (1999: 205)

Rosi Braidotti takes on the key issue of contention in postmodern feminism directly and offers an innovative theoretical position. The death of the subject, she asserts, far from being a metaphor for the void, is a sign of irrepressible theoretical vitality (1991: 2). In *Patterns of Dissonance* she links what she calls the discourse of crisis in contemporary thought and new feminist reflections on subjectivity. The conception of the subject that she proposes is an immensely fruitful one: the nomadic subject. Her argument is that the void left by the exhaustion of the classical version of subjectivity is not an absence or a death, but the historical opportunity to assert the incompleteness and partiality of thought in a positive manner – to open up a new set of possibilities (1991: 140). Central to Braidotti's argument is her thesis that it is no accident that the philosophical crisis of legitimacy arises at the same time as the emergence of the women's movement. But, she asserts, women have different goals from those of the philosophers. Most importantly, women seek to give their struggles a sex-specific character (1991: 211). Feminism has intensified the crisis but is not synonymous with it.

Braidotti fleshes out these themes in her 1994 book, *Nomadic Subjects*. "Nomadic consciousness is an epistemological and political imperative for critical thought at the end of this millennium" (1991: 2). Significantly, Braidotti argues that the starting point for feminist reflections on subjectivity is a new form of materialism that emphasizes embodiment and the sexually differentiated structure of the speaking subject. This constitutes the epistemological project of nomadism. The nomad is a situated, postmodern, culturally differentiated subject, a myth, a political fiction that allows us to move across the established categories (1994a: 4).

Braidotti's nomadic subject is consonant with many of the themes of Butler's work, but fleshes out the parameters of the subject that they both espouse. The nomad is a postmetaphysical, intensive, multiple entity, functioning in a net of interconnectedness (1994a: 36). It is situated and embodied. Braidotti's nomadic subject, furthermore, addresses an issue that was problematic for Butler: politics. Braidotti argues that one need not be settled in a substantive vision of the subject in order to be political (1994a: 35). Echoing Butler, Braidotti argues for a politics of parody in which subjectivity can be explored (1994a: 7). Foundations are not required for political agency and can often be a hindrance to flights of nomadic consciousness (1994a: 35). The key question for feminism, Braidotti argues, is how to reassemble a vision of female subjectivity after the certainties of gender dualism have collapsed (1994a: 99). Her answer is a new kind of female embodied materialism working along the lines of a multiplicity of variables of definition of female subjectivity: race, class, age, sexual preference, and lifestyle (1994a: 156).[4]

Although this was not her intent in 1994, Braidotti's vision is a blueprint for two movements in feminist understandings of the subject that are on the horizon: intersectionality and material feminism. But this is not accidental. Postmodernism, although flawed in many of the ways its critics enumerate, was nonetheless an important step in the evolution of the feminine subject. It brings to the forefront the constitutive force of discourse in defining subjects and the reality they inhabit. And it is consistent with Beauvoir's injunction to transcend previous ways of thought and construct a new feminist approach to knowledge and the subject. The postmoderns provided an important stepping stone in the history of the evolution of the feminine subject. But, like all the conceptions that preceded it, the postmodern feminine subject also left some questions unanswered. It is these questions that would form the springboard to the next conceptions.

II. Race and Ethnicity

In 1988 I was teaching a class in feminist theory at the University of Washington. Almost as an afterthought, I had added a reading about black feminist theoretical approaches to the syllabus, with the intention of devoting one class period to the discussion of race and gender before continuing with the "regular" subject of the class. As the discussion began, a black woman in the class stood up and declared angrily that my way of dealing with the issue of race and gender was totally unacceptable. Race, she claimed, and the differences it entails, changes everything. My strategy of discussing race for one class and then moving on did not take account of the radical changes entailed by introducing racial difference into feminist theory. She angrily stalked out of class.

The young woman's disruption of my classroom certainly got my attention: these sorts of events do not normally occur in the course of my teaching. But it brought home to me the revolutionary consequences entailed by introducing race into feminist theory. My student was right: race changes everything; feminist theory, and, most importantly, our understanding of the subject, must be radically rethought. This rethinking first arose in the political arena with the claim by women of color that the feminist movement was dominated by white, middle-class women. Subsequently this political protest came to affect theoretical discussions as well. Again, women of color have claimed that feminist theory is about white, middle-class women, stating their own voices have been silenced in both theory and practice.

In the 1980s, a spate of books and articles emerged that challenged the hegemony of white feminist thought. Emblematic of these discussions are bell hooks's *Feminist Theory: From Margin to Center* (1984) and Patricia Hill Collins's *Black Feminist Thought* (1990). Notably, hooks claimed that feminism in the US did not emerge from the women most victimized by sexist oppression. The one-dimensional perspective of the feminist movement, she declared, must be corrected with a counter-hegemony. Collins argued that we must place black women's experiences at the center of analysis without privileging those experiences. Other groups of women took up the challenge as well. Chicanas focused on their unique perspective as both non-white and culturally other. Gloria Anzaldua's concept of the borderland brought home the special status of Chicanas in – and out of – the feminist movement (1999). This discussion also spread beyond US borders. Feminists challenged the unitary characterization of "woman" that informed western feminists' discussion of "third world women." Chandra Mohanty argued that we need to counter both the assumption of woman as a coherent group with identical interests, and the lack of understanding of contradictions inherent in women's location in various structures (1991). Thus, from the outset, issues of difference defined these works. "Non-white women," in itself a suspect category, were and are varied and diverse. Issues of class, sexual orientation, and ethnicity multiply differences.

It was unavoidable that the discussions of race and ethnicity and its place in feminism intersected with many of the discussions surrounding the role of postmodernism in feminism. Attention to difference dominates both approaches, but the appropriate relationship between these discussions remains contentious. While some feminist theorists have claimed that postmodern theories are particularly suited to issues of race and ethnicity, feminist theorists of color have countered that the adoption of such theories is yet another form of colonization, one more effort to subsume women of color under a white male discourse.

The stage was set for the discussion of the intersections of race, ethnicity, and gender in feminist theory by Edward Said's pathbreaking *Orientalism* (1978). Although Said is discussing the European "invention" of the Orient, the terms of his discourse are directly relevant to theorizing about women in general and women of color in particular. Said's thesis is that Orientalism is a created body of theory and practice that is parasitic on the cultural hegemony of the west. In this discourse the west is the actor, the Orient the passive reactor; as such, the Orient is identified as feminine, silent, and supine (1978: 138). Said explicitly links the concept of the Orient with concepts identified as "Other" in the hegemonic discourse: women, the insane, the poor (1978: 207). His point is that there is no "essence" of the Orient, but that it is both a discursive construct and a necessary product of the hegemony of the west.

Said's thesis both illuminates and complicates the current feminist dispute about women of color and feminist theory, especially as it relates to postmodernism. On the one hand, Said reveals that the "otherness" of women of color is a constructed, not an essential, category and that it is parasitic both on the hegemonic discourse of white society and on the discourse of white feminist theorists, The very term "women of color" makes no sense without the corresponding concept of "white women." One of the conclusions that seems to follow from this insight is that it would be in the interests of women of color to deconstruct the discourse that marginalizes them, to displace the discourse of center and periphery, self and other. Thus, it would seem that postmodern theories are uniquely applicable to the situation of women of color, women who have been doubly marginalized: by white males in the larger society and white women in the feminist movement. The problem with this neat solution, however, is that in order to effect this displacement, women of color would have to rely on the theoretical constructs of the white European males who created postmodernism. Many women of color find this option unacceptable.

For women of color, their situation is both simple and complex. It is clear that they have been the "Other" in feminist theory – marginalized as different and to a large extent ignored. It has also seemed clear to at least some women of color that it is necessary for them to go their own way rather than attempt to find a place in white feminist theory. It is significant that Audre Lorde is speaking from the perspective of a woman of color when she makes her famous statement: "The *master's tools* will *never* dismantle *the* master's house. They may allow us temporarily to beat him at his own game, but they will never enable us to bring about genuine change" (1981: 99; italics in original). This maxim can be applied to the relationship between white feminist theory and women of color as well. This sentiment has been frequently reiterated. Cherríe Moraga states: "No one can or will speak for us. We must be the ones to define the parameters of what it means to be female and mestizo" (1983: 139). Similarly, Lugones and Spelman (1983) argue that women of color do not recognize themselves in the theories of white feminists.[5] They argue that women with different racial and ethnic identities should not try to fit themselves into these theories but, rather, should work together with white women to jointly create feminist theory.

Barbara Christian (1987) takes this line specifically in relation to literary criticism. She claims that the literary world has been taken over by western philosophers, who have changed literary criticism to suit their own purposes, devaluing and disprivileging those who do not follow in their footsteps. As a result, black and third world critics have been co-opted "into speaking a language and defining their discussion in terms alien to and opposed to our own needs and orientation" (1987: 52). She argues that women of color can and must theorize, but asserts, like Moraga, that it must be in ways that are specific to them:

> For people of color have always theorized – but in forms quite different from the Western form of abstract logic. And I am inclined to say that our theorizing...is often in narrative forms, in the stories we create, in riddles and proverbs, in the play with language, since dynamic rather than fixed ideas seem more to our liking. (1987: 52)

She concludes that what will emerge from this process will not be a "set" theory, a "black feminist literary criticism," but a language that arises from black feminist texts themselves.

Christian's target is theory in general, but other feminist theorists concerned with questions of race and ethnicity have attacked postmodern and poststructuralist theories in particular. Paula Gunn Allen (1986), in her work on the American Indian tradition, specifically criticizes the use of postmodern literary theory in American Indian literary criticism. She claims that American Indians' rejection of western theory is distinct from that of postmodernism, because the former does not constitute a reaction against western tropes. Thus, in the "surrealism" of American Indian literature, dreams and visions do not represent departures from western rationality but are an integral part of a separate oral tradition (1986: 81–91). Likewise, Joyce Joyce (1987), in an argument with Henry Louis Gates on the use of poststructuralism in black literary criticism, argues that treating blackness as a metaphor violates the integrity of black literary criticism. She argues instead that black reactive art is an act of love that sustains the black community.

Feminist women of color have a particular stake in these disputes. On the face of it, rejection of the hegemonic discourse informing postmodernism would seem to be a welcome theoretical refuge for marginalized groups. This is precisely what Jana Sawicki, a (white) postmodern feminist argues. Sawicki's view is that Foucault's politics of difference is particularly applicable to women of color and lesbians because he assumes that difference is not an obstacle to effective resistance (1986: 32). Mae Henderson (1992) argues that Bakhtin's dialogism is an appropriate model for understanding black women's writing, because it defines each group as speaking in its own "social dialect," its own language, values, perspectives, and norms. Gayatri Spivak is perhaps the best-known theorist to unite postmodernism and ethnicity. Despite her advocacy of postmodernism, however, Spivak is ambivalent about the convergence of postmodernism and theorizing ethnicity. In her analysis of the Subaltern Studies Collective (1987: 197–221) she acknowledges an affinity between the imperialist subject and the humanist subject and hence the relevance of the critique of humanism for subaltern studies. Yet she qualifies this by adding that subaltern studies mixes discourse theory with traces of essentialism. And bell hooks offers one of the most positive arguments for uniting postmodernism and theories of ethnicity. Although in her early work she is not explicitly postmodern, in *Yearning* she embraces postmodernism because of its "polyphonic vocality" and its critique of essentialism (1990: 228). In the book she explicitly addresses the charge that postmodernism does not relate to the realities of the lives of black people. Although she concedes that postmodernism unfortunately directs its critical voice primarily to a specialized audience, she nevertheless insists that it is also the contemporary discourse that speaks most directly to questions of heterogeneity and difference. Avoiding theory altogether, she claims, will simply result in the perpetuation of racism.

She advocates the employment of postmodern techniques while at the same time conceding that postmodernism lacks a political program. In the course of presenting her position, she outlines how postmodernism might be employed to address the marginality of black women. Staying on the margins, she argues, nourishes one's will to resist:

> This is an intervention. A message from that space in the margin that is a site of creativity and power, that inclusive space where we recover ourselves, where we move in solidarity to erase the category colonizer/colonized. Marginality as a site of resistance. Enter that space. Let us meet there. Enter that space. We greet you as liberators. (1990: 152)

One of the virtues of hooks's work is that she brings her discussion of postmodernism, ethnicity, and feminism to bear on the discussions of the feminine subject. The issues here are complex. If Said is correct, then it is modernist theories of the subject that have constituted the "otherness" of racial identity by constructing the marginalized other as inferior. Thus it would seem that embracing racial/ethnic identity, declaring that there is an essential subject that is, for example, black, Native American, or Chicana, will perpetuate rather than defeat the modernist hegemony of self and other. But the postmodern move of deconstructing identity has its dangers as well. What is left, many theorists ask, if we deconstruct the otherness of the other? Isn't it necessary to posit a concrete identity on which to build identity politics?

From hooks's viewpoint, this is a danger that can be met and overcome. Like Spivak, she connects essentialist concepts of the self with racism and looks to postmodernism to deconstruct these notions. She argues that the postmodern critique of essentialism provides possibilities for the construction of self and agency that avoid the strictures of essentialism. Furthermore, postmodernism can help define black subjectivity as not unitary but plural (1990: 28–9). In *Talking Back* (1989) hooks illustrates her thesis by describing how she came to be "bell hooks." She explains that as a child she rejected the good little black girl she was supposed to be and, instead, adopted the persona of her outspoken and rebellious great-grandmother, bell hooks. What is significant here is that hooks does not argue that she "discovered" her "real" or "authentic" self in taking on the identity of "bell hooks" but, rather, that she used the elements of subjectivity available to her in her cultural setting. Gates expresses a similar attitude toward subjectivity in his attack on the notion of a transcendent black subject. He maintains that the assumption of an "unassailable integral black self" is false to the black experience (1987: 115–16). Like hooks, he argues that we must deconstruct this essential self.

Although she wants to claim that there is no essence to black subjectivity, hooks nevertheless argues that the construction of the black subject is distinctive. This in itself is an important point. It means that abandoning the concept of essence and arguing for a discursively constituted identity do not necessarily entail abandoning a distinctive definition of identity. Here hooks asserts that the sense of self in black community is a self in relation, a self dependent on others (1989: 30–1). This thesis is echoed in the work of several other black writers. Patricia Collins alleges that, for black women, "Self is not defined as increased autonomy gained by separating oneself from others. Instead, self is found in the context of family and community" (1990: 103). She maintains that black women have fashioned an independent standpoint regarding the meaning of black womanhood, a standpoint that arises out of their common experience. In discussing Afro-American autobiographical writing, Selwyn Cudjoe argues that it avoids "excessive subjectivism and mindless egoism" (1984: 9). She concludes that "the Afro-American autobiographical statement emerges as a *public* rather than a *private* gesture, *me-ism* gives way to *our-ism* and superficial concerns about the *individual subject* usually give way to the *collective subject* of the group" (1984: 10).

Discussions of the issue of race and ethnicity as it relates to gender have brought questions of identity to the forefront. There appear to be advantages, particularly in politics, to defining the subject in essentialist terms: an essentialist subject can be opposed to the hegemonic subject of the dominant discourse. But these writers make a persuasive case that the disadvantages of this move outweigh the advantages. First, positing an essentialist subject denies the multiplicity of subjects that are constructed by the different experiences of non-white women. The experiences of non-white women, "women of color," are not monolithic: many differences divide them; they are subject to different kinds of oppression. Subsuming all non-white women under one concept of identity would deny the specificity of their oppression and impede the political process of overcoming it (Moraga 1981). Second, an essentialist subject is parasitic on the hegemonic discourse that defines "women of color" as "Other" (Trinh T. Minh-ha 1989: 99); it constructs identity using the master's tools. What these writers are suggesting is that identity need not be abandoned if difference is embraced. Rather, as Elizabeth Meese puts it, wholeness and identity require continual negotiations in the field of difference (1990: 48). Difference does not annul identity but, rather, is beyond and alongside it (Minh-ha 1989: 104).

The key issue in this dispute over identity is politics. Feminist women of color seek to posit a subject that can resist the hegemony of the white, middle-class subject, both masculine and feminine. Spivak expresses a common fear in her rejection of the "disappearing subject" of postmodernism on the grounds of political inadequacy (1987: 209). Meese, hooks, and Trinh T. Minh-ha, however, argue that defining subjects as differently constructed does not negate identity but, rather, fosters it. They assert that recognizing that subjects are differently constructed by race, class, and gender does not preclude the movement to end oppression (hooks 1989: 23). Instead, it recognizes that there are different *kinds* of oppression, as well as different subjects that are oppressed. What is required is a "differential consciousness" (Sandoval 1991) that can transform the dominant discourse.

It is significant that the issue of identity and politics as it relates to race has continued to occupy the attention of feminist theorists of race and ethnicity in recent years. These issues take center stage in Moya and Hames-Garcia's *Reclaiming Identity: Realist Theory and the Predicament of Postmodernism* (2000). The title says it all: the authors' goal is to wrest identity, particularly racial identity, from the grips of postmodern theory and redefine it in a realist direction. Impelling their work were two concerns: opposition to what they see as the excesses of widespread constructionism and a commitment to progressive politics. These theorists were united around the conviction that any theory of identity is inadequate unless it allows a social theorist to analyze the epistemic status and political salience of any identity and to evaluate the limits and possibilities of different identities. In her contribution to the volume Paula Moya states the problem very directly:

> In the current theoretical climate within U.S. literary and cultural studies, the feminist scholar who persists in using categories such as race or gender can be presumptively charged with essentialism, while appeals to "experience" or "identity" may cause her to be dismissed as either dangerously reactionary or hopelessly naïve. (2000: 68)

In the context of a critique of Haraway's concept of identity, and particularly the influential figure of the cyborg, Moya argues for an approach to identity that acknowledges how race, class, gender, and sexuality function in individual lives without reducing individuals to these social determinants (2000: 80). What Moya and the other contributors to the volume are attempting to accomplish is to avoid the key problem that has plagued the postmodern concept of identity – the social dupe – without relinquishing the insights gained by the discursive analysis of identity.

To accomplish this goal the authors develop what they call the "postpositivist realist" theory of identity. The authors' discontent with the unreconstructed linguistic determinism of most postmodern theory and their attempt to bring politics back into theory, to look at the practical consequences of the theoretical positions we inhabit is cogently argued and persuasive. Especially insightful is the argument of Linda Alcoff. Both in the article in this volume and in the comprehensive statement of her position in *Visible Identities* (2006), Alcoff elaborates a position that challenges what she calls the "merely linguistic" approach to identity fostered by the postmoderns. The "visible" in the title of her book refers to the visible marks of identity on the body: race and gender operate through the visibility of bodies. Thus identity is not just "What is given to an individual or group, but it is also a way of inhabiting, interpreting and working through, both collectively and individually, an objective social location and group history" (2006: 42).

In order to buttress her position, Alcoff turns to the work of Gadamer. Gadamer's perspective, she asserts, rules out an absolute relativism on identity. No horizon of human being on this earth will be totally incommensurable because all humans share a material life. But there is relativism in the valuation of social practice (2006: 100). In a bold move, Alcoff applies her understanding of the relationship between objective and relative to the dangerous territory of sexed identity and the body. Her thesis is that there is an objective basis of sexed identity: women and men have a different relationship to the possibility of biological reproduction (2006: 172). Relativism enters in the valuation of this relationship. In the end her position is this: identities are discursively constituted; I cannot arbitrarily choose the identity I inhabit. But these identities are also real. The material effects of different identities structure the hierarchy of social relations.[6]

A number of conclusions emerge from this literature. First, the treatment of difference in postmodernism and theories of race and ethnicity, although related, also raise troubling questions. If differences, including racial difference, are linguistically constituted, does this entail that we must give up the "real"? Or, as Alcoff argues, can we incorporate both into a single theory? The second conclusion is that discussions of race and gender raise questions that cannot be answered by existing theories. We need, in a sense, a fresh look at difference. The turn to intersectional theory and feminist materialism represent attempts to provide that new approach.

III. Intersectionality

It is significant that one of the foremothers of black feminist thought, Patricia Hill Collins, raises the issue that would dominate subsequent feminist discussions of difference: intersecting oppressions. In the second edition of *Black Feminist Thought* she asserts that oppression cannot be reduced to one type of oppression and that we must work together to create justice (2009: 21). The focus on intersectional paradigms captured the attention of many feminists as feminist theory moved into the twenty-first century. Most specifically, defining the self as the point of intersection of structures of oppression became the center of feminist discussions.

In her comments on the rise of intersectionality in feminist theory, Mary Hawkesworth defines intersectionality as an analytic tool developed by feminists of color in their struggle to correct the omissions and distortions of feminist analysis caused by the failure to investigate the structuring power of race, class, ethnicity, sexuality, and nationality (2006: 207). Since the nineteenth century, she notes, black women have been analyzing and writing about the intimate interplay of race, gender, class, and sexuality that structure their lives with multiple vectors of power

(2006: 208). As Collins notes, women of color brought to our attention the multiple sources of oppression by revealing that focusing on gender oppression alone was inadequate. The focus on multiple sources of oppression is at the center of intersectional analysis. Intersectional analysts argue that oppression cannot be reduced to one type and that oppressions work together to create injustice (Collins 2009: 2). Collins asserts: "In a context of intersecting oppressions Black feminism requires searching for justice not only for U.S. Black women, but for everyone" (2009: 48). She goes on to argue that because black women are one of the few groups negatively affected by multiple forms of oppression, they are in a better position to see their interrelationship (2009: 233).

Leslie McCall boldly states that "intersectionality is the most important theoretical construction that women's studies, in conjunction with related fields, has made so far" (2005: 1771). Although most contemporary feminist theorists would stop short of this sweeping assessment, there is a consensus among feminists that intersectionality is immensely useful and insightful (Lykke 2010: 50). There is not agreement, however, on how to define the approach and how to articulate a specifically intersectional method. In her work on intersectionality Lykke tries to make up for this omission:

> Intersectionality is a methodological and theoretical tool to analyze how historically specific kinds of power and/or constraining normativity based on discursively, institutionally, and/or structurally constructed socio-cultural categorizations such as gender, ethnicity, race, class, sexuality, age/generation, disability, nationality, Mother tongue and so on interact and in doing so produce different kinds of social inequalities and social relations. (2010: 50)

For Lykke, intersectionality entails the analysis of how individual subjects negotiate the power-laden social conditions in which they are embedded (2010: 51).

As every discussion of intersectionality notes, it was Kimberle Crenshaw's 1989 article that first introduced the term into feminist theory. In her analysis of a legal case involving discrimination against black women Crenshaw focuses on the intersecting vectors of power that subordinate these women. Her thesis is that single-axis analysis erases black women. The operative conceptions of race and sex utilized represent only one subset of a more complex phenomenon (1989: 140). The complexity of this phenomenon came to be realized as intersectional analysis spread beyond its origins in the intersection of race and gender. It soon became obvious that this intersection was only the tip of the iceberg, that many other vectors of domination were also operative. And, thus, a whole new theoretical vista opened up. As did a new politics. Crenshaw notes:

> Through an awareness of intersectionality we can both acknowledge and ground the differences among us and negotiate the means by which these differences will find expression in constructing group politics. (1995: 377)

Much like postmodernism in the 1990s, intersectional analysis has taken feminist theory by storm. Routledge has launched a new series to accommodate this popularity: Routledge Advances in Feminist Studies and Intersectionality. It is tempting to conclude from this title that "feminist studies" and "intersectionality" have in effect merged, a conclusion with which many feminists would concur. In an article published in 2008 Kathy Davis tries to explain the phenomenal rise of intersectional analysis. She notes that any scholar today who neglects differences runs the risk of having her work viewed as theoretically misguided, politically irrelevant, or simply fantastical. But she also notes that despite its popularity there is confusion over whether intersectionality is a theory, a heuristic device, or a research strategy. The main purpose of her argument, however, is not to answer this question but to examine how a theory that is so vague could be so successful. Her conclusion is that intersectionality's focus on difference brings together two strands of feminist thought: understanding the effects of race, class, gender, and women's identity and experience, and analyzing how these factors intersect to produce and transform relations of power (2008: 71). Davis concludes that intersectionality offers a reason to do feminist theory today and assuages our fear that, in an era of differences, theory is superfluous (2008: 72).

The question of what is distinct both methodologically and theoretically in intersectional analysis is a central concern in the discussions of the approach. Collins suggests that it entails a "transversal politics": with the assumption of transversalism, participants bring with them a rooting in their own position but realize that to engage in dialogue across multiple markers of difference they must shift from their own centers (2009: 265). She argues that this results in an understanding of the "matrix of domination" to which subjects are subjected (2009: 246). The theme of multiplicity comes up in many accounts. Jonasdottir, Bryson, and Jones argue that any adequate theory of gender and sexuality requires multiple methods of investigation and interpretive analysis (2011: 4). This entails, they claim, a shift beyond intersectionalities to transsectionalities (2011: 6); Lykke also emphasizes the transformative power of intersectional analysis. It describes forces, she claims, that intra-act rather than interact. Interaction is between discrete phenomena; intra-action transforms the phenomena through interpenetration (2010: 51). The theme of these comments is clear: intersectionality takes the next step in feminist analysis. It goes beyond: it makes visible processes of marginalization that mainstream accounts omit (Hawkesworth 2006: 210); it asks the "other question" (Matsuda 1991: 1189).

Lykke argues that at any given time it is important for feminist analysis to have a nodal point (2010: 86). I think most feminists would agree that, in the early twenty-first century, that nodal point is intersectionality. There is little that I could say here that would add anything significant to the voluminous literature on intersectionality and I will not attempt to do so. But I think it is worth asking at this point what we have gained from the approach. As Lykke herself points out, we have been doing intersectionality for a long time. It is not a stunning insight that identities are complex, that not only gender but race, sexuality, and myriad other factors constitute identity (Sojourner Truth told us this). What intersectionality has done is to bring this insight to the fore and give it a name – which is in itself a positive move for feminist theory. It is also valuable that in terms of feminist analysis intersectionality has spawned what seem like an endless array of case studies. This should come as no surprise. Since the varieties of identities are multiple, their intersections are an exponential function of the multiplicity. Almost any aspect of identity can be analyzed in terms of another aspect: the possibilities of analyses are incalculable.

A less fortunate result of intersectional analysis is the creation of a whole new array of categories in feminist theory. McCall discusses intersectionality in terms of anti-categorical complexity, intercategorical categorical complexity and intra-categorical complexity. Some theorists refer to transsectionality and transversal politics; other categories abound. This tendency has little to recommend it. The last thing that feminism needs today is a list of more categories into which we must fit our analysis. It does not aid our understanding to create even more complicated terms to describe what we study; it obfuscates rather than reveals. Yet this seems to be a distinctive mark of the approach in recent years.

Intersectionality is not without its critics (Hindman 2011; Zack 2005). But, as Davis points out, its sweep is very broad; those who deviate from it can even be accused of "fantastical analysis." I think this is unfortunate on two levels. First, establishing any approach as orthodoxy cuts off exploration of alternative viewpoints. Feminism should not be about finding the "right" approach but, rather, encourage experimenting with multiple approaches in an open environment. For all its virtues, intersectional analysis is not the end point of feminist theory. It is another step along the way. Second, the question of whether intersectionality provides a new perspective on feminist theory is an open one. Does intersectionality have "transformative power" or, as some of its proponents assert, is it merely an extension of what feminists already know: that identities are complex?

The "discovery" of differences between women, along with the realization that ignoring those differences privileges a particular group of women, has changed feminism. We cannot go back to the era of difference; the change is irrevocable. Beauvoir herself and several generations of subsequent theorists could not see beyond a unitary definition of "woman." But the move to differences need not be seen as a repudiation of the era of difference. Rather, emphasizing differences can be interpreted as expanding our understanding of the subject from a feminist perspective. Since Beauvoir's bold assertion that women are made, not born, feminists have been struggling to define "woman" outside the parameters of western thought. One of the defining characteristics of western thought is essential identity. Since Aristotle, "man" and "woman" have been essential identities that create hierarchy within each category. Challenging that conception is an important step in redefining "woman" in the Beauvoirian tradition.

— 6 —

The Material Subject

Reality is what one does not perceive when one perceives it.

Niklas Luhmann

I. The New Materialism

The era of differences in feminist theory was both productive and problematic. Differences proliferated everywhere; as intersectionality demonstrated, there seemed to be no limit to the possible analyses of differences among women. Furthermore, the legacy of postmodernism with its emphasis on language provided feminists with rich opportunities for examining the constitutive power of language. Having rejected groundings, metanarrative, and "woman," feminists found themselves in a limitless space. To some, this situation was an advantage: it meant that nothing was privileged, that we had destroyed the hierarchies that categorized women. Others were not so sure. Were we floundering in difference without any direction or grounding? Had we lost our focus?

Linguistic constructionism/postmodernism created a particular dilemma for feminism. While claiming to deconstruct dichotomies, in particular the dichotomy between the discursive and the material, in practice postmodernism privileged the linguistic and in effect effaced the material. Since, it was argued, language constructs reality, why should we talk about anything but language? But the privileging of language made many feminists uneasy. As Karen Barad put it so succinctly: "Language has been granted too much power. The linguistic turn, the semiotic turn, the interpretive turn, the cultural turn: it seems that at every turn lately every 'thing,' even materiality – is turned into language or some other form of cultural representation" (2007: 132). Turning to the material seemed the obvious remedy, but this move posed a danger for feminists. Modernism's emphasis on the material had been used to define and enforce the subordination of women. As a whole generation of feminist critiques of science demonstrated, science was no friend to feminism. Returning to the materialism of modernity was no solution because it would simultaneously return us to the theories that reinforced patriarchy.

What was needed, it became clear, was a new approach that would accomplish what the postmoderns promised but failed to do: deconstruct the discourse/reality dichotomy. We need to embrace the material, not shun it, but we need a method that acknowledges and builds on the insights of linguistic constructionism. The linguistic constructionists got one thing right: language *does* construct reality. What they got wrong is the idea that language alone constructs reality; other constitutive factors were ignored. The new approach that emerged in the wake of postmodernism complicates our understanding of reality by moving beyond the linguistic and, specifically, bringing the material back into the equation.

This new approach, commonly labeled the "new materialism," is wide-ranging.[1] It embraces not only feminism but philosophy of science, cultural studies, animal studies, and what has come to be called the posthuman. What I will focus on in the following are two trajectories of the new materialism that directly impinge on the feminine subject: feminist studies of the body and posthumanism. I then turn to an issue that the new materialists have not explored fully but that is central to this new understanding of the subject: the ontology of the subject. I develop a new ontology of the subject that can accommodate the contributions of the new materialists.

Underpinning both of these trajectories is the work of two theorists who have come to define the new materialism in feminism: Nancy Tuana and Karen Barad. Nancy Tuana's work has been at the forefront of feminist critiques of science for several decades. From the outset Tuana has been very clear about the necessity of transcending the dualisms that structure philosophical discussions. Since a pathbreaking article in *Hypatia* in 1983, Tuana has made these dualisms the focus of her attention. This early article assessed and rejected the nature/culture dualism. In subsequent work one of her favorite targets has been the sterility of the realism/anti-realism debate. Feminist work in epistemology and science studies, Tuana argues, has begun to identify the need for a close and nuanced examination of the complexities of materiality, specifically the cognitive impact of embodiment and the relationship between human materiality and the more-than human world (2001: 221). The alternative that Tuana suggests is "interactionism," a position that describes the emergent interplay of materiality. What we need now, Tuana argues, is a theory that posits the "coherence of interpretation, practice, phenomena, and materials" (2001: 228). The means of accomplishing this, Tuana claims, is to change our focus from epistemology to ontology. Against the social constructionist account, she argues for a "new metaphysic" that grounds human ways of knowing in patterns of bodily being:

Neither the materiality of the more-than-human world, nor human materiality is an unchanging given. What exists is emergent, issuing from complex interactions between embodiment and the world. (2001: 238)

Tuana's approach constitutes a bold philosophical move. She not only clearly defines the problem facing feminism and critical thought more generally, but she lays out a carefully defined alternative. Her "new metaphysic" addresses the key issues facing both philosophy and feminist theory. At the center of this metaphysics is her emphasis on embodiment. For Tuana, we always know as embodied human beings. This allows her to overcome the dualisms that plagued modernity: nature and culture, human and non-human, the discursive and the material. For Tuana, everything is always in flux; the human, more-than-human, material, and discursive are interacting in a complex mix. The result is a transformation of our understanding of knowledge and the world that is revolutionary.

Equally revolutionary is the work of Karen Barad. Like Tuana, Barad offers an array of concepts to describe her approach. These include "intra-action," "agential realism," "performativity," and "onto-epistem-ology." Beginning in the mid-1990s, Barad published a series of articles that outlined the parameters of her approach. Then, in 2007, she published *Meeting the Universe Halfway: Quantum Physics and the Entanglement of Matter and Meaning*. This book provides the definitive statement of her theory. Her approach offers feminists and science critics a wholly new way to address questions of truth and knowledge. Her theory breaks new ground not only for feminists, but for all theorists concerned with the future direction of knowledge.

Barad begins the book by declaring: "Matter and meaning are not separate elements" (2007: 3). The subject of her book, thus, is "entanglements": to be entangled is not simply to be intertwined with another, but "to lack an independent, self-contained existence...individuals emerge through and as a part of their entangled intra-relating" (2007: ix). The thesis that Barad develops throughout her book is that quantum physics can show us how entanglement works; it can lead us out of the morass that takes absolutism and relativism as the only two possibilities (2007: 18). Central to Barad's account is what she calls "agential realism." Agential realism as Barad defines it provides a powerful alternative to the dominant orthodoxy of linguistic constructionism. Barad's assertion is that postmodernism and poststructuralism claim to deconstruct dichotomies such as nature/culture and material/discursive, but in fact they fail to do so, instead privileging the culture/discourse side of the dichotomies. From this perspective Barad's theory does what postmodernism and poststructuralism only claim to do: it overcomes these dichotomies and provides a framework that "takes as its central concern the nature of materiality, the relationship between the material and the discursive, the nature of 'nature' and 'culture,' the relationship between them, the nature of agency, and the effects of boundary, including the nature of exclusions that accompany boundary projects" (1998: 89). In her book Barad makes it clear that her commitment to agential realism entails an attack on representationalism, the characterization of language as representing reality. Agential realism, she claims, shifts the focus from the nature of representation to the nature of discursive practices, examining how discursive practices are related to material phenomena (2007: 45).

II. Body Studies

Tuana's "interactionism," Barad's "intra-action" and "agential realism," and the "new materialism" of feminist science studies are beginning to transform feminist approaches to knowledge. This transformation is evident in the feminist science studies cited above, but it has also made deep inroads into an area that has always been central to feminist analysis: the body. For feminism, the body is unavoidable, but it is also problematic. Women's bodies are the point of intersection between patriarchal structures and women's lives. It is women's bodies that feel the pain those structures create and it is also women's bodies that have been constructed as the cause of women's inferiority. Dealing with women's bodies has thus always been a necessary aspect of feminist analysis, but also one of the most difficult.

With the advent of linguistic constructionism in feminist theory, however, the body became problematic in an entirely new way. Judith Butler's *Bodies That Matter* (1993a) released a firestorm of critique that brought the status of the body in feminist theory after postmodernism to the forefront. Critics of Butler have attacked her from many directions, but one critique stands out: the claim that despite the aspiration of postmodernism to deconstruct dichotomies, Butler's approach to the body in effect reifies the modernist dichotomy of the body as either a brute given or a representational effect (Bray and Colebrook 1998: 42). Feminists expressed widespread discontent with what they saw as Butler's privileging of discourse over materiality in her analysis of the body. Many began to explore how to avoid this theoretical impasse.

Susan Bordo has been both a consistent defender of the materiality of the body and a critic of the strictly linguistic approach to the body attributed to Butler.[2] But Bordo's position is far from a simplistic materialism. Instead, in works like *Unbearable Weight* (1993) her analyses of anorexia and bulimia as "cultural diseases" merge culture, nature, and biology into an indistinguishable mix. In recent years the attempt to find an alternative to linguistic constructionism, an attempt that picks up many of the themes of Bordo's work, has fueled a new approach to the body that radically alters the terms of the debate. Many feminists are now arguing that we should not be forced to choose between discourse and materiality, culture and nature. Rather, we should devise an approach to the body that overcomes these dualisms, that defines the body as a "complex and dynamic configuration of events that includes the material and the corporeal" (Bray and Cole-brook 1998: 44). Proponents of this approach to the body define the body as a "transformer," a complex interplay of highly constructed social and symbolic forces (Braidotti 2002: 20–2). This approach, they argue, constitutes a "healthy and exciting new era in feminist philosophy" (Kukla 2006: vii).

The feminist theorist who is most closely associated with this new approach to the body is Elizabeth Grosz. Her 1994 book, *Volatile Bodies*, stakes out what is at issue very clearly. At the outset Grosz states that we need to think about bodies in a non-dualistic way, to displace the centrality of mind in discussions of the subject and make the subject a corporeal being. But it is not enough only to avoid the dualisms that have defined the body in western thought; we also need to avoid essentialism. Grosz argues that the means to accomplish this requires that we rethink one of the pillars of feminist thought: the sex/gender distinction. Against decades of social constructionist thought, she asserts: "Gender is not an ideological superstructure added to a biological base" (1994: 58). Grosz's argument is that unless we can transcend this dichotomy that has grounded so much feminist thought, we will not be able to transform our approach to the body.

One of Grosz's most effective means of addressing this issue is her argument that masculine and feminine gender cannot be neutrally attributed to bodies of either sex. Theorists of the sex/gender distinction defined bodies as blank slates on which gender is inscribed. Grosz counters this with the point that the same message inscribed on a male or female body does not have the same meaning (1994: 156). Her argument is that bodies matter, but they are not the only aspect that matters. Like the other feminist theorists of the new materialism, Grosz is trying to include the material without excluding the discursive. Subjectivity, she asserts, is fully material, but it is a materiality extended to include the operations of language, desire, and significa-tion (1994: 210).

Grosz elaborates on these themes in *Space, Time, and Perversion: Essays on the Politics of Bodies* (1995). The specific object of her critique here concerns the effects of linguistic constructionism on discussions of the body. Her contention is that after *Gender Trouble* the dominant trend in feminist theory has been to focus on discourse at the expense of bodies. Bodies entail biologism and essentialism, the traps of modernism. Grosz wants to reverse this by providing a non-biologistic, non-reductive account of the body. She boldly asserts that sexual difference is the ontological condition of human bodies. Human bodies are always sexed bodies. But this is not all there is to the story. The sex assigned to a body has a great deal to do with the kind of social subject the body will be (1995: 85). The body, Grosz concludes, is incomplete: "it is indeterminate, amorphous, a series of uncoordinated potentialities that require social triggering, ordering, and long term 'administration'" (1995: 104).

Grosz's attempt to approach the body in radically different terms is echoed in the work of other contemporary feminist theorists. Like Grosz, Moira Gatens emphasizes sexual difference, challenging the neutrality of the body implicit in much gender theory. The connection between femininity and the female body, masculinity and the male body, she asserts, is not arbitrary (1996: 4). There are two kinds of bodies: male and female. Her thesis is that the same behavior will have different significance when acted out by male or female bodies (1996: 8–9). In order to formulate her alternative approach to the body, Gatens turns to the work of Spinoza. Unlike other theorists in the western tradition, Spinoza presents a non-dualistic philosophy in which the body is the ground of human action. Building on Spinoza's work, Gatens develops a conception of the body that focuses on what Barad calls the intra-action of bodies and culture. For Gatens, bodies exist, but what they are at any given time is always historical and cultural: "Past contingencies become the material of present necessities" (1996: 103). Bodies are always in interconnection with other body complexes. Gatens concludes that it is only within these complex assemblages that sexed bodies are produced as socially and politically meaningful bodies (1996: 149).

What the new feminist theorists of the body have accomplished constitutes a new era in feminist theory: an ontology of the body. The emphasis of these theories is that bodies *exist*, but that they exist in intra-action with a complex array of forces (Colebrook 2000). Grosz and Gatens's exploration of this ontology stays almost exclusively within the realm of theory. Other feminists exploring the ontology of the body, however, have moved their analyses into the real world that bodies inhabit. A good example of this is Annemarie Mol's analysis in *The Body Multiple: Ontology in Medical Practice* (2002). Mol calls her approach "ontological politics," a position based on the assumption that the conditions of possibility (the real) are not given but enacted (1999: 75). In her book Mol examines how medicine "enacts" the objects of its concern and treatment, how it creates an ontological politics. Instead of focusing on objects in her analysis, Mol focuses instead on practices. Her thesis is that objects are "enacted" in practices; they come into being and disappear in the practices within which they are manipulated (2002: 5).

For Mol, reality multiplies along with objects; the two are linked in the practices in which they exist. Unlike previous science studies, Mol's focus is ontological, not epistemological. But her ontology is not given in the order of things. It is, instead, brought into being through practices. The specific subject of Mol's analysis is atherosclerosis. She analyzes the treatment and experience of this disease from the perspective of doctors, patients, relatives of patients, and others in the healthcare system. But Mol is careful to distinguish her approach from perspectival interpretation. Unlike a perspectival approach, Mol's analysis foregrounds practices, materialities, events. In practices, objects are enacted. The result is what she calls "ontology-in-practice." The theoretical significance of her work, Mol hopes, is to shift the understanding of objects as the focus of various perspectives to following them as they are enacted in a variety of practices. Her question is not how science represents, but how it intervenes (2002: 152).

Mol's book is a striking illustration of how the shift to ontology alters the theoretical landscape of feminism. Mol is very clear in her rejection of epistemology and representationalism. For Mol, knowledge is no longer primarily referential but a practice that interferes with other practices (2002: 153). But she is also clear that the shift to ontology does not entail a return to modernity: "If practice becomes our entrance into the world, ontology is no longer a monist whole. Ontology-in-practice is multiple" (2002: 157). Different enactments of, in this case, a disease, entail different ontologies. Mol's goal is to analyze modes of coordination, distribution, and inclusion that allow different versions of a single object to exist (2002: 180). For Mol, everything is continually in flux, but it is a flux that is grounded in real bodies, a real disease, and real lives. Mol's analysis illustrates how what we might call the new ontology gives us a new way to understand knowledge and the world.[3]

Elizabeth Grosz summarizes the significance of feminists' new approach to the body in *The Nick of Time*: "If the body is to be placed at the center of political theory and struggle, then we need to rethink the terms in which the body is understood" (2004: 3). With this statement Grosz introduces another aspect of the new materialism that feminists are developing. For Grosz, the new terms in which the body should be understood can only be formulated by addressing an issue that has been off-limits in feminist theory since the rise of linguistic constructionism: biology. Grosz sets out to transgress these limits. The goal of *The Nick of Time* is to explore how the biological prefigures and makes possible the various permutations of life that constitute natural, social, and cultural existence (2004: 1). As Grosz is well aware, feminism's relationship to biology is highly problematic. Biological essentialism has been identified as one of the root causes of sexism from the advent of feminism. Thus approaching this subject is fraught with multiple dangers. But it is Grosz's contention that we must bring biology back into feminist theory if we are to develop the political critiques that feminism needs to further its cause.

What Grosz proposes is an understanding of biology that enables rather than limits. Biology, she asserts, is a system of differences that engenders historical, cultural, social, and sexual differences. It does not limit social, political, and personal life, but makes them possible (2004: 1). In order to elaborate her conception of the relationship between nature and culture, Grosz turns to a theorist who has been anathema to feminists because of his alleged biological determinism: Darwin. Grosz's interpretation of Darwin contests this characterization. For Grosz, Darwin's understanding of the relationship between culture and nature is that "culture produces the nature it needs to justify itself, but nature is also that which resists by opening according to its own logic and procedures" (2004: 72).

Grosz's purpose, however, is much more than a reinterpretation of Darwin. Grosz wants feminism to embrace what she calls "a politics of affirmation of difference" (2004: 72). Central to that goal is a reconfiguration of nature as dynamic, of matter as culturally productive. Grosz sees Darwin's work as facilitating rather than hindering her project. Along with the other new materialists, she is arguing that we need a new way of knowing that focuses on ontology rather than epistemology, the real rather than the production of knowledge (2004: 18). These themes carry over into Grosz's next book, appropriately titled *Time Travels* (2005). Here her attempt is to elaborate on the new conception of ontology that she sketched in the previous book. Again, she looks to Darwin. Darwin's "ontology," she claims, defines life and matter as the two orientations in the universe. What we can learn from Darwin is that human practices such as language are never adequate to life and matter. They try to contain them, but they always and necessarily escape (2005: 40–2).

Another theorist who begins with a consideration of feminist approaches to the body and moves on to an exploration of the broader framework of such analyses is Elizabeth Wilson. Wilson's premise is that despite intensive scrutiny of the body in recent feminist literature, certain fundamental aspects of the body, specifically biology and materiality, have been foreclosed (1998: 16). Like Grosz, Wilson believes that this foreclosure has both theoretical and political consequences: "Critiques premised on a primarily oppositional relation to the sciences or premised on antibiologism, antiessentialism or antirationalism are losing their critical and political purchase" (1998: 200). While Grosz turns to biology, and particularly the biology of Darwin, to make her point, Wilson turns to neurology. A feminist analysis of neuropsychology, she claims, will enable those studying feminist psychology to rethink the nature of feminist psychology and the politics of feminist intervention in general (1998: 67). In order to accomplish this, Wilson turns to what might seem a curious theoretical source: Derridean deconstruction. Wilson uses Derrida to examine psychology as a science under erasure, a science radically at odds with the binaries that seek to control it (1998: 88). But despite this significantly different strategy, Wilson ends up occupying the same theoretical space as Grosz. She concludes that the feminist emphasis on gender has meant that the possibility of thinking biology as "other than an excluded, distant, and foundational use has been foreclosed in the majority of feminist projects" (1998: 54).

Several of the theorists discussed above make reference to the issue of sexual difference in their analyses. This is not an issue limited to feminist studies of the body. It is, rather, an overarching concern that informs all contemporary discussions of the feminine subject. It is also fundamentally connected with the Beauvoirian questioning of "woman" with which I began this inquiry. Irigaray, furthermore, put this issue at the center of her analysis of woman. She understood that central to the identity of "woman" in western thought has been a particular understanding of sexual difference, and specifically bodily sexual difference. The feminist effort to redefine "woman," therefore, must challenge this fundamental definition. As Grosz puts it, sexual difference is the question of our age because it is not adequately represented in knowledge practices or values in social or psychic life. The question of sexual difference has the power to force and transform all subjects, cultures, knowledges, and practices (2011: 103). Wilson echoes this in her statement that "Sexual difference founded on compulsory heterosexuality is itself the key technology and perpetuation of western man and the assurance of this project as a fantastic lie" (1998: 352).

By bringing the body back into the analysis, the new materialists' approach to sexual difference has transformed these discussions. Linguistic constructionists were, in a sense, afraid of the body. Focusing solely on the linguistic construction of sexual difference, they avoided the materiality of the body because that materiality had, historically, been used to define sexual difference in masculine terms. By bringing the body back in, the new materialists have effected a transformation of "woman" not as a masculine defined body, but as a phenomenon produced by language, science, technology, and apparatuses. The question of sexual difference is the question of our age because we must think of it outside the confines of western thought – not as foundational or oppositional, but as the product of an array of factors not limited to language.[4]

III. Posthumanism

One of the, if not most central, dichotomies informing our definition of the human subject is that between the human and the non-human. Since Aristotle the distinction between the human and non-human worlds has been at the root of humans' self-definition, a definition that places humans firmly above the natural world. Challenging this dichotomy goes to the heart of what it means to be a subject. It also goes to the heart of feminists' attempts to redefine the subject. Women's association with nature entails that they share in the subordination of the natural world. The new materialists' challenge to this dichotomy thus has deep feminist implications.

Discussions of the posthuman move in several different directions. One is an outgrowth of Bruno Latour's insistence on the agency of the non-human world. Latour advances the thesis that the non-human world possesses agency, that it *acts*, and that this action is very much a part of our common existence. This thesis has had repercussions across the intellectual spectrum. Latour talks about a "politics of things," bringing the non-human into our political order (1999). Andrew Pickering (1995) talks about how, in scientific experiments, nature "punches back." Environmentalists call for a new ethics that includes the non-human.

Stacy Alaimo's work has been definitive in the discussions of the non- or posthuman. In *Bodily Natures* (2010) her thesis is that emphasizing the material connection of human corporeality with the more-than-human world allows us to form ethical and political positions that can contend with numerous twenty-first-century realities in which human and environment are not separate (2010: 2). In order to effect this emphasis, she develops the unique concept of "trans-corporeality." The trans-corporeal is the place where corporeal theories, environmental theories, and science studies meet in productive ways (2010: 3). Trans-corporeality, as a descendant of Darwinism, insists that the human is always the stuff of the messy, contingent, emergent mix of the material world (2010: 11). Alaimo's goal in the book is to trace how trans-corporeality ruptures ordering knowledge practices (2010: 17).

Focusing on multiple chemical sensitivity as the quintessential example of trans-corporeality, Alaimo argues for a posthuman environmental ethics in which the interchange between the human corporeality and the more-than-human world resist the ideological forces of disconnection (2010:

142). In this ethics the human becomes a site of emergent material intra-actions inseparable from the very stuff of the rest of the world; it denies the human the sense of separation from the interconnected, mutually constitutive actions of material reality (2010: 156–7). She concludes: "We need an ethics not circumscribed by the human but accountable to the material world that is never merely an external place but always the very substance of ourselves and others" (2010: 158).

Many of these themes are echoed in Jane Bennett's *Vibrant Matter* (2010). Bennett argues that women, because of their close association with nature, have a special place in this new conception of knowledge. Connecting with the feminist analyses of the body, she advocates a method that attends to the non-human forces operating inside and outside the human body (2010: xiv). Developing a vocabulary and syntax for the active powers issuing from non-subjects will give "short shrift" to the otherwise important topic of subjectivity (2010: ix). Her goal is to develop a theory of the self as an impure, human, non-human assemblage. The efficacy of agency, formerly limited to the human, is distributed across an ontologically heterogeneous field (2010: 23). She concludes: "There was never a time when human agency was anything other than an interfolding network of humanity and non-humanity; today this mingling has become harder to ignore" (2010: 31).

Katherine Hayles develops another approach to the posthuman in *How We Became Posthuman* (1999). Like the other theorists of the posthuman, Hayles focuses on agency, arguing that agency is not central to the posthuman subject. But, unlike the theorists of the posthuman who emphasize the material world and our interaction with it, Hayles turns away from the material to the disembodiment of information technology. The posthuman, she argues, entails envisioning humans as information- processing machines with fundamental similarities to complex computers (1999: 246). Hayles defines the posthuman subject specifically in opposition to the liberal subject of humanism. This adds an important dimension to the other critiques of the subject of humanism, a dimension with explicit political implications. The posthuman, Hayles argues, signals the end to a certain conception of the human, a conception that only applies to a fraction of humanity who had the wealth, power, and leisure to conceptualize themselves as autonomous beings through agency and choice (1999: 286). Hayles's critique has explicit feminist implications as well – the liberal subject she describes is, obviously, masculine. She envisions a non-sexist, non-hierarchical democratic politics that eschews the autonomous subject of humanism.[5]

IV. The Ontology of the Subject

Thanks to the discussions of the subject from the material feminists, we now see the female body as trans-corporeal, as an intra-action between nature and culture. But there is an important gap in this literature. We now have an ontology of the body, but do we have an ontology of the subject? We are more than our bodies – we are persons with identities, we are "I's." What can we say about the ontology of the subject, the "I"? Can we develop an ontology of the subject without falling prey to one of the traps of modernism: the mind/body dualism? This is an incredibly difficult topic and one which few theorists, feminists or otherwise, have attempted to analyze. But it is a topic that must be dealt with in the context of the material feminists' claim that everything is not constituted by language. The problem is this: in the case of the subject it seems abundantly obvious that we *are* wholly constituted by language. Positing an "I" apart from linguistic constitution is highly problematic and seems to necessitate a return to the essential subject of modernism. But the other alternative is equally unacceptable: that language wholly constitutes us and we are, in a sense, social dupes. This issue has been at the center of the critique of linguistic constructionism. Addressing it is imperative if we are to complete the agenda of material feminism.[6]

An ontology of the subject must be able to describe the interaction of the multiple factors that constitute subjectivity: the linguistic, the material, the cultural, the racial, sexual preference and many others. Perhaps the best understanding of this interaction is provided by a concept used by the philosopher of science, Andrew Pickering: the mangle. What we call scientific knowledge, Pickering argues, is a mangle composed of disparate elements. None alone is constitutive; each contributes unique elements. The process of the construction mangles the elements, mixes everything up. This concept will guide me in my attempt to define the ontology of the subject.

The thesis I advance here will seem, on the face of it, counter-intuitive: that our best guide in exploring the subject today is in the work of Judith Butler. Although Butler's work has been identified with the extreme constructivist pole of the debate, I will argue that in her recent work she approaches the constitution of the subject from a perspective that is unique and uniquely helpful in trying to understand the complexity of subject constitution. I will not argue that Butler has repudiated her previous position but, rather, that she has complicated and enhanced it by looking at subjects from a broader perspective than that which she takes in *Gender Trouble*. The Butler of *Gender Trouble* is, in a sense, narrowly focused. She wants to extract feminism from what she sees to be the deleterious effects of the sex/gender distinction. She also wants to reveal the errors of grounding feminism in the identity "woman." The later Butler that I use here is more comprehensive. Having made these points she moves on to a deeper analysis of the consequences of her position for feminist theory.

Butler's approach to the subject in *Gender Trouble* is not exceptional in the claim that gender is socially constructed and therefore not "real," but, rather, in the claim that sex cannot be distinguished from gender. The social construction of gender had become a staple of feminist literature by the time *Gender Trouble* was published. What sets Butler's theory apart is that she eliminates the ground on which most discussions of gender had rested: the reality of sex. For Butler, sex, like gender, is a social construction and, even more provocatively, it is *produced* by gender.[7] To many of Butler's critics this seemed to go too far. If we remove the ground of biological sex the result is that "there is no there there," no doer behind the deed. We are then left with a social dupe who cannot act and has no grounding in "reality."

I will not dispute whether this is a plausible reading of *GT*. What I want to assert is that, even at this early stage, Butler introduces perspectives that challenge a reading of her subject as a social dupe. Early in the book she asks: if there is no recourse to a person that escapes the matrix of power, then where can we look for the possibility of the subversion of that power? Her answer is that:

> If the regulatory fictions of sex and gender are themselves multiply contested sites of meaning, then the very multi-plicity of their construction holds out the possibility of a disruption of their univocal posturing. (1990: 32)

Both sex and gender are socially produced, but that social production simultaneously creates the possibility of dis-ruption. There is slippage in the construction process and this slippage opens the door to other articulations of sex and gender. Expanding on this point at the end of the book, Butler argues that the coexistence and convergence of discursive injunctions produce the possibility of recon-figurations and redeployments. Thus, although there is no self prior to this convergence, the subject can take up the "tools" where they lie (1990: 145).

Butler's goal in *Bodies That Matter* is, at least ostensibly, to answer some of the questions posed by the critics of *GT*, particularly questions relating to the subject. In doing so, she explores dimensions of the subject that were only latent in *GT*. Specifically, she confronts the issue that was at the heart of the criticisms of *GT*: how do we understand the constitutive and compelling status of gender norms without falling into the trap of cultural determinism (1993a: x)? The discussion that follows centers around two themes that structure not only this discussion but Butler's subsequent work as well: the "I" and the outside.

The "I," she declares, neither proceeds nor follows the process of gendering but emerges within the matrix of gender relations themselves (1993a: 7). This "I" (which is always in scare quotes) is not a simple entity. In a discussion of Althusser, Butler asserts that the "I" that is produced through the accumulation and convergence of calls of identity cannot extract itself from the historicity of these claims. The "I" is violating and enabling at the same time. The "I" who would oppose its construction is at the same time drawing from that construction to articulate its opposition (1993a: 122). This formulation also accounts for the issue of agency: the "I" draws its agency in part through being implicated in the very relations of power it seeks to oppose (1993a: 123).

The strategy that Butler employs in this analysis is articulated in a passage immediately preceding this discussion. What is required, she asserts, is to shift the terms of the debate from construction vs essentialism to the more complex question of how deep-seated constitutive constraints can be posed in terms of symbolic limits in their intractability and contestability (1993a: 94). It follows that "There is no subject prior to its construction, and neither is the subject determined by those constructions" (1993a: 124). In perhaps her most revealing comment, Butler admits that in making these formulations she brackets the "I," but then comments, "I am still here" (1993a: 123).

The same deconstructive impulse informs Butler's discussion of the "outside." There is an outside to what is constructed by discourse, but it is not an absolute outside, an ontological thereness (1993a: 8). The task, she asserts, is to refigure this necessary outside as a future horizon, one in which the violence of exclusion is perpetually in the process of being overcome (1993a: 53). It follows that, as with the "I," the dichotomy is breached: language and materiality are not opposed "for language both is and refers to that which is material and what is material never fully escapes from the process by which it is signified" (1993a: 68).

These two themes come together in Butler's discussion of an issue that will become a central theme of her later work: the abject. The constitution of the "I" always necessarily depends on exclusion and, specifically, the exclusion of the domain of the abject. Those who are not yet subjects form the constitutive outside of the domain of the subject (1993a: 3). Butler will have much to say about this exclusion in her subsequent work. What is important at this point, however, is that the domain of the "I" is bounded by the abject. Some are excluded from this domain that is constituted and regulated by sexual norms. Those who are excluded lack subjectivity; they are not "I's" in the full sense.

It is undeniable that, for Butler, language is necessarily imbricated in the constitution of the subject. Her critics and defenders are undoubtedly correct on this point. But it should be clear from the above analysis that this does not lead to linguistic monism or determinism. It should also be clear that, from the outset, Butler is aware that the subject is more than language, that the "I" is not simply a product of culture but, rather, a complex mix of power, agency, and subjectification. Tracing the development of the subject in Butler's work leads to the conclusion that, after GT and BTM, she realizes the difficulty of the problem she has raised and turns her attention to exploring that problem in more detail in her subsequent work. This is what sets Butler's work apart from the social constructionist position with which she is identified. Unlike other social constructionists, who make vague references to "reality" beyond discourse, Butler confronts the complexity of the problem head on and takes on the difficult task of defining a subject that is constituted conjointly by language, power, and materiality. In other words, "It must be possible to claim that the body is not identifiable apart from the linguistic coordinates that establish it without claiming that the body is nothing other than the language by which it is known" (2001: 256).

A. Subjects and subjectification

Based primarily on a reading of *GT* and *BTM*, Butler's position on the subject has come to be emblematic of what Lois McNay (2000) calls the "negative paradigm" in feminist theory. My analysis of her early works, however, reveals that Butler's understanding of the subject is much more complex and multifaceted than the "negative paradigm" allows. This complexity becomes more pronounced in her subsequent work. What emerges from this work is an understanding of the subject that, although not abandoning the constructed subject, presents the subject as a confluence of disparate forces that transcends the material/ discursive dichotomy.

The central thesis that Butler develops in this work is what she calls the paradox of the subject. This theme will structure the various discussions of the subject that will occupy her in the books that follow *GT* and *BTM*. The paradox revolves around her claim that power is what we oppose *and* what forms us as subjects (1997b: 1). The subject is "neither fully determined by power nor fully determining of power (but significantly and partially) both" (1997b: 17). She continues to insist, as she did in *GT*, that subjects are formed through subjection to power. What she emphasizes in her later work, however, is that this process is not complete, that the subject that is determined by power is not *completely* determined. Her task, then, is to explicate how that paradox operates, to explain how subjectification is not always subordinating.[8]

In her attempt to explore the paradox of the subject, Butler finds an ally in Foucault. Both Butler and Foucault argue that there is no outside to power, that the self forms itself within the context of power:

> The self forms itself but it forms itself within a set of formative practices that are characterized as modes of subjectification. That the range of its passable forms is determined in advance by such modes of subjectification does not mean that the self fails to form itself, that the self is fully formed. On the contrary, it is compelled to form itself, but to form itself within forms that are already more or less in operation and underway. (Butler 2001: 226)

The paradox of the subject is expressed here in terms of the character of power: it is both all encompassing and fragile at the same time. The "desubjugation" of the subject, Butler asserts, marks precisely the fragility and the transformability of power (2001: 222). Along with Foucault, Butler claims that we make ourselves, but it is a self-making that is never fully self-inaugurated. The self delimits itself but it is always through norms that are already in place (2001: 225).

In "Contingent Foundations: Feminism and the Question of 'Postmodernism'," Butler takes on this paradox very directly: "But to claim that the subject is constituted is not to claim that it is determined; on the contrary, the constituted character of the subject is the very precondition of its agency" (1995a: 46). The subject constituted by the relations of power can be turned against itself, enabling a "purposive and significant reconfiguration of cultural and political relations" (1995a: 46). The paradox of power is that the power that constitutes us is at the same time the power that gives us the means to resist and the agency to employ those means. Actions can inaugurate effects that had not been foreseen. The question we should be asking ourselves, Butler argues, is where are the possibilities of reworking the matrix of power by which we are constituted?

Butler answers this question in various ways in her post-*GT* writings. In "Competing Universalities" she articulates her thesis in terms of speech. Speech becomes something else by virtue of having been broken open by the unspeakable: "The unspeakable speaks, or the unspeakable speaks the unspeakable into silence" (2000a: 158). In her contribution to *Feminist Contentions* she explores how agency can be understood from this perspective. Agency, she asserts, is found at the juncture where discourse is renewed; the subject is open to formations that are not fully constrained in advance. Agency is the effect of discursive relations which, for that reason, do not control its use (1995b: 135–7).[9]

This, then, is the paradox of power: the subject is neither a ground nor a product, but the position from which we weigh the possibilities of resignification (1995a: 47). Power provides its own possibility of being reworked. We are within power and it is from this position that we resist power. Far from being unconcerned with agency and resistance, Butler is almost obsessed with the issue. Unlike her critics, however, Butler refuses to locate agency outside of power. Butler's position is that we find agency, along with everything else, inside of power. More specifically, agency appears at the juncture where discourse is renewed. Subjects are not constituted once and for all, but again and again; the subject is open to formulations that are not fully constrained in advance (1995b: 135).

B. Ontology

Butler's exploration of norms, particularly as they relate to Foucault's work, continues to occupy her attention in *Undoing Gender* (2004c) and *Giving An Account of Oneself* (2005). On one hand, her discussion continues the theme of the paradox of power: norms define us but also provide the possibility of going beyond them. Norms, she asserts, are not static entities "but incorporated and interpreted features of existence that are sustained by the idealizations furnished by fantasy" (2000: 152). The subject produced through operations of power is not "always already trapped": resistance is not precluded (2000: 151). In giving an account of myself, I tell a story that is defined by its relations to norms, but this does not obviate moral agency (2005: 8).

But Butler's discussion of norms in these contexts also begins to explore a new aspect of the subject that she has not addressed specifically in her previous work: ontology. In *Undoing Gender* she asserts that norms have a double role: we need norms in order to live, and to live well, but norms also constrain us and do violence to us (2004c: 206). Norms tell us what kind of bodies and sexualities will be considered real and true; they give us an ontology. In *Giving an Account of Oneself*, Butler argues that norms decide in advance who will and will not be a subject. Thus, as I give an account of myself, I do so in terms of an ethical code already in place, an ethical code that defines who is a legitimate subject and who is not. It follows that to call into question a regime of truth is to call into question the basis of my own ontological status (2005: 22–3). I can give an account of myself, accept moral responsibility for my actions, only in terms of a moral code that precedes me and, most importantly, defines my existence. Norms are what we need to live, but challenging these norms, moving outside the ontological space they create, will efface us (2004c: 217).

The discussion of ontology marks a change in Butler's approach to the subject. But one must be very careful here in assessing this change. Butler is not positing an a priori realm of subjectivity, an essential "I." Rather, she is beginning to talk about a realm of the "I" that partially escapes subjectification. As she puts it in the introduction to the second edition of *GT*: "I am not outside the language that structures me, but neither am I determined by the language that makes this 'I' possible" (1999: xxvi).

In her attempt to explore this ontological space, Butler turns to what seems to be an obvious topic: the psyche. But the psyche, like ontology itself, is dangerous territory. It is all too tempting to reify both ontological and psychic reality as a given. To offset this danger, she makes it clear from the outset that it is a "significant theoretical mistake" to take the "internality" of the psychic world for granted (1999: xvi). The unconscious is not a psychic reality purified of social content but, rather, like the conscious mind, the unconscious is an "ongoing psychic condition" in which norms are registered in both normalizing and non-normalizing ways. And here, also, norms can be undone: subjects can pervert norms in identifications and disavowals that are not always consciously or deliberately performed (2000b: 153). The danger here, Butler argues, is to give psychic reality an independent ontological status. The ideals of personhood are socially produced; the emotions produced by the unconscious cannot be understood outside their social formation. "The specificity of the psyche does not imply its autonomy" (2000b: 154).

Butler's approach to the psyche, then, parallels her approach to the subject itself. Subjects exist; there is a reality to the "I." But we cannot discuss that reality apart from the discursive constructs that constitute it. What Butler seems to be saying about the psyche is that, as humans, we possess a conscious and unconscious mind; in that sense psychoanalysts are correct. But they are not correct in assuming that the unconscious is a realm of ontological reality, prior to social norms that form the ground of our identity. Her thesis is that both the conscious and the unconscious are constituted by those norms; neither is independent of the social. But, as with the subject, this is not all there is to it. Norms can fail, be undone, be perverted in both the conscious and the unconscious. Norms provide the possibility of their own transformation. Norms can be resignified and thus mobilized in unseen ways; power can be self-subverting (Thiem 2008: 81). Butler's perspective, although at odds with most psychoanalytic theories, is nevertheless a view consistent with her overall approach to subjectivity.

Butler's discussion of the psyche is closely related to an issue that occupies her attention in *Undoing Gender*

(2004c), *Precarious Life* (2004b), and other works from this period: what I will call the necessity of identity. From the perspective of *GT* and even *BTM* this seems like a departure for Butler. The thesis of *GT* is that we must eschew identity because it is the vehicle of women's oppression. Butler is famous for her anti-identity stance. It seems blatantly contradictory to attribute to her a theory that posits identity as necessary. But I think that Butler's concern with the necessity of identity is less a departure than a shift in focus. As Butler's concern with the subject deepens and takes on more complexity, she is forced to consider aspects of the subject that were not evident in her earlier investigations. And one of those aspects is the apparent fact that, for most of us, identity is a necessity for a livable life.

It is noteworthy that Butler's interest in this issue appears long before she became the famous author of *GT*. In an article originally published in 1987, Butler explores Foucault's approach to power and the body. She argues that Foucault redefines the body not as a substance, thing, or set of drives, but a site of transfer of power itself. It follows that, for Foucault, the subject is not merely the passive recipient of power but is also a site of agency and resistance. Agreeing with Foucault, Butler argues that although this relationship seems contradictory, it is better understood as complex. But there is another aspect to this relationship that Butler mentions, almost in passing, toward the end of the article: "Power attaches a subject to its own identity. Subjects appear to require this self-attachment, this process by which one becomes attached to one's subjecthood" (2004a: 190).

This is a very peculiar statement, particularly in light of Butler's other discussions of identity. This "requirement," however, is a major theme of *Undoing Gender* and *Precarious Life*. She begins with the thesis that has informed her discussion of norms throughout her work: "I cannot be who I am without drawing on the sociality of norms that precede and exceed me" (2004c: 32). But she then proceeds to seriously complicate this perspective. Echoing her earlier thesis, Butler argues that identity, some form of stability, is a necessity for a "livable life." But what if none of the identities available in the norms of my society fit me? What if these identities fail to offer me a way of being? Sometimes, she asserts, "a normative conception of gender can undo one's personhood, undermining the capacity to persevere in a livable life" (2004c: 1). The consequence of this is that, in this case, I cannot "be." I am denied an ontology, a being, and, because I must have an identity to lead a livable life, I am denied that as well. It follows that "For those who are still looking to become possible, possibility is a necessity" (2004c: 31).

These passages add another dimension to Butler's previous discussion of norms. In those discussions she argues that, although norms define us, they do not wholly determine us: there is, in a sense, some wiggle room in the deployment of norms. What we get here is a darker picture. Norms allow us to "be," but for some subjects being is not a possibility. If we ask "What, given the contemporary order of being, can I be?" and that answer is negative, then I am denied what she calls "possibility." In *Undoing Gender* Butler discusses this in the context of transsexuals; in *Precarious Life* she refers to the prisoners at Guantánamo Bay. But the problem is the same. If, in both of these cases, these persons are not classified as human within existing norms, they are denied an ontology, they have no possibility.

Implicit in these discussions is an assumption that, although Butler never addresses it explicitly, is central to her argument. In *Undoing Gender* she states that if gender comes from elsewhere, then gender undoes the "I" who is supposed to bear it and that undoing is part of the very meaning and comprehensibility of that "I" (2004c: 16). It is easy to misinterpret this passage. Butler is not positing an "I" prior to the assignment of gender; this would be antithetical to her whole corpus. But it is significant, and hugely so, that there are two entities here: the "I" that is defined by gender norms and the "I" that is the recipient of those norms. The two are not identical. Butler insists that the "undoing," that is, resistance to gender, is implicit in the gender norms themselves, but it is still the case that there is an "I" that resists. And, furthermore, it is the case that the tension between the norms and a norm's recipient is what subjectivity is all about:

> The "I" is the moment of failure in every narrative effort to give an account of oneself. It remains the unaccounted for and, in a sense, constitutes the failure that the very project of self-narration requires. Every effort to give an account of oneself is bound to encounter this failure and to founder upon it. (2005: 79)

I think it is undeniable that Butler is offering what amounts to an ontology of the subject in these passages.[10] It is an ontology that departs radically from the ontology of the essentialist subject prior to discourse, but it is an ontology nonetheless. I would even go so far as to say that, for Butler, there *is* a there there, a subject who resists norms and "undoes" gender. But it is a subject who cannot be thought outside the norms that constitute it. The resistance itself is performed inside those norms and is made possible by them. And, most importantly, it is a subject whose ontology, whose being, is dependent on those norms.[11] Two important passages reveal the elements of Butler's position on ontology:

> I see myself as working within discourses that operate through ontological claims – "there is no doer behind the deed" – and recirculating the "there is" in order to produce a counterimaginary to the dominant metaphysics. Indeed, I think it is crucial to recirculate and resignify the ontological operators, if only to produce ontology itself as a contested field. (1998: 279)

> We might reread "being" as precisely the potentiality that remains unexhausted by any particular interpellation. Such a failure of interpellation may well undermine the capacity

of the subject to "be" in a self-identical sense, but it may also mark the path toward a more open, basic even more ethical kind of being, one of or for the future. (1997b: 131)

The picture that emerges from this ontological view of the subject is more negative than that of Butler's earlier work. In her earlier view of the subject resistance was possible within the normative framework constituting gender. And, certainly, this option is still open to most subjects. Butler's ontological investigations, however, raise a problem that the earlier analysis had not addressed explicitly: what if norms make it impossible for the subject to *be* at all, preclude an identity for certain kinds of subjects? The only option for these non-subjects is to challenge the norms that confer recognition, that grant being to some subjects but not to others. What is required, Butler declares, is nothing less than to challenge what it means to be human.

In *Precarious Life* she takes on this challenge. She declares that it is "an ongoing task of human rights to reconceive the human when it finds that its putative universality does not have universal reach" (2004b: 91). We must, in the name of the human, allow the human to become something other than is traditionally assumed. We must embrace the rearticulation of the human, not to know in advance the form of our humanness. In politics, Butler argues, this demands a double path: simultaneously using the language of entitlement to assert the human while subjecting our categories to critical scrutiny (2003b: 17–23). And the key to this is what Butler calls "cultural translation": "translation will compel each language to change in order to apprehend the other, and this apprehension, at the limit of what is familiar and parochial, will be the occasion of both an ethical and a social translation" (2003b: 24).[12]

But how do we change our conception of the human? How do we extend the category of the human to include the excluded? Butler's answer to this question in her recent work revolves around a discussion of kinship. Discussions

surrounding gay marriage and the question of how feminists, and particularly non-heterosexual feminists, should
regard it stimulated Butler to look at issues of legitimacy,
the state, and personhood. Legitimizing gay marriage
would have the effect of expanding our norms of acceptable personhood, a goal apparently consistent with Butler's statements about extending the realm of the human.
But only apparently. It also has the effect of granting the
state the power to define what is legitimate and what is
illegitimate in the realm of the sexual. Does the turn to the
state, she asks, make it more difficult to argue in favor of
the viability of alternative kinship arrangements? Does the
turn to the state signal the end of a radical sexual culture
(2002: 231)?

These are difficult questions for feminists and particularly for Butler. One aspect of the problem, however, is
clear. Legitimizing gay marriage does extend the realm of
acceptable personhood. The problem is that it has two
unacceptable consequences. First, it acknowledges state
power as the agent of legitimation. Second, it does nothing
to change the delegitimization of other, more radical, forms
of sexual relations. Butler is not happy with the first consequence, but it is the second that she wants to pursue.
There are realms outside the legitimate and the illegitimate
in sexual relations that are not yet thought of as a domain.
These "non-places" are foreclosed by the campaign for gay
marriage. It is this domain that should command our
attention. Butler asserts that "we should all be pursuing
and celebrating sites of uncertain ontology and difficult
nomination" (2002: 235). But how do we do this politically? How does one think politics from the site of unrep-
resentability (2002: 232–4)?

We need, Butler concludes, a critical challenge to the
norms of recognition supplied by state legitimation. It is
this conclusion that causes Butler to turn to the issue of
kinship. Historically, marriage is inseparable from kinship,
from the definition of who is legitimate and who is illegitimate, who belongs to whom. Every culture has kinship

rules and in most cases those rules are fundamental to the norms that define it. Thus challenging kinship entails challenging the basic structure of society. Butler sites recent work in anthropology that is doing precisely this. "Postkinship" studies in anthropology no longer situate kinship as the basis of culture, but conceive it as one cultural phenomenon interlinked with other phenomena (2002: 250).

The turn to kinship provides the "critical challenge" that Butler is looking for. New kinship and sexual relations can compel a rethinking of culture itself. A more radical social transformation than that made possible by the legitimation of gay marriage is to refuse to allow kinship to be reduced to family or sexuality to marriage (2002: 254–5). Calling into question traditional forms of kinship displaces the central place of biological and sexual relations. New forms of association give sexuality a separate domain apart from kinship, allowing for durable ties outside the conjugal frame and opening sexuality to social articulations that do not always imply binding relations or conjugal ties. Sexuality outside the field of monogamy, she concludes, may open us to a different sense of community (2003a: 206).

In *Undoing Gender* Butler goes into more detail on the radical potential of rethinking kinship. Once more citing "postkinship" studies in anthropology, she asserts that new kinship and sexual arrangements compel a rethinking of culture itself. When relations that bind are no longer traced to heterosexual procreation then the homology between nature and culture is broken. This is the point of Butler's analysis in *Antigone's Claim* (2000b). Antigone is denied a livable life, and, eventually, any life at all because her kinship ties are deemed illegitimate.[13] Kinship provides a unique link between nature and culture in human society. The biological relationships that define kinship are at the same time "natural" and at the root of cultural arrangements. Challenging kinship, thus, challenges the norms that define not only sexual relations but the realm of the human itself.

Butler further develops her understanding of the ontology of the subject in *Frames of War: When is Life Grievable?* (2009). What, she asks, are the frames through which we apprehend a life as lost or injured? What, ontologically, is a life? Her answer is that the being of life is constituted through selective means. She then explores the conditions under which it becomes possible to apprehend a life or a set of lives as precarious. As in her discussion of kinship, Butler argues that in order to make broader claims about rights of protection we need a new bodily ontology, one that rethinks precariousness, vulnerability, injurability, and the claims of language and social belonging (2009: 1–2).

Once more Butler makes it clear that the ontology she defines does not refer to the fundamental structure of being. It does not exist outside of political organization and interpretation. The "being" of the body is defined by norms and social and political association. It follows that maximizing precariousness for some minimizes it for others. The ontology of the body is not separate from the social: "Rather, to be a body is to be exposed to social craft and form, and that is what makes the ontology of the body a social ontology" (2009: 3).

The ambiguity of the subject position is, again, the focus of Butler's analysis. If the normative conditions for the production of a subject produce a historically contingent ontology, "In what sense, then, does life always exceed the normative conditions of its recognizability" (2009: 4). Once more, Butler's answer is that we need new norms that allocate recognition differently. What makes change and resistance possible is that the production of norms that define bodies is partial and is "perpetually haunted by its ontologically uncertain double." Every normative instance is haunted by its own failure (2009: 7).

Butler's themes here are consistent with her discussion of the "I": subjects are constituted but not wholly so. Furthermore, the material and the discursive merge in the subject: the differential distribution of precariousness is at once a material and perceptual issue. She asserts that it would be difficult, if not impossible, to decide whether the failure to regard leads to material reality or vice versa (2009: 23). The goal of my book, Butler asserts, is to reorient politics on the left toward a consideration of precarity as a promising site for coalitional exchange (2009: 28). Precariousness cuts across identity categories and multicultural maps and provides the possibility of an alliance focused on opposition to state violence (2009: 32). Echoing the theme of *Gender Trouble*, Butler argues that the key to contemporary politics must be not the identity of the subject, but the question of how power forms the field in which subjects become possible. We must call into question the framework that silences certain subjects (2009: 163).

Butler concludes with an argument that speaks both to the critics of her alleged linguistic constructionism and to the new materialists: performativity is a more useful term than construction because performative effects may become material effects and are part of the process of materialization. Performativity entails a shift from metaphysics to ontology and offers an account of ontological effects that allows us to rethink materiality itself (2009: 168). And, finally, the boundary of who I am is the boundary of the body, but the boundary of the body never fully belongs to me (2009: 54).

V. Butler's Material Subject

That Judith Butler has been identified as the founding mother of linguistic constructionism in feminist theory, particularly as it relates to the subject, is established orthodoxy among feminists. She represents the "negative paradigm" in the subject debates that still occupy feminists. One of the purposes of the foregoing analysis has been to challenge this assessment. Particularly in her post-*GT* writing, Butler defines a subject who resists, who possesses agency, who participates in her subjectification. This subject is far from the social dupe that her critics have assigned to her.

A more important purpose of my analysis, however, is to explore the complexities of Butler's analysis and to suggest an affinity between her position and that of the "new materialists." Like these theorists, Butler integrates power and subjectivity, the material and the linguistic, into her theory. As Butler explores issues of resistance and agency, she does not abandon her constructivist position but, rather, integrates the discursive as an element, but not the only element, of her theory. This is evident in several aspects of her recent work. First, in *Frames of War* she replaces "construction" with "performativity" to emphasize the material connection. Second, her exploration of post-kinship studies has a decidedly "new materialist" slant. Third, her turn to "precarity" is an explicit recognition of the material. As material beings we are all, in various ways, precarious – dependent on social and political norms for our material existence.

Although Butler is unlikely to be identified by herself or other feminists as a new materialist, her work provides an important contribution to this perspective. She is doing what the new materialists have failed to do – articulating the "thereness" of the subject without relinquishing its discursive construction. The result is a striking and strikingly complex understanding of the subject. Subjects are constituted by social norms but this constitution is not complete. The performance of those norms opens up the possibility of resistance. Norms do not fully constrain subjects; there are openings – interstices – that can be exploited. Agency, likewise, is not antithetical to constitution. Agency is a product of constitution not precluded by it. What this comes to is what Karen Barad calls an intraaction. The norms that constitute the subject, give it its ontology, provide the possibility of a subject that constitutes itself. The material existence of the subject, a result of constitution, or, better, performativity, then becomes the ground of agency and resistance.

Although Butler has less to say about this material existence than the other authors who embrace this perspective,
it is an important element of her analysis. Perhaps her most
effective discussion of how the discursive, normative, and
material intra-act in the constitution of the subject is her
analysis of Venus Xtravaganza in *Bodies That Matter*. For
Venus, gender is marked by race and class: "Gender is the
vehicle for the phantasmatic transformation of that nexus
of race and class, the site of its articulation" (1993a: 130).
What *Paris Is Burning* suggests, Butler concludes,

> is that the order of sexual differences is not prior to
> that of race or class in the constitution of the subject;
> indeed, the symbolic is also and at once a racializing set of
> norms, and that norms of realness by which the subject is
> produced are racially informed conceptions of "sex."
> (1993a: 130)

All the elements in the mix that constitute Venus's subjectivity have both a material and a discursive component,
but none can be isolated and analyzed apart from the
others.[14]

Venus Xtravaganza's life – and death – also exemplifies
Butler's understanding of resistance. Resistance only works
for some of us, those who are recognized as subjects and
who thus have an ontology, a being. For those of us, like
Venus, who are denied personhood, denied a being by the
norms that govern what is human and what is not, a
livable life is, quite simply, impossible. It is my being as a
subject that allows me to exploit the elements of my constitution to act as an agent and, most importantly, to resist.
But if I am not constituted as a subject, this option is not
open to me. My only hope is that the norms which exclude
me from the human will change, will become more open
and inclusive. Failing this, I cannot *be*.

Butler's discussion of kinship speaks to this possibility.
Kinship is the central element defining who counts as a
subject and who does not. It constitutes the material

ground of subjectivity. If kinship can be destabilized, delinked from nature and biology, the definition of the human would correspondingly open up. But, as Butler freely admits, such a destabilization challenges the foundational norms of a society. As a consequence, the possibility of such change is very remote. What is important is that we recognize what is at stake here. Addressing the exclusion of some subjects from the realm of being must become our foremost political priority. This is her thesis in *Frames of War*. Our politics must be oriented around broadening the norms that define human life, who counts as grievable and who doesn't. And this politics must be ontological.

One of the ongoing criticisms of Butler's work is that her writing is impenetrable, that her theories are unnecessarily complex. My counter is that, particularly with regard to the subject, that complexity is necessary. The "new materialism" that, I am arguing, is compatible with Butler's position, is difficult to articulate because it describes the complicated intra-action of the material, the discursive, and a host of other elements. Applying this perspective to the subject is perhaps the greatest challenge facing this perspective. For subjects, the connection between the discursive and the ontological is more intimate than that of any other entity. Subjects can only "be" within a discursive realm that grants them an ontology. Trying to understand how this operates is a uniquely difficult theoretical task.

What we have, then, is the subject as mangle. For Butler, the discourses that constitute the subject are a central aspect of the mangle, but not the only one. Subjects are not outside language but neither are they wholly determined by language. Subjects have bodies that are raced and sexed but these elements, as in the case of Venus Xtravaganza, cannot be neatly separated from the discursive. Subjects are mangles in the sense that they are constituted by distinct elements that intra-act to constitute the "I." My argument here is that defining the subject as a mangle in this sense is the best description of the ontology of the subject available in contemporary feminist theory.

VI. Defining the Feminine Subject

Simone de Beauvoir's exploration of "woman" led women on a journey that has not yet come to a conclusion. The enormity of the task facing women was not clear from the outset. When Beauvoir declared that women do not fit into the western tradition and that we must define her as a subject apart from that tradition, neither she nor subsequent feminists realized how difficult and far-reaching that task would be. Without guidance from the tradition that quite literally constitutes our cultural understandings, feminists were cast adrift. "Jamming the theoretical machinery" as Irigary put it, would prove to be a daunting task.

My goal here has been to trace that journey toward a new definition of "woman." My thesis has been that each new approach to the question has built on rather than repudiated previous conceptions, adding something new while relying on the past. No one approach has gotten "woman" right, although many have claimed to do so. Each has contributed to the definition without reaching a conclusion. Although there have undoubtedly been conflicts along the way, it would be short-sighted of us to let these conflicts define the journey. Each approach has jammed the theoretical machinery in a different, although productive, way. What we have discovered is that there is a lot of theoretical machinery to jam and that it has exerted an almost insurmountable influence on our thought. Liberal and Marxist feminists are evidence of this. But they are also evidence of the transformative power of feminism. Introducing women changes, and transforms, the tradition.

The focus of many feminist discussions of the subject has been issues of philosophy and epistemology. As Beauvoir made very clear, the western tradition provided no place for women: the masculine is the standard of knowledge and truth. Women were excluded from this realm and, if included at all, defined as inferior. This definition is, in a sense, hardwired into the tradition. It began with the Greeks and is alive and well today. Thus it is appropriate that the feminist theorists who followed Beauvoir should concentrate on these issues. Until the feminine subject can extricate herself from these conceptions we cannot move forward.

A key component of this tradition has been and continues to be politics. Aristotle excluded women from politics on the grounds of their inferiority. It was women's alleged deficiency in reason that constituted the barrier to women's participation in politics. As a result, the politics of the feminine subject has always been a difficult issue. Beauvoir had little to say about politics, but those who followed her understood that the political subject was defined in masculine terms and for women to enter the political sphere as equals this definition must be jettisoned. Irigaray wanted to define two political subjects, one masculine, one feminine, but it was soon clear why this definition was problematic: differences other than gender must be regarded as politically relevant as well.

The feminine definition of the relational subject constituted a huge step forward in the effort to redefine the political subject. The relational subject challenged the hegemony of the rational, autonomous subject that grounds the masculine political subject. The ethics of care that evolved from the theories of the relational subject make it clear that a very different politics is dictated by this subject. A politics of care inspired by maternal practice would radically transform politics as we know it. Although this transformation has not occurred, there are signs that some political realms are becoming more receptive to a care ethics.

The intent of my discussion of liberalism and Marxism was to demonstrate the impossibility of fitting women into existing definitions of politics. The most valuable aspect of these discussions is the work of Carol Pateman.

Pateman's concept of the veiled identity of the masculine political subject reveals very precisely why women can never be equal in the political sphere. Pateman sketches, but only sketches, what another kind of political subject might look like. The embodied subject she posits is a subject that embraces rather than rejects difference. It is a subject that does not abandon differences of race, gender, sexuality, and myriad others, but rather brings them into the political arena, a move prohibited by liberalism. Feminist theorists' turn to differences reinforces Pateman's conception. We now realize that we must pull the veil away from the masculine subject and create a political world in which differences matter.

Material feminism reinforces these themes and adds another dimension: the environment. Their insight is that the politics that emerges from feminist theory must be an eco-politics, a politics that takes political account of the material world in which we live. It must be a politics that deconstructs the human/non-human dichotomy, a politics in which we see matter, in Jane Bennett's terms, as vibrant rather than inert. A feminist material politics, thus, would be a politics inclusive of the material world.

So, then, where does this leave us? Beauvoir set us on a path that has not yet reached a conclusion. Nor will it. The material feminists who are in ascendancy today offer a complex and unique definition of "woman." In the spirit of Beauvoir they have defined a new approach to knowledge, politics, and the subject that deconstructs the categories of modernism. This conception is exciting and promising. But we should not be seduced into thinking that it is a conclusion. What we do know is that the material feminists will provide the springboard for the next iteration of "woman." What that iteration will be has yet to be articulated.

Notes

Chapter 1 Simone de Beauvoir and the Beginnings of the Feminine Subject

1 In the posthumous pre-World War II diaries some of these ideas surface as well. But for my purposes *The Ethics of Ambiguity* offers a more sustained argument.
2 It is also a major theme of her fiction.
3 There are also distinct parallels in this discussion to Foucault's technology of the self (Kruks 2006).
4 See especially Deutscher (2008) for a comprehensive analysis of Beauvoir's relationship to the thought of her day.
5 See also Imbert (2004), Tidd (1999), and Weiss (2006).
6 It should be noted, however, that this is only one aspect of Sartre's complex work.
7 See Lundgren-Gothlin (1996); Gothlin (2003); Gatens (2003); Daigle (2006); Vintges (2006); Bergoffen (1997). Linda Zerilli argues that although Beauvoir begins by posing the question of woman's freedom as a subject question, she later casts it as a question of transforming woman's condition in the world (2005: 11).
8 Moi argues that Butler wrongly interprets Beauvoir as espousing the sex/gender distinction (1999: 68).
9 See Alaimo and Hekman (2008), Hekman (2010), and Barad (2007).

10 See also Le Doeuff (1991). In a recent article Margaret Simons (2010) identifies what she calls an "impasse" in Beauvoir scholarship. She claims that in her posthumously published diaries Beauvoir makes it clear that she is, indeed, a philosopher and that her intention from the outset was to answer philosophical questions. Simons further claims that Beauvoir's assertions in her memoirs and interviews that she is not a philosopher misrepresent those intentions. The unanswered question in Beauvoir scholarship, Simons argues, is why she gave up philosophy in the late 1950s. The argument I present here addresses this question. Beauvoir abandoned philosophy because she found it inadequate to the issue that commanded her attention: the situation of women. She moved away from the philosopher's concern with eternal truths as she began to explore the situated truths of women's existence.

Chapter 2   Difference I:
The "French Feminists"

1 See Mitchell (1974) for an elaboration of this argument.

Chapter 3   Difference II:
Radical Feminism and the Relational Self

1 See Adrienne Rich *Of Woman Born* (1976), and Mary O'Brien, *The Politics of Reproduction* (1981).
2 For a detailed account of Gilligan and her critics, see my *Moral Voices/Moral Selves* (1995).

Chapter 4   Continuing the Tradition:
Liberalism and Marxism

1 In *Is Multiculturalism Bad for Women?* (1999), Okin seems to move back to a more liberal stance. She talks about women having the opportunity to live as fulfilling and as freely chosen lives as men can. But then, more consistent with her other works, she insists that education, even religious education, must be taught in a non-sexist way. Once more, this requires an intrusion into individuals' private lives.

2 Commentators on Nussbaum's work, and Nussbaum herself, have discussed whether feminism demands a comprehensive liberalism in Rawls's sense. Nussbaum claims that her liberalism is political, not comprehensive (1999a: 110; Cudd 2004).

3 Phillips argues that Nussbaum's position leads to an "illiberal liberalism" (2001: 261).

4 See Baehr (2004).

5 For an early discussion of the problem of difference, see Hartsock (1983a). She argues that in our society some empirical differences are reified into an ontologically significant "Difference" by the ruling class. She asserts that feminists should reject this construction of "Difference" and, rather, use empirical differences as sources of creativity and power. I find this to be an insightful and useful discussion of difference that has been unfortunately neglected in current discussions.

6 See Bordo (1990) for a cogent statement of this problem.

7 Bar On (1993) offers an excellent account of the epistemological problems entailed by the claim to epistemic privilege and that of the center/margin dichotomy.

8 See also Kathi Weeks (1998) for a more recent defense of feminist standpoint theory.

9 See also Jackson (2001) and Hennessy and Ingraham (1997). Weeks (2012) develops an innovative feminist interpretation of Marxism focused on the problem of work.

Chapter 5   From Difference to Differences: Postmodernism, Race, Ethnicity, and Intersectionality

1 I will use the terms "postmodernism" and "poststructuralism" interchangeably in the following.

2 See Butler's reply to these criticisms in "Merely Cultural" (1997a).

3 A possible exception is Fraser and Nicholson 1990).

4 See also de Lauretis's eccentric subjects (2007).

5 This was made clear not only by her, but by others at the NWSA convention in Akron that broke the NWSA apart.

6 For an extended discussion of these issues, see my *The Material of Knowledge* (2010).

Chapter 6   The Material Subject

1 Other suggestions are "postconstructionism" (Lykke), "porous viscosity," (Tuana), "intra-action" (Barad).
2 See her exchange with Butler in Bordo (1998).
3 For a compatible analysis, see Emily Martin's *Flexible Bodies* (1994). In *Philosophy in the Flesh* (1999), George Lakoff and Mark Johnson advance an argument that attacks the mind/body dualism from a different perspective. Lakoff and Johnson assert that the mind is inherently embodied, that abstract concepts are largely metaphysical and that those metaphors are rooted in the facts of our bodily existence. They take on nothing less than the entire tradition of western philosophy, suggesting that their insights provide the basis for the redefinition of that tradition. Like the theorists discussed here, they reject representationalism. Their alternative is a theory of truth rooted in the facts of our bodily existence. Although it is doubtful that philosophers will take up Lakoff and Johnson's radical suggestion, they nevertheless represent another indication of the discontent with the dualism of modernist thought that characterizes many contemporary discussions.
4 For a detailed analysis of these issues, see Hekman (2010).
5 See Wolfe (2010) for a comprehensive overview of posthumanism.
6 Although I will focus here on Judith Butler's work, Rosi Braidotti has raised similar issues in her discussion of the subject. Her "nomadic subject" provides an alternative foundation for ethical and political subjectivity (1994a).
7 It is curious that Butler reverses her position on de Beauvoir's approach to sex/gender. In an article published in 1987, Butler claims that de Beauvoir, like herself and Wittig, takes the position that both sex and gender are fictions (1987: 134; also see 1986: 44–5). In *GT*, however, Butler places Beauvoir, along with other social constructionists, in the camp of those adhering to the sex/gender distinction.
8 Amy Allen provides an excellent discussion of this point in *The Politics of Our Selves* (2008: 81).

 9 For compatible interpretations of Butler, see Olson and
   Worsham (2007), and Weeks (1998). For a conception of
   the subject similar to Butler's, see Smith (1988).
10 Chambers and Carver claim that there is no ontological turn
   in Butler but that ontological questions always dominated
   her work (2008: 93).
11 Kathi Weeks (1998) defines her approach to the subject as
   pursuing a specific version of the ontological model of the
   subject located in a reading of Butler.
12 Lloyd criticizes Butler's ontological assumptions, arguing
   that she does not sufficiently examine her position
   (2008: 105).
13 See Loizidou (2007).
14 Butler's discussion of Rodney King's beating is another
   example of the intra-action of the material and discursive in
   her work (1993b).

Bibliography

Ahmed, Sara 2006. *Differences that Matter: Feminist Theory and Postmodernism*. Cambridge: Cambridge University Press.

Ahmed, Sara and Jackie Stacey, eds, 2001. *Thinking Through the Skin*. New York: Routledge.

Ahmed, Sara et al., eds 2000. *Transformations: Thinking Through Feminism*. New York: Routledge.

Alaimo, Stacy 2010. *Bodily Natures: Science, Environment, and the Material Self*. Bloomington: Indiana University Press.

Alaimo, Stacy and Susan Hekman, eds, 2008. *Material Feminisms*. Bloomington: Indiana University Press.

Alcoff, Linda 2006. *Visible Identities: Race, Gender, and the Self*. New York: Oxford University Press.

Allen, Amy 2008. *The Politics of Our Selves*. New York: Columbia University Press.

Allen, Paula Gunn 1986. *The Sacred Hoop: Recovering the Feminine in American Indian Traditions*. Boston: Beacon Press.

Althusser, Louis 2006. *Philosophy of the Encounter: Later Writings 1978–82*, ed. Francois Matheron and Oliver Corpet. London: Verso.

Anzaldua, Gloria 1999. *Borderlands/La Frontera: The New Mestiza*, 2nd edn. San Francisco: Aunt Lute Books.

Bacal, Howard and Kenneth Newman 1990. *Theories of Object Relations: Bridges to Self Psychology*. New York: Columbia.

Baehr, Amy, ed. 2004. *Varieties of Feminist Liberalism*. Lanham: Rowman and Littlefield.

Barad, Karen 1998. Agential realism: feminist interventions in understanding scientific practices. In Mario Biagoli, ed., *The Science Studies Reader*, New York: Routledge, 1–11.

Barad, Karen 2007. *Meeting the Universe Halfway: Quantum Physics and the Entanglement of Matter and Meaning*. Durham: Duke University Press.

Bar On, Bat-Ami 1993. Marginality and epistemic privilege. In Linda Alcoff and Elizabeth Potter, eds, *Feminist Epistemologies*. New York: Routledge, 83–100.

Barvosa, Edwina 2008. *Wealth of Selves: Multiple Identities, Mestiza Consciousness and the Subject of Politics*. College Station: Texas A&M Press.

Bauer, Nancy 2001. *Simone de Beauvoir: Philosophy and Feminism*. New York: Columbia University Press.

Beauvoir, Simone de 1948. *The Ethics of Ambiguity*. New York: Philosophical Library.

Beauvoir, Simone de 1962. *The Prime of Life*, trans. Peter Green. Cleveland: The World Publishing Co.

Beauvoir, Simone de 1964. *Force of Circumstances*, trans. Richard Howard. New York: Harper Colophon Books.

Beauvoir, Simone de 1972. *The Second Sex*. New York: Penguin.

Beauvoir, Simone de 1974. *All Said and Done*, trans. P. O'Brien. New York: Putnam.

Beauvoir, Simone de 2010. *The Second Sex*, trans. Constance Borde and Sheila Malovany-Chevallier. New York: Knopf.

Beck-Gernsheim, Elizabeth, Judith Butler, and Lidia Puigvert 2003. *Women and Social Transformation*. New York: Peter Lang.

Belenky, Mary et al. 1986. *Women's Ways of Knowing*. New York: Basic Books.

Bell, Vikki 2008. From performativity to ecology: on Judith Butler and matters of survival. *Subjectivity* 25: 395–412.

Benhabib, Seyla 1992. *Situating the Self: Community and Postmodernism in Contemporary Ethics*. New York: Routledge.

Benhabib, Seyla 1995. Feminism and postmodernism: an uneasy alliance. In Seyla Benhabib et al., eds, *Feminist Contentions*. New York: Routledge, 17–34.

Bennett, Jane 2010. *Vibrant Matter: A Political Ecology of Things*. Durham: Duke University Press.

Bergoffen, Debra 1997. *The Philosophy of Simone de Beauvoir: Gendered Phenomenology, Erotic Generosities*. Albany: University of New York Press.

Bordo, Susan 1990. Feminism, postmodernism, and gender skepticism. In Linda Nicholson, ed., *Feminism/Postmodernism*. New York: Routledge, 133–56.

Bordo, Susan 1993. *Unbearable Weight: Feminism, Western Culture and the Body*. Berkeley: University of California Press.

Bordo, Susan 1998. Bringing body to theory. In Donn Welton, ed., *Body and Flesh*. Oxford: Blackwell, 84–97.

Braidotti, Rosi 1991. *Patterns of Dissonance*. New York: Routledge.

Braidotti, Rosi 1994a. *Nomadic Subjects: Embodiment and Sexual Difference in Contemporary Feminist Theory*. New York: Columbia University Press.

Braidotti, Rosi 1994b. Of bugs and women: Irigaray and Deleuze on the becoming-woman. In Carolyn Burke, Naomi Schor, and Margaret Whitford, eds, *Engaging with Irigaray*. New York: Columbia University Press, 111–37.

Braidotti, Rosi 2002. *Metamorphoses: Toward a Materialist Theory of Becoming*. Cambridge: Polity.

Braidotti, Rosi 2010. The politics of "life itself." In Diana Cooley and Samantha Frost, eds, *New Materialisms*. Durham: Duke University Press, 201–18.

Brake, Elizabeth 2004. Rawls and feminism: what should feminists make of liberal neutrality? *Journal of Moral Philosophy* 1/3: 293–309.

Bray, Elizabeth and Claire Colebrook 1998. The haunted flesh: corporeal feminism and the politics of (dis)embodiment. *Signs* 24/1: 35–67.

Brodribb, Somer 1992. *Nothing Mat(t)ers: A Feminist Critique of Postmodernism*. North Melbourne, Australia: Spinifex Press.

Brown, Lyn Mikel and Carol Gilligan 1992. *Meeting at the Crossroads: Women's Psychology and Girls' Development*. Cambridge: Harvard University Press.

Burke, Carolyn, Naomi Schor, and Margaret Whitford, eds, 1994. *Engaging with Irigaray*. New York: Columbia University Press.

Butler, Judith 1986. Sex and gender in Simone de Beauvoir's *Second Sex. Yale French Studies* 72: 35–49.

Butler, Judith 1987. Variations on sex and gender: Beauvoir, Wittig, Foucault. In Seyla Benhabib and Drucilla Cornell, eds, *Feminism as Critique*. Cambridge: Polity, 128–42.

Butler, Judith 1990a. *Gender Trouble: Feminism and the Subversion of Identity*. New York: Routledge.

Butler, Judith 1990b. Performative acts and gender constitution: an essay in phenomenology and feminist theory. In Sue-Ellen Case, ed., *Performing Feminisms: Feminist Critical Theory and Theatre*. Baltimore: Johns Hopkins University Press, 270–82.

Butler, Judith 1993a. *Bodies That Matter: On the Discursive Limits of Sex*. New York: Routledge.

Butler, Judith 1993b. Endangered/Endangering: schematic racism and white paranoia. In Robert Gooding-Williams, ed., *Reading Rodney King/Reading Urban Uprising*. New York: Routledge, 15–22.

Butler, Judith 1995a. Contingent foundations: feminism and the question of "postmodernism." In Seyla Benhabib et al., eds, *Feminist Contentions: A Philosophical Exchange*. London: Routledge, 35–57.

Butler, Judith 1995b. For a careful reading. In Seyla Benhabib et al., eds, *Feminist Contentions: A Philosophical Exchange*. London: Routledge, 127–43.

Butler, Judith 1996. Universality in culture. In Joshua Cohen, ed., *For Love of Country*. Boston: Beacon Press, 44–52.

Butler, Judith 1997a. Merely cultural. *Social Text* 52/53: 265–77.

Butler, Judith 1997b. *The Psychic Life of Power*. Stanford: Stanford University Press.

Butler, Judith 1998. How bodies come to matter. *Signs* 23: 275–86.

Butler, Judith 1999. *Gender Trouble*, 2nd edn. New York: Routledge.

Butler, Judith 2000a. Competing universalities. In Judith Butler, Ernesto Laclau, and Slavoj Žižek, *Contingency, Hegemony, Universality*. London: Verso, 136–81.

Butler, Judith 2000b. *Antigone's Claim: Kinship between Life and Death*. New York: Columbia Press.

Butler, Judith 2001. What is critique? An essay on Foucault's virtue. In David Ingram, ed., *The Political: Readings in Continental Philosophy*. London: Blackwell, 212–28.

Butler, Judith 2002. Is kinship always already heterosexual? In Wendy Brown and Janet Halley, eds, *Left Legalism/Left Critique*. Durham: Duke University Press, 229–58.

Butler, Judith 2003a. Global violence, sexual politics. In *Queer Ideas*. The Center for Gay and Lesbian Studies. New York: The Feminist Press, 199–214.

Butler, Judith 2003b. The question of social transformation. In Elizabeth Beck-Gernsheim et al., *Women and Social Transformation*. New York: Peter Lang, 1–28.

Butler, Judith 2003c. Transformative encounters. In Elizabeth Beck-Gernsheim et al., *Women and Social Transformation*. New York: Peter Lang, 81–98.

Butler, Judith 2004a. Bodies and power revisited. In Dianna Taylor and Karen Vintges, eds, *Feminism and the Final Foucault*. Urbana: University of Illinois Press, 183–94.

Butler, Judith 2004b. *Precarious Life: The Power of Mourning and Violence*. New York: Verso.

Butler, Judith 2004c. *Undoing Gender*. New York: Routledge.

Butler, Judith 2005. *Giving an Account of Oneself*. New York: Fordham University Press.

Butler, Judith 2009. *Frames of War: When is Life Grievable?* New York: Verso.

Butler, Judith and Gayatri Spivak 2007. *Who Sings the Nation-state? Language, Politics, Belonging*. New York: Seagull.

Card, Claudia, ed. 2003. *The Cambridge Companion to Simone de Beauvoir*. Cambridge: Cambridge University Press.

Chambers, Samuel and Terrell Carver 2008. *Judith Butler and Political Theory: Troubling Politics*. New York: Routledge.

Chodorow, Nancy 1978. *The Reproduction of Mothering*. Berkeley: University of California Press.

Christian, Barbara 1987. The race for theory. *Cultural Critique* 6: 51–63.

Cimitile, Maria and Elaine Miller, eds, 2007. *Returning to Irigaray: Feminist Philosophy, Politics, and the Question of Unity*. Albany: SUNY Press.

Cixous, Helene 1976. The laugh of the Medusa, *Signs* 1/4: 875–93.

Cixous, Helene 1980. The laugh of the Medusa. In Elaine Marks and Isabelle de Courtivron, eds, *New French Feminisms*. Amherst: University of Massachusetts Press, 245–64.

Cixous, Helene and Catherine Clement 1986. *The Newly Born Woman*, trans. Betsy Wing. Minneapolis: Minnesota University Press.

Colebrook, Claire 2000. From radical representation to corporeal becomings. *Hypatia* 15/2: 76–93.

Collins, Patricia Hill 1990. *Black Feminist Thought*. Boston: Unwin Hyman.

Collins, Patricia Hill 2009. *Black Feminist Thought: Knowledge, Consciousness, and the Politics of Empowerment*. New York: Routledge.

Conley, Verena 1992. *Helene Cixous*. Toronto: University of Toronto Press.

Coole, Diana and Samantha Frost, eds, 2010. *New Materialisms*. Durham: Duke University Press.

Cornell, Drucilla 1999. *Beyond Accommodation: Ethical Feminism, Deconstruction, and the Law*. Lanham: Rowman and Littlefield.

Crenshaw, Kimberle 1989. Demarginalizing the intersection of race and sex. *University of Chicago Legal Forum* 1980: 139–67.

Crenshaw, Kimberle 1995. Mapping the margins: intersectionality, identity politics, and violence against women of color. In Kimberle Crenshaw et al., eds, *Critical Race Theory*. New York: The New Press, 357–83.

Cudd, Ann 2004. The paradox of liberal feminism. In Amy Baehr, ed., *Varieties of Feminist Liberalism*. Lanham: Rowman and Littlefield, 37–61.

Cudjoe, Selwyn 1984. Maya Angelou and the autobiographical statement. In Mari Evans, ed., *Black Women Writers*. New York: Doubleday, 6–24.

Daigle, Christine 2006. The ambiguous ethics of Beauvoir. In Christine Daigle, ed., *Existentialist Thinkers and Ethics*. Montreal: McGill-Queen's University Press, 120–41.

Davis, Kathy 2008. Intersectionality as a buzzword: a sociology of science perspective on what makes a feminist theory successful. *Feminist Theory* 9/1: 67–85.

DeLanda, Manuel 2002. *Intensive Science and Virtual Philosophy*. New York: Continuum.

Delphy, Christine 1984. *Close to Home: A Materialist Analysis of Women's Oppression*, trans. Diana Leonard. Amherst: University of Massachusetts Press.

Deutscher, Penelope 2002. *Politics of Impossible Difference: The Later Work of Luce Irigaray*. Ithaca: Cornell University Press.

Deutscher, Penny 2008. *The Philosophy of Simone de Beauvoir: Ambiguity, Conversion, Resistance*. New York: Cambridge University Press.

Diamond, Irene and Lee Quinby 1988. Introduction. In Irene Diamond and Lee Quinby, eds, *Feminism and Foucault: Reflections on Resistance*. Boston: Northeastern University Press, ix–xx.

Digeser, Paul 1995. *Our Politics, Our Selves? Liberalism, Identity and Harm*. Princeton: Princeton University Press.

Di Stefano, Christine 1990. Dilemmas of difference: feminism, modernity and postmodernism. In Linda Nicholson, ed., *Feminism/Postmodernism*. New York: Routledge, 63–82.

Duras, Marguerite 1980. From an interview. In Elaine Marks and Isabelle de Courtivron, eds, *New French Feminisms*. Amherst: University of Massachusetts Press, 174–76.

Ebert, Teresa 1996. *Ludic Feminism and After: Postmodernism, Desire, and Labor in Late Capitalism*. Ann Arbor: University of Michigan Press.

Eisenstein, Zillah 1981. *The Radical Future of Liberal Feminism*. New York: Longman.

Eisenstein, Zillah 1990. Constructing a theory of capitalist patriarchy and socialist feminism. In Karen Hansen and Ilene Philipson, eds, *Women, Class and the Feminist Imagination*. Philadelphia: Temple University Press, 114–45.

Engels, Friedrich 1985. *The Origins of the Family, Private Property and the State*. Harmondsworth: Penguin.

Evans, Mary 1985. *Simone de Beauvoir: A Feminist Mandarin*. London: Tavistock.

Firestone, Shulamith 1970. *The Dialectic of Sex: The Case for Feminist Revolution*. New York: William Morrow.

Flax, Jane 1990. *Thinking Fragments: Psychoanalysis, Feminism, and Postmodernism in the Contemporary West*. Berkeley: University of California Press.

Flax, Jane 1993. *Disputed Subjects: Essays on Psychoanalysis, Politics, and Philosophy*. New York: Routledge.

Foucault, Michel 1993. About the beginnings of the hermeneutics of the self. *Political Theory* 21/2: 198–227.

Fraser, Nancy 1992. Introduction. In Nancy Fraser and Sandra Lee Bartky, eds, *Revaluing French Feminism*. Bloomington: Indiana University Press, 1–24.

Fraser, Nancy and Linda Nicholson 1990. Social criticism without philosophy: an encounter between feminism and postmodernism. In Linda Nicholson, ed., *Feminism/Postmodernism*. New York: Routledge, 19–38.

Freud, Sigmund 1961. Some psychical consequences of the anatomical distinction between the sexes. In James Strachey, ed., *The Standard Edition of the Complete Psychological Works of Sigmund Freud*, vol. 19. New York: W.W. Norton, 248–58.

Friedman, Susan Stanford 1995. History: reflections on feminism, narrative, and desire. In Diane Elam and Robyn Wiegman, *Feminism Beside Itself*. New York: Routledge, 11–54.

Frye, Marilyn 1983. *The Politics of Reality*. Freedom, CA: The Crossings Press.

Gallop, Jane 1982. *The Daughter's Seduction*. Ithaca: Cornell University Press.

Gallop, Jane 1988. *Thinking Through the Body*. New York: Columbia University Press.

Gatens, Moira 1996. *Imaginary Bodies: Ethics, Power and Corporeality*. New York: Routledge.

Gatens, Moira 2003. Beauvoir and biology: a second look. In Claudia Card, ed., *The Cambridge Companion to Simone de Beauvoir*. Cambridge: Cambridge University Press, 266–85.

Gates, Henry Louis 1987. *Figures in Black*. New York: Oxford University Press.

Gauthier, Xaviere 1980. Why witches? In Elaine Marks and Isabelle de Courtivron, eds, *New French Feminisms*. Amherst: University of Massachusetts Press, 199–203.

Gilligan, Carol 1982. *In a Different Voice*. Cambridge, MA: Harvard University Press.

Gilligan, Carol 1987. Moral orientation and moral development. In Eva Kittay and Diane Meyers, eds, *Women and Moral Theory*. Totowa, NJ: Rowman and Littlefield, 19–33.

Gilligan, Carol 1988. Remapping development: creating a new framework for psychological theory and research. In Carol Gilligan et al., eds, *Mapping the Moral Domain*. Cambridge, MA: Harvard University Press, 3–19.

Gilligan, Carol 1990a. Joining the resistance: psychology, politics, girls, and women. *Michigan Quarterly Review* 24/9: 501–36.

Gilligan, Carol 1990b. Preface. In Carol Gilligan et al., eds, *Making Connections*. Cambridge, MA: Harvard University Press, 6–29.

Gilligan, Carol 1990c. Prologue. In Carol Gilligan et al., eds, *Making Connections*. Cambridge, MA: Harvard University Press, 1–5.

Gilligan, Carol 1991. Women's psychological development: implications for psycho-theory. In Carol Gilligan et al., eds, *Women, Girls, and Psychotherapy: Reframing Resistance*. New York: Harrington Park Press, 5–31.

Gilligan, Carol 2009. Simone de Beauvoir and practical deliberation. *PMLA* 124/1: 199–205

Gilligan, Carol 2011. *Joining the Resistance*. Cambridge: Polity.

Gilligan, Carol, Nona Lyons, and Trudy Hanmer, eds 1990. *Making Connections: The Relational Worlds of Adolescent Girls at Emma Willard School*. Cambridge, MA: Harvard University Press.

Gothlin, Eva 2003. Reading Simone de Beauvoir with Martin Heidegger. In *The Cambridge Companion to Simone de Beauvoir*. Cambridge: Cambridge University Press, 45–65.

Grosholz, Emily, ed. 2004. *The Legacy of Simone de Beauvoir*. New York: Oxford University Press.

Grosholz, Emily 2009. Simone de Beauvoir and practical deliberation. *PMLA* 124/1: 199–205.

Grosz, Elizabeth 1989. *Sexual Subversions: Three French Feminists*. Sydney: Allen and Unwin.

Grosz, Elizabeth 1994. *Volatile Bodies: Toward a Corporeal Feminism*. Bloomington: Indiana University Press.

Grosz, Elizabeth 1995. *Space, Time, and Perversion: Essays on the Politics of Bodies*. New York: Routledge.

Grosz, Elizabeth 2004. *The Nick of Time*. Durham: Duke University Press.

Grosz, Elizabeth 2005. *Time Travels*. Durham: Duke University Press.

Grosz, Elizabeth 2011. *Becoming Undone: Darwinian Reflections on Life, Politics, and Art*. Durham: Duke University Press.

Hansen, Karen and Ilene Philipson 1990. *Women, Class, and the Feminist Imagination*. Philadelphia: Temple University Press.

Haraway, Donna 1990. A manifesto for cyborgs: science, technology, and socialist feminism in the 1980s. In Linda

Nicholson, ed., *Feminism/Postmodernism*. New York: Routledge, 190–233.

Haraway, Donna 1991. *Simians, Cyborgs, and Women: The Reinvention of Nature*. New York: Routledge.

Haraway, Donna 2008. *When Species Meet*. Minneapolis: University of Minnesota Press.

Hartley, Christie and Lori Watson 2010. Is feminist political liberalism possible? *Journal of Ethics and Social Philosophy* 5/1: 1–21.

Hartmann, Heidi 1981. The unhappy marriage of Marxism and feminism: toward a more progressive union. In Lydia Sargent, ed., *Women and Revolution*. Boston: South End Press, 1–41.

Hartsock, Nancy 1981a. Fundamental feminism: prospect and perspective. In Charlotte Bunch, ed., *Building Feminist Theory*. New York: Longman, 32–43.

Hartsock, Nancy 1981b. Difference and domination in the women's movement: the dialectic of theory and practice. In Amy Swerdlow and Hanna Lessinger, eds, *Class, Race, and Sex: The Dynamics of Control*. Boston: G.K. Hall, 157–72.

Hartsock, Nancy 1983a. The feminist standpoint: developing the ground for a specifically feminist historical materialism. In Sandra Harding and Merrill Hintikka, eds, *Discovering Reality: Feminist Perspectives on Epistemology, Metaphysics, Methodology, and the Philosophy of Science*. Dordrecht: Reidel, 283–310.

Hartsock, Nancy 1983b. *Money, Sex, and Power: Toward a Feminist Historical Materialism*. Boston: Northeastern University Press.

Hartsock, Nancy 1987. Rethinking modernism: minority vs. majority theories. *Cultural Critique* 7: 187–206.

Hartsock, Nancy 1989–90. Postmodernism and political change: issues for feminist theory. *Cultural Critique* 14: 15–33.

Hartsock, Nancy 1990. Foucault on power: a theory for women? In Linda Nicholson, ed., *Feminism/Postmodernism*. New York: Routledge, 157–75.

Hartsock, Nancy 1998. *Feminist Standpoint Theory Revisited and Other Essays*. Boulder: Westview Press.

Hawkesworth, Mary 2006. *Feminist Inquiry: From Political Conviction to Methodological Innovation*. New Brunswick: Rutgers University Press.

Hayles, N. Katherine 1999. *How We Became Posthuman: Virtual Bodies in Cybernetics, Literature and Informatics.* Chicago: University of Chicago Press.

Hearn, Jeff 2010. Global/transnational gender/sexual scenarios. In Anna Jonasdottir et al., eds, *Sexuality, Gender, and Power.* New York: Routledge, 209–26.

Hekman, Susan 1990. *Gender and Knowledge: Elements of a Postmodern Feminism.* Cambridge: Polity.

Hekman, Susan 1995. *Moral Voices/Moral Selves.* Cambridge: Polity.

Hekman, Susan 1997. Truth and method: feminist standpoint theory revisited. *Signs* 22/2: 341–65.

Hekman, Susan 1999. *The Future of Differences.* Cambridge: Polity.

Hekman, Susan 2004. *Private Selves/Public Identities.* University Park: The Pennsylvania State Press.

Hekman, Susan 2010. *The Material of Knowledge: Feminist Disclosures.* Bloomington: Indiana University Press.

Henderson, Mae 1992. Speaking in tongues. In Judith Butler and Joan Scott, eds, *Feminists Theorize the Political.* New York: Routledge, 144–66.

Hennessy, Rosemary 1993. *Materialist Feminism and the Politics of Discourse.* New York: Routledge.

Hennessy, Rosemary 1997. Introduction. In Rosemary Hennessy and Chrys Ingraham, *Materialist Feminism: A Reader in Class, Difference, and Women's Lives.* New York: Routledge, 1–14.

Hennessy, Rosemary and Chrys Ingraham 1997. *Materialist Feminism: A Reader in Class, Difference, and Women's Lives.* New York: Routledge.

Hindman, Matthew Dean 2011. Rethinking intersectionality: toward an understanding of discursive marginalization. *New Political Science* 33/2: 189–210.

Hird, Myra and Celia Roberts 2011. Feminism theorizes the nonhuman. *Feminist Theory* 12/2: 109–17.

Hirsch, Marianne and Evelyn Fox Keller, eds, 1990. *Conflicts in Feminism.* New York: Routledge.

Hirschmann, Nancy 1989. Freedom, recognition, and obligation: a feminist approach to political theory. *American Political Science Review* 83: 1227–44.

Hirschmann, Nancy 2003. *The Subject of Liberty: A Feminist Theory of Freedom.* Princeton: Princeton University Press.

hooks, bell 1984. *Feminist Theory: From Margin to Center*. Boston: South End Press.

hooks, bell 1989. *Talking Back: Thinking Feminist Theory, Thinking Black*. Boston: South End Press.

hooks, bell 1990. *Yearning: Race, Gender and Cultural Politics*. Boston: South End Press.

Imbert, Claude 2004. Simone de Beauvoir: a woman philosopher in the context of her generation. In Emily Grosholz, ed., *The Legacy of Simone de Beauvoir*. New York: Oxford University Press, 3–21.

Irigaray, Luce 1985a. *Speculum of the Other Woman*, trans. Gillian Gill. Ithaca: Cornell University Press.

Irigaray, Luce 1985b. *This Sex Which Is Not One*, trans. Catherine Porter. Ithaca: Cornell University Press.

Irigaray, Luce 1987. Sexual difference. In Toril Moi, ed., *French Feminist Thought*. New York: Blackwell, 118–29.

Irigaray, Luce 1989. The gesture in psychoanalysis. In Teresa Brennan, ed., *Between Feminism and Psychoanalysis*. New York: Routledge, 127–38.

Irigaray, Luce 1993a. *An Ethics of Sexual Difference*. Ithaca: Cornell University Press.

Irigaray, Luce 1993b. *Je, Tu, Nous: Toward a Culture of Difference*, trans. Alison Martin. New York: Routledge.

Irigaray, Luce 1993c. *Sexes and Genealogies*. New York: Columbia University Press.

Irigaray, Luce 1994. *Thinking the Difference*. New York: Routledge.

Irigaray, Luce 2001. *Democracy Begins Between Two*, trans. Kirsteen Anderson. New York: Routledge.

Irigaray, Luce 2002. *Between East and West: From Singularity to Community*. New York: Columbia University Press.

Jack, Dana 1991. *Silencing the Self: Depression and Women*. Cambridge, MA: Harvard University Press.

Jackson, Stevi 2001. Why a materialist feminism is (still) possible – and necessary. *Women's Studies International Forum* 24/3–4: 283–93.

Jaggar, Alison 1983. *Feminist Politics and Human Nature*. Totowa, NJ: Rowman and Allanheld.

Jardine, Alice 1985. *Gynesis: Configurations of Women and Modernity*. Ithaca: Cornell University Press.

Johnston, Adrian 2008. *Zizek's Ontology: A Transcendental Materialist Theory of Subjectivity*. Evanston: Northwestern University Press.

Jonasdottir, Anna, Valerie Bryson, and Kathleen Jones 2011. Introduction. In Jonasdottir et al., eds, *Sexuality, Gender, and Power: Intersectionality and Transnational Perspectives*. New York: Routledge, 1–8.

Jones, Ann Rosalind 1981. Writing the body: toward an understanding of *L'Ecriture Feminine*. *Feminist Studies* 7/2: 247–63.

Joyce, Joyce 1987. The black canon: reconstructing black American literary criticism. *New Literary History* 18/2: 355–44.

Keller, Catherine 1986. *From a Broken Web: Separation, Sexism, and Self*. Boston: Beacon Press.

Kirby, Vicki 2006. *Judith Butler: Live Theory*. New York: Continuum.

Kittay, Eva and Diane Meyers, eds, 1987. *Women and Moral Theory*, Totowa, NJ: Rowman and Littlefield.

Kohlberg, Lawrence 1981. *The Philosophy of Moral Development*. San Francisco: Harper and Row.

Kristeva, Julia 1980. *Desire in Language*, ed. Leon Roudiez. New York: Columbia University Press.

Kristeva, Julia 1984. *Revolution in Poetic Language*, trans. Margaret Waller. New York: Columbia University Press.

Kristeva, Julia 1986a. *The Kristeva Reader*, ed. Toril Moi. New York: Columbia University Press.

Kristeva, Julia 1986b. Women's time. In *The Kristeva Reader*, ed, Toril Moi. New York: Columbia University Press, 187–213.

Kristeva, Julia 1987. *In the Beginning Was Love: Psychoanalysis and Faith*. New York: Columbia University Press.

Kristeva, Julia 2000. *Crisis of the European Subject*. New York: Other Press.

Kritzman, Lawrence 2009. Simone de Beauvoir, the paradoxical intellectual. *PMLA* 124/1: 206–13.

Kruks, Sonia 1990. *Situation and Human Existence: Freedom, Subjectivity and Society*. London: Unwin Hyman.

Kruks, Sonia 2001. *Retrieving Experience: Subjectivity and Recognition in Feminist Politics*. Ithaca: Cornell University Press.

Kruks, Sonia 2006. Reading Beauvoir with and against Foucault. In Lori Marso and Patricia Moynagh, eds, *Simone de Beauvoir's Political Thinking*. Urbana: University of Illinois Press, 55–71.

Kruks, Sonia 2010. Simone de Beauvoir: engaging discrepant materialisms. In Diana Coole and Samantha Frost, eds, *New Materialisms*. Durham: Duke University Press, 258–80.

Kukla, Rebecca 2006. Introduction: maternal bodies. *Hypatia* 21/1: vii–ix.

Kymlicka, Will 1999. Liberal complacencies. In Susan Moller Okin, *Is Multiculturalism Bad for Women?* Princeton: Princeton University Press.

Laden, Simon 2003. Radical libersl, reasonable feminists: reason, power and objectivity in MacKinnon and Rawls. *Journal of Political Philosophy* 11/2: 133–52.

Lakoff, George and Mark Johnson 1999. *Philosophy in the Flesh*. New York: Basic Books.

Latour, Bruno 1999. *Pandora's Hope*. Cambridge, MA: Harvard University Press.

Lauretis, de, Teresa 2007. *Figures of Resistance: Essays in Feminist Theory*. Urbana: University of Illinois Press.

Le Doeuff, Michele 1987. Women and philosophy. In Toril Moi, ed., *French Feminist Thought*. New York: Blackwell, 181–209.

Le Doeuff, Michele 1991. *Hipparchia's Choice: An Essay Concerning Women, Philosophy, etc.*, trans. Trista Selous. Oxford: Blackwell

Lloyd, Moya 2007. *Judith Butler: From Norms to Politics*. Cambridge: Polity.

Lloyd, Moya 2008. Towards a cultural politics of vulnerability. In Terrell Carver and Samuel Chambers, eds, *Judith Butler's Precarious Politics*. New York: Routledge, 92–105.

Loizidou, Elena 2007. *Judith Butler: Ethics, Law, Politics*. New York: Routledge-Cavendish.

Lorde, Audre 1981. The master's tools will never dismantle the master's house. In Cherrie Moraga and Gloria Anzaldua, eds, *This Bridge Called My Back*. New York: Kitchen Table Press, 98–101, p. 98.

Lugones, Maria and Elizabeth Spelman 1983. Have we got a theory for you! Feminist theory, cultural imperialism and the demand for the woman's voice. *Women's Studies International Forum* 6/6: 573–81.

Lundgren-Gothlin, Eva 1996. *Sex and Existence: Simone de Beauvoir's The Second Sex.* London: Athlone.

Lykke, Nina 2010. *Feminist Studies: A Guide to Intersectional Theory, Methodology and Writing.* New York: Routledge.

McCall, Leslie 2005. The complexity of intersectionality. *Signs* 30/3: 1771–1800.

MacKinnon, Catherine 1987. *Feminism Unmodified: Discourses on Life and Law.* Cambridge: Oxford University Press.

MacKinnon, Catherine 1989. *Toward a Feminist Theory of the State.* Cambridge, MA: Harvard University Press.

McNay, Lois 2000. *Gender and Agency: Reconfiguiring the Subject in Feminist Social Theory.* Cambridge: Polity.

Mann, Bonnie 2006. *Women's Liberation and the Sublime: Feminism, Postmodernism, Environment.* New York: Oxford University Press.

Marcus, Isabel and Paul Spiegelman 1985. Feminist discourse, moral values and the law – a conversation: the 1984 James MacCormick Mitchell lecture. *Buffalo Law Review* 34: 11–87.

Marks, Elaine and Isabelle de Courtivron 1980. Introduction. In Elaine Marks and Isabelle de Courtivron, *New French Feminisms.* Amherst: University of Massachusetts Press, 3–9.

Marks, Elaine and Isabelle de Courtivron, eds, 1980. *New French Feminisms.* Amherst: University of Massachusetts Press.

Martin, Biddy 1998. Feminism, criticism, and Foucault. In Irene Diamond and Lee Quinby, eds, *Feminism and Foucault.* Boston: Northeastern University Press, 3–19.

Martin, Emily 1994. *Flexible Bodies.* Boston: Beacon Press.

Marx, Karl 1970. *Contribution to the Critique of Political Economy*, ed. Maruice Dobb, trans. S. W. Ryazanskaya. New York: International Publishers.

Matsuda, Mari 1991. Beside my sister, facing the enemy: legal theory out of coalition. *Stanford Law Review* 43/6: 1183–92.

Meese, Elizabeth 1990. *(Ex)tensions: Refiguring Feminist Criticism.* Urbana: University of Illinois Press.

Meyers, Diana Tietjens 1989. *Self, Society, and Personal Choice.* New York: Columbia University Press.

Meyers, Diana Tietjens 1994. *Subjection and Subjectivity: Psychoanalytic Feminism and Moral Philosophy.* New York: Routledge.

Meyers, Diana Tietjens 2004. *Being Yourself: Essays on Identity, Action, and Social Life*. Lanham, MD: Rowman and Littlefield.

Minh-ha, Trinh T. 1989. *Women, Native, Other: Writing Postcoloniality and Feminism*. Bloomington: Indiana University Press.

Mitchell, Juliet 1974. *Psychoanalysis and Feminism*. New York: Vintage Books.

Mitchell, Kaye 2008. Unintelligible subjects: making sense of gender, sexuality, and subjectivity after Butler. *Subjectivity* 25: 413–31.

Mohanty, Chandra 1991. Under Western eyes: feminist scholarship and colonial discourse. *Boundary 2* 12/3: 333–59.

Moi, Toril 1985. *Sexual/Textual Politics: Feminist Literary Theory*. London: Methuen.

Moi, Toril 1987. *French Feminist Thought: A Reader*. New York: Blackwell.

Moi, Toril 1999. *What is a Woman?: And Other Essays*. New York: Oxford University Press.

Moi, Toril 2008. *Simone de Beauvoir: The Making of an Intellectual Woman*, 2nd edn. New York: Oxford.

Mol, Annemarie 1999. Ontological politics. In John Law and John Hassard, eds, *Actor Network Theory and After*. Oxford: Blackwell, 74–89.

Mol, Annemarie 2002. *The Body Multiple: Ontology in Medical Practice*. Durham: Duke University Press.

Moody-Adams, Michele 1991. Gender and the complexity of moral voices. In Claudia Card, ed., *Feminist Ethics*. Lawrence: University Press of Kansas, 195–212.

Moraga, Cherrie 1981. La Guera. In Cherrie Moraga and Gloria Anzaldua, eds, *This Bridge Called My Back*. Watertown, MA: Persephone Press, 27–34.

Moraga, Cherrie 1983. *Loving in the War Years*. Boston: South End Press.

Morris, Meaghan 1988. *The Pirate's Fiancee: Feminism, Reading, Postmodernism*. New York: Verso.

Moya, Paula 2000. Postmodernism, "realism" and the politics of identity. In Paula Moya and Michael Hames-Garcia Berkeley, eds, *Reclaiming Identity*. Berkeley: University of California Press, 67–101.

Moya, Paula and Michael Hames-Garcia, eds, 2000. *Reclaiming Identity*. Berkeley: University of California Press.

Nash, Jennifer 2008. Rethinking intersectionality. *Feminist Review* 89/1: 1–15.

Nicholson, Linda 1990. *Feminism/Postmodernism*. New York: Routledge.

Noddings, Nel 1984. *Caring*. University of California Press.

Nussbaum, Martha 1999a. A plea for difficulty. In Susan Moller Okin, *Is Multiculturalism Bad for Women?* Princeton: Princeton University Press, 105–14.

Nussbaum, Martha 1999b. *Sex and Social Justice*. New York: Oxford University Press.

Nussbaum, Martha 2000. *Women and Human Development*. New York: Cambridge University Press.

Nussbaum, Martha 2004. The future of feminist liberalism. In Amy Baehr, ed., *Varieties of Feminist Liberalism*, Lanham: Rowman and Littlefield, 103–32.

Nye, Andrea 1986. Preparing the way for a feminist praxis. *Hypatia* 1: 101–16.

O'Brien, Mary 1981. *The Politics of Reproduction*. Boston: Routledge.

Okin, Susan Moller 1979. *Women in Western Political Thought*. Princeton: Princeton University Press.

Okin, Susan Moller 1989. *Justice, Gender, and the Family*. New York: Basic Books.

Okin, Susan Moller 1994. Political liberalism, justice, and gender. *Ethics* 105/1: 23–43.

Okin, Susan Moller 1998. Humanist liberalism. In Nancy Rosenblum, ed., *Liberalism and the Moral Life*. Cambridge: Harvard University Press, 39–53.

Okin, Susan Moller 1999. *Is Multiculturalism Bad for Women?* Princeton: Princeton University Press.

Oliver, Kelly 1993. *Reading Kristeva: Unraveling the Double Bind*. Bloomington: Indiana University Press.

Olson, Gary and Lynn Worsham 2007 Changing the subject: Judith Butler's politics of radical resignification. In Gary Olson and Lynn Worsham, eds, *The Politics of Possibility*, Boulder and London: Paradigm Publishers, 5–42.

Pateman, Carole 1988. *The Sexual Contract*. Stanford: Stanford University Press.

Pateman, Carole 1989. *The Disorder of Women*. Cambridge: Polity.

Phillips, Anne 1991. *Engendering Democracy*. University Park: Penn State Press.

Phillips, Anne 2001. Feminism and liberalism revisited: has Martha Nussbaum got it right? *Constellations* 8/2: 249–66.

Piaget, Jean 1965. *The Moral Judgment of the Child*. New York: Free Press.

Pickering, Andrew 1995. *The Mangle of Practice: Time, Agency, and Science*. Chicago: University of Chicago Press.

Pilardi, Jo-Ann 1991. Philosophy becomes autobiography: the development of the self in the writings of Simone de Beauvoir. In Hugh Silverman, ed., *Writing and the Politics of Difference*. Albany: Suny Press, 145–62.

Quick, James 1992. Pronoun "she": Luce Irigaray's fluid dynamics. *Philosophy Today* 36/3: 199–209.

Rawls, John 1971. *A Theory of Justice*. Cambridge, MA: Harvard University Press.

Reed, Evelyn 1971. *Problems of Women's Liberation: A Marxist Approach*. New York: Pathfinder Press.

Rich, Adrienne 1976. *Of Woman Born: Motherhood as Experience and Institution*. New York: W.W. Norton.

Riley, Denise 1988. *"Am I That Name?" Feminism and the Category of "Women" in History*. Minneapolis: University of Minnesota Press.

Rosenblum, Nancy 2009. Okin's liberal feminism as a radical political theory. In Debra Satz and Rob Reich, eds, *Toward a Humanist Justice: The Political Philosophy of Susan Moller Okin*. New York: Oxford University Press, 15–40.

Rowbotham, Sheila 1973: *Women's Consciousness, Man's World*. Harmondsworth: Penguin.

Ruddick, Sarah 1989. *Maternal Thinking*. Boston: Beacon Books.

Said, Edward 1978. *Orientalism*. New York: Vintage.

Sandoval, Chela 1991. U.S. third world feminism: the theory and method of oppositional consciousness. *Genders* 10: 1–24.

Sargent, Lydia 1981. *Women and Revolution: A Discussion of the Unhappy Marriage of Marxism and Feminism*. Boston: South End Press.

Sartre, Jean-Paul 1984. *Being and Nothingness*. New York: Washington Square Press.

Satz, Debra and Rob Reich, eds, 2009. *Toward a Humanist Justice: The Political Philosophy of Susan Moller Okin*. New York: Oxford University Press.

Sawicki, Jana 1986. Foucault and feminism. Toward a politics of difference. *Hypatia* 1/2: 23–36.

Sawicki, Jana 1990. *Disciplining Foucault: Feminism, Power, and the Body*. New York: Routledge.

Schor, Naomi 1994. This essentialism which is not one. In Carolyn Burke, Naomi Schor, and Margaret Whitford, eds, *Engaging with Irigaray*. New York: Columbia University Press, 57–78.

Schwartzman, Lisa 2008. Can liberalism account for women's "adaptive preferences?" *Social Philosophy Today* 23: 175–86.

Segal, Lynne 2008. Judith Butler: identities, who needs them? *Subjectivity* 25: 381–94.

Shildrick, Margrit 1997. *Bodies and Boundaries: Feminism, Postmodernism and (Bio)ethics*. New York: Routledge.

Shildrick, Margrit 2010. Confronting an impasse: reflections on the past and future of Beauvoir scholarship. *Hypatia* 25/4: 909–26.

Simons, Margaret 1999. *Beauvoir and the Second Sex: Feminism, Race, and the Origins of Existentialism*. Lanham, MD: Rowman and Littlefield.

Simons, Margaret 2010. Confronting an impasse: reflecting on the past and future of Beauvoir scholarship. *Hypatia* 25/4: 909–26.

Singer, Linda 1990. Interpretation and retrieval: rereading Beauvoir. In Azizah al-Hibri and Margaret Simons, eds, *Hypatia Reborn*. Bloomington: Indiana University Press, 323–35.

Sinopoli, Richard and Nancy Hirschmann 1991. Feminism and liberal theory. *American Political Science Review* 85/1: 221–33.

Smith, Dorothy 1990. *The Conceptual Practices of Power*. Boston: Northeastern University Press.

Smith, Paul 1988. *Discerning the Subject*. Minneapolis: University of Minnesota Press.

Spelman, Elizabeth 1988. *Inessential Woman*. Boston: Beacon Press.

Spivak, Gayatri 1987. *In Other Worlds: Essays in Cultural Politics*. New York: Methuen.

Stern, Lori 1990. Conceptions of separation and connection in female adolescents. In Carol Gilligan et al., eds, *Making Connections*. Cambridge: Harvard University Press, 73–87.

Thiem, Annika 2008. *Unbecoming Subjects: Judith Butler, Moral Philosophy, and Critical Responsibility*. New York: Fordham University Press.

Thurman, Judith 2010. Introduction. Simone de Beauvoir, *The Second Sex*, trans. Constance Borde and Sheila Malovany-Chevallier. New York: Knopf.

Tidd, Ursula 1999. *Simone de Beauvoir: Gender and Testimony*. Cambridge: Cambridge University Press.

Tronto, Joan 1993. *Moral Boundaries*. New York: Routledge.

Tuana, Nancy 1983. Re-fusing nature/nurture. *Hypatia*. Special issue of *Women's Studies International Forum* 6/6: 45–56.

Tuana, Nancy 2001. Material locations. In Nancy Tuana and Sandi Morgen, eds, *Engendering Rationalities*. Bloomington: Indiana University Press, 221–43.

Vintges, Karen 1996. *Philosophy as Passion in the Thinking of Simone de Beauvoir*. Bloomington: Indiana University Press.

Vintges, Karen 2006. Simone de Beauvoir: a feminist thinker for the twenty-first century. In Margaret Simons, ed., *The Philosophy of Simone de Beauvoir: Critical Essays*. Bloomington: Indiana University Press, 214–27.

Weedon, Chris 1987. *Feminist Practice and Poststructuralist Theory*. New York: Blackwell.

Weeks, Kathi 1998. *Constituting Feminist Subjects*. Ithaca: Cornell University Press.

Weeks, Kathi 2012. *The Problem With Work: Feminism, Marxism, Antiwork Politics, and Postwork Imaginaries*. Durham: Duke University Press.

Weir, Allison 1996. *Sacrificial Logics: Feminist Theory and the Critique of Identity*. New York: Routledge.

Weiss, Gail. 2006. Challenging choices: an ethic of oppression. In Margaret Simons, ed., *The Philosophy of Simone de Beauvoir: Critical Essays*. Bloomington: Indiana University Press, 241–61.

Wendell, Susan 1987. A (qualified) defense of liberal feminism. *Hypatia* 2/2: 65–93.

Whitford, Margaret 1991. *Luce Irigaray: Philosophy in the Feminine*. London: Routledge.

Wiegman, Robyn 2000. Feminism's apocalyptic futures. *New Literary History* 31/4: 805–25.

Wilson, Elizabeth 1998. *Neural Geographics: Feminism and the Microstructure of Cognition*. New York: Routledge.

Wolfe, Cary 2010. *What is Posthumanism?* Minneapolis: University of Minnesota Press.

Young, Iris 1981. Beyond the unhappy marriage: a critique of dual systems theory. In Lydia Sargent, ed., *Women and Revolution*, Boston: South End Press, 43–69.

Young, Iris 1985. Humanisim, gynocentrism, and feminist politics. *Hypatia*, special issue of *Women's Studies International Forum* 8: 173–83.

Young, Iris 1997. *Intersecting Voices*. Princeton: Princeton University Press.

Zack, Naomi 2005. *Inclusive Feminism: A Third Wave Theory of Women's Commonality*. Lanham, MD: Rowman and Littlefield

Zakin, Emily 2007. Between two: civil identity and the sexed subject of democracy. In Maria Cimitile and Elaine Miller, eds, *Returning to Irigaray: Feminist Philosophy, Politics, and the Question of Unity*. Albany: SUNY Press, 173–205.

Zerilli, Linda 1992. A process without a subject. *Signs* 18/1: 111–35.

Zerilli, Linda 2005. *Feminism and the Abyss of Freedom*. Chicago: University of Chicago Press.

Žižek, Slavoj 1999. *The Ticklish Subject: The Absent Center of Political Ontology*. New York: Verso.

Žižek, Slavoj 2006. *The Parallax View*. Cambridge: MIT Press.

Index

abject/exclusion 166
adolescence 5, 66–8
Afro-American
    autobiographical
    writing 137–8
agency
  autonomy 162
  Butler 122, 165, 169
  Hayles 161–2
  intra-action 180–1
  non-human 160
  resistance 169, 180
  self 136
  subject 120, 122
agential realism 150, 151
Alaimo, Stacy 160–1
Alcoff, Linda 140, 141
All Said and Done
    (Beauvoir) 23
Allen, Paula Gunn 134
alterity: *see* Other
Althusser, Louis 4, 165
American Indian tradition
    134

Antigone's Claim (Butler)
    177
Anzaldua, Gloria 131
Aristotelian-Marxist
    liberalism 88–9
Aristotle 88–9, 146, 159,
    184
atherosclerosis 155–6
Austin, J. L. 52, 53
autonomy
  Collins 137
  education 91
  Gilligan 60–1, 62, 63, 68,
    69–70
  humanism 162
  liberalism 88, 89–90
  masculine norms 22, 49,
    56, 57–8, 62–3, 70–1,
    184
  object relations 54
  self 62, 63, 70, 89–90

Bakhtin, Mikhail 135
Bar On, Bat Ami 188n7

Barad, Karen 148, 149, 150–1, 154, 180
Bauer, Nancy 25
Beauvoir, Simone de 14, 94–5
  Butler on 22–3, 186n8, 189n7
  criticisms of 18–19
  existentialism 21, 22
  freedom 7, 8
  French feminists 27–30, 35, 45–7
  masculinism 2, 9–10, 18–19, 49
  neutral person myth 128
  and new materialism 24, 25–6
  Other 9–10, 11, 12, 13–14, 17, 23, 115, 116, 122–3
  philosophical tradition of west 3–4, 9, 16–17, 19, 24–5, 45–6, 77, 81, 115, 183–4
  and Sartre 19–20
  on woman 122–3, 158, 183
  woman made not born 96, 115–16, 146
  works
    All Said and Done 23
    The Ethics of Ambiguity 6–9, 186n1
    The Prime of Life 20
  Young on 48, 49
  see also The Second Sex
Being and Nothingness (Sartre) 21
Belenky, Mary 49, 72–3
Benhabib, Seyla 125–6
Bennett, Jane 161, 185

Bettelheim, Bruno 58–9
Beyond Accommodation (Cornell) 128
biology/body 6, 156–7
bisexuality 43
black feminism 130–1, 142
Black Feminist Thought (Collins) 131, 141
black literary criticism 134–5
black womanhood 137, 141–2
Bodies That Matter (Butler) 121–2, 152, 164–5, 166, 172, 181
Bodily Natures (Alaimo) 160–1
body 14, 15
  biology 6, 156–7
  boundary 179
  complexities 152–3, 154–5
  culture 154
  feminist studies 149, 151–9
  Foucault 172
  gender 22–3
  linguistic constructionism 154, 159
  materiality 121
  ontology of 155, 178
  patriarchy 152
  sexual difference 154, 158, 159
  as situation 21–2
  writing 43–4
The Body Multiple (Mol) 155
Bordo, Susan 125, 152
Braidotti, Rosi 127, 128–9, 153, 189n6
Bray, Elizabeth 152, 153
Brown, Lyn Mikel 67–8, 69

Bryson, Valerie 144
Butler, Judith
  agency 122, 165, 169
  and Beauvoir 22–3, 186n8,
    189n7
  criticism of 120, 152
  and Foucault 167–8
  gender 118, 119–20,
    121–2
  "I" 165, 166, 170, 173–4,
    178–9
  identity 118, 172, 173
  kinship 175–8, 181–2
  linguistic constructionism
    179–80
  material subject 179–83
  new materialism 180
  norms 121–2, 169–70,
    171, 172–4
  ontology of body 178
  ontology of subject 174–5
  Other 123
  and outside 165–6
  on Paris is Burning 181
  performance 122
  politics 120–1
  psyche 170–1
  sex/gender 119
  sexual difference 121, 181
  social constructionism
    166–7
  subject 163, 166–9,
    182–3
  subjectivity 123
  unconscious 171
  woman 118
  works
    Antigone's Claim 177
    Bodies That
      Matter 121–2, 152,
      164–5, 166, 172, 181
    "Competing
      Universalities" 168–9
    "Contingent
      Foundations" 168
    in Feminist Contentions
      169
    Frames of War 178, 180,
      182
    Gender Trouble 23,
      117–23, 154, 163–5,
      166, 170, 172
    Giving An Account of
      Oneself 169–70
    Precarious Life 172,
      173, 175, 178–9
    Undoing Gender 169–
      70, 171–2, 173, 177

capitalism 82, 96, 97, 98–9,
    103
care, ethic of 60, 65–6, 71–2,
    73–5, 184
Caring (Noddings) 72
Cartesian cogito: see
    Descartes, René
center/periphery
    dichotomy 107–8,
    133, 188n7
Chicana feminism 131
child care 82, 84, 98
Chodorow, Nancy 49, 54–5,
    56
chora 38–9, 40
Christian, Barbara 133–4
Cimitile, Maria 36
citizenship 35, 36, 47, 93–5,
    112
civil relationships 35–6
civil society 92–4
Cixous, Hélène 4, 41–5, 46
  on Beauvoir 28

on Freud 30, 42–3
works
"Laugh of the Medusa"
44
The Newly Born Woman
42
class 10, 94, 96, 97–8,
107–8, 181, 188n5
Clement, Catherine 42
Colebrook, Claire 152, 153,
155
Collins, Patricia Hill 109,
131, 137, 141, 142,
144
Conley, Verena 42
consciousness
body 14
differential 139
materiality 104, 105
nomadic 129
oppression 98
Other 10
public 49
Sartre 20
social 96
consciousness-raising 99
Cornell, Drucilla 127–8
Courtivron, Isabelle de 28
Crenshaw, Kimberle 143
Cudjoe, Selwyn 137
culture: *see* nature/culture
cyborgs 116, 139

Daly, Mary 50
Darwin, Charles 157
Davis, Kathy 143–4, 145
deconstruction 45, 115–16,
120–1, 133, 136, 158
Delphy, Christine 97–8
*Democracy Begins Between
Two* (Irigaray) 35, 36

Derrida, Jacques 115,
158
Descartes, René
cogito 7, 20
ego 40
freedom 22
subject 27, 40, 115
detachment 66, 68–9
determinism
biological 157
cultural 121, 165
linguistic 140, 166
Di Stefano, Christine 125,
127
The Dialectic of Sex
(Firestone) 51
Diamond, Irene 123
difference
Cixous 43
feminism 113–14
feminist standpoint
theory 109
Foucault 135
gender 62, 63, 80
Gilligan 59–60
Grosz 157
Hartsock 104–5, 107,
109–10, 188n5
identity 138–9
intersectionality 143–4,
147
object relations theory
104–5
politics 112
postmodernism 107, 114,
141
racial 130, 132, 141
resistance 135
truth 109–10
see also diversity; sexual
difference

discourse 116, 140, 148,
    152, 154
Disputed Subjects (Flax) 124
diversity 36, 109, 111,
    113–14
    see also difference
domination
    freedom from 78
    intersectionality 141, 143
    matrix of 144
    by men 48, 51, 53, 73
    reality 101–2
    white middle-class 131
drag 119, 120, 122
Duras, Marguerite 28–9

eating disorders 152
Ebert, Teresa 126–7
ego 40
Eisenstein, Zillah 78–9, 86,
    88, 99
embodiment 21, 25, 94, 129,
    149–50
Engels, Friedrich 96
entanglements 150–1
environment 160, 185
epistemology 72–3, 101–2,
    149–50, 156, 157
    see also knowledge
equality 79, 82, 87–8
Erikson, Erik 58–9
essentialism 154
    Beauvoir 14, 15, 30
    biological 10–11, 14, 15,
        156–7
    Bordo 125
    Butler 165
    charges of 139
    hooks 136
    Spivak 135
    subject 138

The Ethics of Ambiguity
    (Beauvoir) 6–9, 13,
    21, 186n1
*An Ethics of Sexual
    Difference* (Irigaray)
    34–5
Evans, Mary 14
exclusion 166
existentialism 2, 7, 8, 11,
    18–19, 21, 22
exploitation 98, 102

family law 85, 86
family/politics 82, 83, 84
feminine subject
    Butler 117
    Cixous 45
    defined 183–5
    hooks 136
    Irigaray 37
    Kristeva 38
    material feminism 127–8
    object relations theory
        54–5
    postmodernism 115, 116,
        130
    redefined 38, 42, 47
feminine syntax 34, 37, 42,
    46
femininity 13, 15, 30, 44, 48,
    154
feminism 1–2, 3, 100–1
    body studies 149, 151–9
    difference 113–14
    knowledge 124, 151–2
    liberalism 77, 78–9
    Marxism 77–8, 95–112
    postmodernism 110,
        114–30
    poststructuralism 114,
        118, 123, 151

race 105–6, 107–8
transformative 183
see also specific feminisms
Feminism Unmodified
(MacKinnon) 51–2
Feminist Contentions (ed.
Benhabib) 169
*Feminist Politics and Human
Nature* (Jaggar) 80,
100
feminist science
studies 151–2
feminist social criticism 107,
125
feminist standpoint theory
188n8
Hartsock 101–9
male supremacy 102, 103
object relations theory
103–5
patriarchy 102
reality 108–9
situated knowledge 109
*Feminist Theory: From Margin
to Center* (hooks) 131
Firestone, Shulamith 51
Flax, Jane 124
Flexible Bodies (Martin)
189n3
Foucault, Michel 115, 123,
135, 167–8, 172
Frames of War (Butler) 178,
180, 182
Fraser, Nancy 28
fraternity 92
freedom 7, 8–9, 20, 21, 22,
186n7
French feminists 27–30, 45–7
see also Cixous, Hélène;
Irigaray, Luce;
Kristeva, Julia

Freud, Sigmund
Cixous on 30, 42–3
detachment 68–9
Irigaray on 30, 31
Kristeva on 46
moral development 58
subjectivity 38
on women 53, 75–6
Friedan, Betty 78
Frye, Marilyn 50, 52–3, 82

Gadamer, Hans Georg 140
Gatens, Moira 154–5
Gates, Henry Louis 134, 137
Gauthier, Xaviere 29
gay marriage 176
gender
body 22–3
Butler 118, 119–20, 121–2
hierarchy 112, 113, 118,
128, 146
"I" 173–4
identity 119, 120, 128
justice 83–4
performativity 122
sex 23, 98, 119, 144, 153,
163–4, 189n7
social construction
of 163–4
socialization 84
gender differences 62, 63, 80
gender roles 55–6, 67–8,
119, 165
Gender Trouble (Butler)
criticisms of 117–18,
120–1
gender/sex 23, 163
Grosz on 154
identity 170, 172
new introduction 117–18,
170

Gender Trouble (Butler) (cont.)
   real 121
   subject 163–5, 166
Gilligan, Carol 4–5, 76
   adolescent girls 15, 66–8
   autonomy 60–1, 62, 63,
      68, 69–70
   care 60, 65–6, 71–2, 74–5,
      184
   coherentist scientific
      method 62
   decision-making process
      56–7
   difference 59–60
   moral development 56–7,
      62–5, 71
   multiplicity 64
   object relations 103–5, 111
   relational self 49, 62–3, 70
   relationships 68–9
   works
      In a Different Voice
         57–69, 70, 71
      *Meeting at the
         Crossroads* 69–71
*Giving An Account of
   Oneself* (Butler)
   169–70
Grosholz, Emily 19
Grosz, Elizabeth 33, 153,
      154, 155, 156–7, 159
Guantánamo Bay prisoners
   173
gynesis 29
gynocentrism 48

Habermas, Jürgen 125
Hansen, Karen 110
Haraway, Donna 116–17,
   139
Harding, Sandra 109

Hartmann, Heidi 98–9
Hartsock, Nancy 100–4
   difference 104–5, 107,
      109–10, 188n5
   disappearance of subject
      108
   feminist standpoint theory
      101–9
   modernism 107
   object relations theory
      103–5, 111
   postmodernism 111, 125
   principled relativism 108,
      111
   relational self 105–6
   ruling classes 107–8
   subjectivity 125
   on woman 124–5
   works
      "The Feminist
         Standpoint" 103–4
      Money, Sex, and Power
         101–2
      "Rethinking Modernism"
         106
Hawkesworth, Mary 141,
   144
Hayles, Katherine 161–2
Hegel, G. W. F. 76
Hekman, Susan 10, 80
Henderson, Mae 135
Hennessy, Rosemary 110–11
Hindman, Matther Dean 145
historical materialism 14,
      103, 126–7
hooks, bell 131, 135–6, 137
How We Became Posthuman
   (Hayles) 161–2
human capabilities theory 87
human nature 17, 18, 74
human rights 175

humanism 135, 161–2
human/non-human 150,
    159–60, 161, 185
Hypatia 149

"I" (Butler) 165, 166, 170,
    173–4, 178–9
identity 2, 3, 40
  blurred 37, 45
  Butler 118, 172, 173
  civil 35–6
  deconstruction 120–1,
    136
  difference 138–9
  discourse 140
  gender 119, 120, 128
  in *Gender Trouble* 170,
    172
  Haraway 139
  multiple 114, 145
  Other 13–14
  politics 118, 138
  race/gender/ethnicity 136,
    138, 140
  social 8–9
identity politics 94, 114
In a Different Voice (Gilligan)
    57–69, 70, 71
Inessential Woman
    (Spelman) 113–14
inferiority 71, 116, 184
interactionism 149–50, 151
interpellation 174–5
intersectionality 5, 130,
    141–6, 147
intra-action 151, 154, 155,
    161, 162, 180–3
Irigaray, Luce 27
  on Beauvoir 28, 35
  deconstruction 45
  diversity 36

dual citizenship 35, 36, 47
feminine syntax 34
on Freud 30, 31
jamming theoretical
    machinery 4, 32, 34,
    40, 49, 183
language 31–2
legacy of 37
mimicry 31
Other 30
phallocracy 29
politics 35–7, 46–7
psychoanalysis 29–30, 46
subject 35, 41
woman 158–9
works
  *Democracy Begins
    Between Two* 35, 36
  *An Ethics of Sexual
    Difference* 34–5
  Sexes and Genealogies
    34–5
  *Speculum of the Other
    Woman* 30–1
  *This Sex Which Is Not
    One* 31–2, 33
*Is Multiculturalism Bad for
    Women?* (Okin)
    187n1

Jaggar, Alison 80, 100
Jardine, Alice 29
Johnson, Mark 189n3
Jonasdottir, Anna 144
Jones, Kathleen 144
jouissance 42–3
Joyce, Joyce 134–5
justice 65–6, 71–2, 83–4
*Justice, Gender, and the
    Family* (Okin) 82–3,
    85–6

Kant, Immanuel 76, 86, 87
King, Rodney 190n14
kinship 175–8, 181–2
knowledge 20
  feminism 124, 151–2
  masculine 184
  postmodernism 109
  scientific 163
  situated 109
  transformed 98
  truth 150
  see also epistemology
Kohlberg, Lawrence 56–7,
    62, 63–4, 68, 75
Kristeva, Julia 4, 27
  on Beauvoir 28
  chora 38, 39
  drives 38–9
  and Freud 46
  Other 38
  poetic language 39–40
  psychoanalysis 29–30, 38
  semiotic/symbolic 38, 39,
    40
  thetic phase 38, 39
  woman as subject 37–8, 41
  works
    Revolution in Poetic
      Language 38–40
    "Woman's Time" 41
Kruks, Sonia 8, 20, 21, 22
Kukla, Rebecca 153

labor 97–8, 102–3, 188n9
labor division 83, 97, 102
Lakoff, George 189n3
language
  Cixous 43–4
  common stock of words 52
  Irigaray 31–2
  poetic 39–40

reality 148
subject 182–3
woman 32
see also linguistic
  constructionism
Latour, Bruno 160
Le Doeuff, Michele 29,
    187n10
lesbians 52, 135
liberal feminism 86–7, 88,
    90, 91, 93
liberalism 5
  autonomy 88, 89–90
  civil society 92–3
  criticisms 78–81
  defenses 81–91
  equality 87–8
  family law 85, 86
  and feminism 77, 78–9
  neo-Aristotelian 89
  Nussbaum 87, 88–9,
    188n2
  Pateman 91–2
  public/private spheres 50,
    86, 94
  radical feminism 88
  Rawls 83
  transformation of 91–5
life plan 90–1
linguistic constructionism
    148, 151, 154, 159,
    162–3, 179–80
linguistic turn 5–6, 148
  see also language
literary criticism 133–4,
    139
Lorde, Audre 77, 133
Ludic Feminism
    (Ebert) 126–7
Lugones, Maria 133
Luhmann, Niklas 147

Lundgren-Gothlin, Eva 19
Lykke, Nina 142, 144–5

McCall, Leslie 142, 145
MacKinnon, Catherine 51–2, 80, 83, 86, 99
McNay, Lois 167
male supremacy 102, 103
Marcus, Isabel 66
marginalization 99, 133, 135, 136
Marks, Elaine 28
marriage contract 98
Martin, Emily 189n3
Marx, Karl 95–6
Marxism 5
  and feminism 77–8, 95–112
  labor 97, 188n9
  MacKinnon on 99
  postmodernism 126–7
  proletariat 102
  radical feminism 99
Marxist feminism 99–100, 125
masculine hegemony 59, 71
masculinism
  Beauvoir 2, 9–10, 18–19, 49
  and gynocentrism 48
  moral development 61
  thought traditions 6
  transformed 111
material feminism
  and Beauvoir 25, 26
  contemporary 111
  environment 185
  feminine subject 127–8
  and intersectionality 130
  ontology of subject 162
  postmodernism 110

material subject
  body studies 151–9
  and Butler 179–83
  and feminine subject 183–5
  new materialism 147–51
  ontology of subject 162–79
  posthumanism 159–62
  see also new materialism
material turn 6, 24, 25–6, 129, 148
materiality
  body 121
  consciousness 104, 105
  discourse 152
  epistemology 102
  Marxist feminism 125
  subjectivity 153
  see also new materialism
Maternal Thinking (Ruddick) 73
Matsuda, Mari 144
Meese, Elizabeth 138
Meeting at the Crossroads (Brown and Gilligan) 69–71
Meeting the Universe Halfway (Barad) 150–1
Merleau-Ponty, Maurice 25
Meyers, Diana 89–90, 91
Mill, John Stuart 76, 78, 79–80, 86, 95
Miller, Elaine 36
mimesis 128
mimicry 31
Minh-ha, Trinh T. 138
modernism
  categories
    deconstructed 185
    essentialism 154

modernism (cont.)
  Gilligan 66
  Hartsock on 107
  mind/body dualism 162
  patriarchy 148
  and postmodernism 127
  subjectivity 27
Mohanty, Chandra 131
Moi, Toril 8, 9, 20, 21–2,
    186n8
Mol, Annemarie 155
Money, Sex, and Power
    (Hartsock) 101–2
Moraga, Cherrie 133, 134,
    138
Moral Boundaries (Tronto)
    73–4
moral development
  fairness/care 65
  Freud 58
  Gilligan 56–7, 62–5, 71
  Kohlberg 56–7, 68, 75
  masculine hegemony 59
  masculinism 61
  maturity 60, 68–9
  woman 60–2, 70, 76
mother–daughter
    relationship 36
motherhood 15, 49, 51
mothering 55–6, 102
Moya, Paula 139–40
multiplicity
  female subjectivity
    129
  gender/sexuality 144,
    164
  Gilligan 64
  Hartsock 107, 108
  identity 114, 145
  resistance 119
  subject 129, 138

nature/culture 43, 116, 149,
    151, 157
neuropsychology 158
new materialism 147–51
  and Beauvoir 24, 25–6
  and Butler 180
  epistemology/ontology 157
  intra-action 182
  sexual difference 159
The Newly Born Woman
    (Cixous and
    Clement) 42
The Nick of Time
    (Grosz) 156–7
Nietzsche, Friedrich 115
Noddings, Nel 49, 72
Nomadic Subjects (Braidotti)
    129
non-humans 150, 159–60,
    161, 185
norms
  Butler 121–2, 169–70,
    171, 172–4
  masculine autonomy 22,
    49, 56, 57–8, 62–3,
    70–1, 184
  resistance 174
  sexual relationships 177
  subject 180
Nussbaum, Martha 81, 86–9,
    188n2
  "The Future of Feminist
    Liberalism" 88–9
  Sex and Social Justice 86–7
  *Women and Human
    Development* 88

object relations theory
  autonomy 54
  difference 104–5
  feminist standpoint 103–5

Gilligan 57, 63, 70
Hartsock 103–5, 111
relational self 54–6, 105–6
situated knowledge 109
Okin, Susan Moller 83, 84,
    85, 86
"Human Liberalism"
    84–6
*Is Multiculturalism Bad
    for Women?* 187, ch.
    4, n1
*Justice, Gender, and the
    Family* 82–3, 85–6
*Women in Western Political
    Thought* 81–2, 85
Oliver, Kelly 40
ontology
    of body 155, 178
    epistemology 149–50, 157
    politics 155
    Sartre 19–20
    of subject 149, 162, 174–5
    truth 170
ontology-in-practice 155–6
oppression
    black feminism 142
    consciousness 98
    different kinds of 139
    exploitation 98, 102
    intersectionality 141, 142
    non-white women 138
    politics 50
    reality 105
Orientalism (Said) 132
*The Origins of the Family,
    Private Property and
    the State* (Engels) 96
Other
    Beauvoir 9–10, 11, 12,
        13–14, 17, 23, 115,
        116, 122–3

    Butler 123
    Irigaray 30
    Kristeva 38

Paris is Burning 181
parody 129
pastiche 119–20
Pateman, Carole
    citizenship 94–5
    civil society 92–4
    liberal feminism 93
    on liberalism 91–2
    politics 111–12, 184–5
    public/private spheres 92
    on Rawls 93
patriarchy
    body 152
    capitalism 96, 97, 98–9
    equality 79
    feminist standpoint
        theory 102
    modernism 148
    motherhood 51
Patterns of Dissonance
    (Braidotti) 128–9
performativity 122, 180
personal/political 49–53, 85,
    89
personhood 88–9, 171, 176,
    181
phallocracy 29, 30, 33, 52–3
phenomenology 18–19
Philipson, Ilene 110
Phillips, Anne 91
philosophical tradition of the
    west 11–12, 15, 18
    Beauvoir 3–4, 9, 16–17,
        19, 24–5, 45–6, 77,
        81, 115, 183–4
    Irigaray 31, 158–9
    Okin 81–2

philosophical tradition of the
west (cont.)
  postmodernism 114
  Tuana 150
Philosophy in the Flesh
  (Lakoff and
  Johnson) 189n3
Piaget, Jean 58, 62, 75
Pickering, Andrew 25, 26,
  160, 163
Pilardi, Jo-Ann 19
Plato 30, 31, 38, 40, 76
politics
  Aristotle 184
  Butler 120–1
  care 74–5
  difference 112
  equality 82
  family 82, 83, 84
  identity 118, 138
  Irigaray 35–7, 46–7
  ontology 155
  oppression 50
  Pateman 111–12, 184–5
  of resistance 118, 120
  transversal 144
The Politics of Reality
  (Frye) 52
pornography 51–2
posthumanism 149,
  159–62
post-kinship studies 177
postmodern feminism 114–
  15, 116, 118, 127
postmodernism
  difference 107, 114, 141
  feminine subject 115, 116,
  130
  feminism 110, 114–30
  Hartsock 111, 125
  knowledge 109

linguistic constructionism
  148
literary theory 134
marginality 136
material feminism 110
modernism 127
philosophical tradition
  114
resistance 126–7
subjectivity 115–16, 117
woman 5–6
poststructuralism 114, 118,
  123, 151
power 118, 122, 123, 168,
  169–70, 172
Precarious Life (Butler) 172,
  173, 175, 178–9
The Prime of Life (Beauvoir)
  20
principled relativism 108,
  111
production modes 97, 98
proletariat 96, 97, 102
psyche 170–1
psychoanalysis 14, 28,
  29–30, 38, 45–6
public/private spheres 50, 82,
  84, 86, 92, 94

quantum physics 151
Quest 100–1
Quick, James 37
Quinby, Lee 123

race 105–6, 107–8, 130–41
racism 106, 135, 136
radical feminism 49–53, 88,
  99
*The Radical Future of Liberal
  Feminism* (Eisenstein)
  78–9

Rawls, John
  life plan 90–1
  and Meyers 90
  Nussbaum on 87, 88
  Okin on 83, 84, 85, 86
  Pateman on 93
  A Theory of Justice 91–2
reality
  dominant groupings 101–2
  feminist standpoint
      theory 108–9
  language 148
  object relations
      theory 103–4
  oppression 105
  socially constructed 100,
      101–2
*Reclaiming Identity: Realist
    Theory and the
    Predicament of
    Postmodernism*
    (Moya) 139–40
Reed, Evelyn 96
relational self 49, 53–6,
    62–3, 70–1, 105–6,
    137
relativism
  Alcoff 140
  Barad 151
  black women's
      standpoint 109
  Hartsock 108, 110, 111
  principled 108, 111
representationalism 156,
    189n3
*The Reproduction of
    Mothering* (Chodorow)
    54–5
resistance
  adolescent girls 67
  agency 169, 180

difference 135
  Foucault 123
  marginalization 136
  multiplicity 119
  norms 174
  politics of 118, 120
  postmodernism 126–7
  power 123
  Venus Xtravaganza 181
Returning to Irigaray
    (Cimitile and Miller)
    36
*Revolution in Poetic
    Language* (Kristeva)
    38–40
Routledge Advances in
    Feminist Studies and
    Intersectionality 143
Rowbotham, Shelia 97
Ruddick, Sarah 49, 73, 74
ruling classes 107–8,
    188n5

Said, Edward 132, 136
Sandoval, Chela 139
Sartre, Jean-Paul 2, 7, 19–20,
    21
Sawicki, Jana 123, 135
science 60–2, 149, 163
The Second Sex (Beauvoir)
    1–2
  citizenship 94–5
  inferiority 71
  monism rejected 26
  objectives 28
  One/Other 9–10, 23
  phallocracy 29
  Sartrean existentialism 19
  social identity 8–9
  subject 20
  transcendence 23–4

self
  adolescence 67
  agency 136
  autonomous 62, 63, 70,
    89–90
  cyborgs 116
  hooks on 137
  human/non-human 161
  intersectionality 141
  liberal 86
  mature 60, 68–9
  power 168
  socially constructed 85,
    89–91
  see also relational self
semiotic 38–9, 40
sex
  biological given 10–11
  class 96
  gender 23, 98, 119, 144,
    153, 163–4, 189n7
Sex and Social Justice
  (Nussbaum) 86–7
Sexes and Genealogies
  (Irigaray) 34–5
sexism 156–7
sexual contract 92
sexual difference
  body 154, 158, 159
  Butler 121, 181
  Gatens 154
  Grosz 154, 157, 159
  Irigaray 33, 34, 37
  new materialism 159
  Wilson 159
sexual equality 80, 82, 84
sexual relations 176, 177
sexuality 33, 49, 50–1, 96,
    99, 144, 177
Shildrick, Margrit 124
signification 7, 8, 38–9, 40

Signs 44
Simons, Margaret 21,
    187n10
Singer, Linda 25
situation, as concept 9, 21–2,
    25
Smith, Dorothy 100, 109
social constructionism
  Butler 166–7
  gender 163–4
  reality 100, 101–2
  self 85, 89–91
  subject 95–6, 100, 115
socialist feminism 99, 100
socialization 84, 90
Space, Time, and Perversion
  (Grosz) 154
Speculum of the Other
  Woman
  (Irigaray) 30–1
speech 40, 129, 169
Spelman, Elizabeth 113–14,
    133
Spiegelman, Paul 66
Spinoza, Baruch 154
Spivak, Gayatri 135, 136
Stanton, Elizabeth Cady 78
Stern, Lori 69
Subaltern Studies
    Collective 135
subject
  agency 120, 122
  ambiguity 6–7, 9, 178
  autonomy 184
  Butler 163, 166–9,
    182–3
  Cartesian 27, 40, 115
  complexities 172, 182
  death of 108, 115, 116,
    127, 128
  essentialist 138

in *Gender Trouble* 163–5,
    166
human/non-human 159–60
intra-action 182–3
Irigaray 35, 41
Kristeva 41
language 182–3
liberal 80, 81, 161–2
masculine, displaced 56
multiplicity 129, 130
nomadic 128–9, 189n6
norms 180
posthuman 161–2
postmodern 115–16, 117
power 169–70
redefined 35, 124, 160
relational 53–6, 58, 184
socially constructed 95–6,
    100, 115
speaking 40, 129, 169
subjectification 167–9
transcendental 120, 121,
    137
woman as 33, 37–8
see also feminine subject;
    material subject;
    ontology of subject
subject-in-process 39–40, 41
subjectivity
    abstract 19–20
    black 137
    Braidotti 128, 129
    Butler 123
    collective 138
    constructed 110–11
    embodied 21, 25
    female 129
    freedom 8–9
    Freud 38
    Hartsock 125
    kinship 181–2

materiality 153
modernism 27
parody 129
postmodernism 115–16,
    117
woman 10, 17
super-ego 75

Talking Back (hooks) 137
A Theory of Justice
    (Rawls) 91–2
thetic phase 38, 39
Thinking Fragments
    (Flax) 124
"third world women" 131
This Sex Which Is Not One
    (Irigaray) 31–2, 33
Thurman, Judith 1
Tidd, Ursula 8
Time Travels (Grosz) 157
time/space 33, 41, 103
transcendence 11, 16, 23–4,
    40, 120, 121, 137
trans-corporeality 160–1,
    162
transsexuals 173
Tronto, Joan 49, 73–4
truth
    difference 109–10
    knowledge 150
    masculine 184
    method 58, 59–60, 61,
        62
    ontology 170
Truth, Sojourner 145
Tuana, Nancy 149–50,
    151

Unbearable Weight
    (Bordo) 152
unconscious 171

Undoing Gender (Butler) 169–70, 171–2, 173, 177
unspeakable 169

Vibrant Matter (Bennett) 161
Vintges, Karen 19
Visible Identities (Alcoff) 140
Volatile Bodies (Grosz) 153

Weedon, Chris 123
Weeks, Kathi 188n8, 190n11
Wendell, Susan 91
western thought: *see* philosophical tradition
white feminism 131, 133
Wilson, Elizabeth 158, 159
Wollstonecraft, Mary 78, 79, 95
woman
  Beauvoir 122–3, 158, 183
  black 137, 141–2
  Butler 118
  Hartsock 124–5
  in history 29
  as inferior 71, 116, 184
  Irigaray 158–9
  made not born 51–2, 96, 115–16, 119, 146
  as Other 9–10, 12, 13–14, 17, 23, 30, 38, 115, 116, 122–3
  postmodernism 5–6

redefined 26, 27, 29, 46, 111, 159
  as subject 33, 37–8
  subjectivity 10, 17
  third-world 131
  see also female body; philosophical tradition of the west
Women and Human Development (Nussbaum) 88
Women in Western Political Thought (Okin) 81–2, 85
women of color
  diversity 138
  feminist 133–4, 135, 138
  identity politics 114
  oppression, multiple 142
  as Other 132–3
  white domination 131, 132, 133
  see also black feminism
Women's Way of Knowing (Belenky) 72–3
writing the body 43, 44

Yearning (hooks) 135–6
Young, Iris Marion 48, 49, 99

Zack, Naomi 145
Zerilli, Linda 186n7

- Cortes
- Stage 6, Kohlbert
- Marilyn Frye